Understanding Indian Society

Understanding Indian Society

The Non-Brahmanic Perspective

Edited by
S.M. Dahiwale

RAWAT PUBLICATIONS
Jaipur and New Delhi

ISBN 81-7033-894-8 (hardcover)
ISBN 81-316-0026-2 (paperback)

Reprinted 2006

Published by
Prem Rawat for *Rawat Publications*
Satyam Apts., Sector 3, Jawahar Nagar, Jaipur 302 004 (India)
Phone: 0141 265 1748 / 7006 Fax: 0141 265 1748
E-mail: info@rawatbooks.com
Website: www.rawatbooks.com

New Delhi Office
4858/24, Ansari Road, Daryaganj, New Delhi 110 002
Phone: 011-23263290

Typeset by Rawat Computers, Jaipur
Printed at Chaman Enterprises, New Delhi

Contents

Preface

This book is the outcome of the papers presented at the seminar organised under the UGC Special Assistance Programme in the Department of Sociology, University of Pune. The theme of the seminar was *Understanding Indian Society: Perspective from Below*. The sub-title 'Non-Brahmanic Perspective' was proposed by me, but it was not acceptable to Professor T.K. Oommen who was invited to deliver his inaugural address and so in the seminar and his address/paper title, the word *Below* was kept. However, the word *Below* has a Marxian connotation. In the Indian context, since there is a long history of two opposing forces, i.e. Brahmanic and non-Brahmanic, the word *non-Brahmanic* seems to me appropriate.

Sociologists and social anthropologists have developed Indological, structural-functional and Marxian approaches to understand the Indian society. Despite a distinctive history of non-Brahmanic traditions from the times of Buddha to the post-independent Ambedkar social scientists have made non-Brahmanic traditions a part of broader Hinduism. In British India, a number of social reformers in their regions had launched anti-systemic movements to threaten the hegemony of upper-caste Hindus. There are several issues of identity, power, conversion, gender inequality and social justice, which have not been addressed properly. And, since the last decade, the militant Hindus, with their political support, have become aggressive to implement the agenda of pan-Hinduism. In this background, the attempt is made through this book to reveal the other side of reality of Indian society.

For the fruition of this book, the invited scholars for the seminar have responded with their papers and some of them have taken pains to revise their papers. I am grateful to all the contributors to this volume. Professor U.B. Bhoite has been kind to go through the minute details of *Introduction* and gave comments for revising the draft. I acknowledge my deep thankfulness to him. Also, I would like to thank my friend C.R. Das, who had gone through my drafts and offered his sincere comments. I thank Malati Shendge, who was kind enough to suggest important readings. I wish to express my appreciation to the editorial team of the publisher for making constructive comments and useful suggestions. I record my thanks to Sanjivani Bhalchim and Yogesh Dhumal for their sincere cooperation in getting the typescript ready. Finally, I wish to remain grateful to Shri Kailash Rawat for accepting the manuscript for publication.

S.M. Dahiwale

Contributors

S.M. Dahiwale is former Professor of Sociology, University of Pune, Pune. In addition to two books *Emerging Entrepreneurship among Scheduled Castes of Contemporary India* (1989) and *Rural Poverty and Slums* (1997), he has published over twenty articles in reputed journals. He has also served as a member of the Maharashtra State Backward Classes Commission (1992-99).

T.K. Oommen is a retired Professor of Sociology, Jawaharlal Nehru University, New Delhi. He has served as President of the International Sociological Association (1990-94) and President of the Indian Sociological Society (1998-99). He is the recipient of prestigious V.R.R.V. Rao Prize in Sociology (1981), the G.S. Ghurye Prize in Sociology and Anthropology (1985) and the Swami Pranavananda Award in Sociology (1997). Professor Oommen has published over a dozen books including *Pluralism, Equality and Identity: Comparative Studies* (2002).

Surinder S. Jodhka is Associate Professor at Centre for the Study of Social System, Jawaharlal Nehru University, New Delhi. He has been a recipient of the Charles Wallace India Trust Fellowship in Social Anthropology. He has been a Visiting Fellow at Queen's University of Belfast, Northern Ireland, and South Asian Visiting Scholar at Queen Elizabeth House, University of Oxford. He published extensively on agrarian studies and social identities in various Indian and international journals.

Gail Omvedt was Professor of Sociology at the University of Pune, Pune (1997-98). She is a well-known sociologist. She has published over a dozen books and over sixty articles in national and international journals. Her major books include *Cultural Revolt in a Colonial Society: The Non-Brahman Movement in Western India* (1976), *Dalits and the Democratic Revolution: Dr. Ambedkar and the Dalit Movement* (1994), *Dalit Visions: The Anti-Caste Movement and the Construction of an Indian Identity* (1995).

S.P. Punalekar is a retired Professor from the Centre for Social Studies, Surat. He is the author of seven books. He has completed over three dozen research studies and published over hundred papers in reputed journals and periodicals.

Ambrose Pinto S.J. is Executive Director of the Indian Social Institute, New Delhi. He has authored several papers for various journals.

S.M. Michael is Professor of Sociology, University of Mumbai, Mumbai. Since 1976, he has been pursuing research in Anthropology and Indian Culture. He has, to his credit, several books and research articles.

Lancy Lobo is Director of the Centre for Culture and Development, Vadodara. Earlier, he was Director of the Centre for Social Studies, Surat. He has published several articles in reputed journals.

Padma Velaskar is Professor of Education at Tata Institute of Social Sciences, Mumbai. She has several published papers to her credit.

Satish Deshpande is a Researcher at the Institute of Economic Growth, Delhi. His interests include the socio-cultural aspects of economic phenomena—caste and class inequalities in relation to social policy.

1

Introduction

S.M. Dahiwale

In contemporary literature on social and religious movements, the word, *non-Brahman*, is often used. The Phuleian (after Mahatma Phule) or the Ambedkarian approach has been followed for having adopted the analysis of the non-Brahman/ backward classes/Dalit movement in India. Since the 1980s, Sharad Patil became well known for his use of the trilogy of Marx, Phule and Ambedkar in his historical analysis of Indian society. His trilogy is termed as the non-Brahmanic interpretative methodology. According to Patil, the non-Brahmanic stream means the end of the slavery of class, caste and women. Following Patil's perspective, the Women's Studies Centre at the University of Pune organised a seminar on Non-Brahmanic Feminist History Writing on September 24-25, 1998, and published the presented papers in the form of a book (Bhagwat and Pardeshi, 1998). The writers in the book have been critical of Indian history from the non-Brahmanic perspective and reiterated the observations made by Patil, Phule and Ambedkar in their writings. The scholars in the book affirm that the notion of purity worked in exercising the dominance of Brahmans in the hierarchies of caste, gender and culture. But the understanding of the larger Indian society, which is made of several religious groups, castes, gender, and is full of dynamics, requires a comprehensive definition of the non-Brahmanic perspective. *It perceives the practices, which are non-Vedic, non-Shastric, non-caste, non-patriarchal or having equalitarian character, and a number of attempts made to bring about change/transformation towards the equalitarian order through protest/resist/action movements against the Brahmanic hegemony.* In this volume, since T.K. Oommen's paper deals with the perspective 'from below', it is necessary to give some clarification about his construction/use of the term, *below*, and my standpoint on using the 'non-Brahmanic perspective'. Oommen's construction is largely based on empirical observations comprehending the localised religious practices, prevalent gender equalitarian practices and social justice in the Dalit-bahujan society. It is certainly non-Brahmanic in its formulation. The use of the term, below, denotes the western influence, especially that of Marxian literature. Considering the history of change from Vedic religion to Hindu religion, the growth of caste, the adapted patriarchal practices amongst lower caste Hindus, etc., on one hand, and the history of both egalitarian religious movements in ancient and medieval India and social reform movements in British India on the other hand, the term non-Brahmanic is used in opposition to the Brahmanic and differentiating from it. As the ex-untouchable castes were regarded outside the *varna* (caste) society, these were kept away from the process of sanskritisation and these castes have not been made free from their age-old disabilities in the countryside even today. And how the peasant/intermediate (dominant today) castes had to struggle in medieval and British India for claiming Kshatriya status and for performing Vedic rites is a well-known historical fact, but these are sanskritised today. In post-Independent India, because of the power politics, the peasant castes have become the agents of Brahman *dharma*. This is to say that the term, below, connotes a class category, while the term, non-Brahmanic, signifies the historical categories of religion, caste and gender. Accordingly, attention is focussed here on the important aspects of both early and later religions, religious movements, untouchability, social movements, gender and identity.

Indian society is composed of people of a variety of religions, sects, castes and tribes. It has a preponderance of 82.72 percent Hindus (Census 2001), who belong to the Hindu religion having a history of about 2,000 years. Hinduism has no monolithic character of having a single founder, a single sacred text, a single god or a well-defined doctrine. It has a caste system in which one's superior/inferior status is determined by birth. Historically, the outsiders have used the word, Hindu, to refer to the people living in the Indus valley. Since the pre-Vedic times, the history of Indian society has been a history of wars, oppositions, protests, conflicts and movements in various forms. Many tribes from outside invaded India, but the Aryan tribe culturally, socially and politically dominated the indigenous tribes.

The Aryan Invasion and the Rise of the Vedic Religion

Sources in Vedic literature lead to the inference that the original home of the Aryans was the Arctic region (between North Germany and Scandinavia/north of Siberia), but they later settled down in the plains of Central Asia (Tilak, 1956:275, 380, 388, 390). The names of both Iran and Ireland signify them as the lands of the Aryans (Trautmann, 1977:13). From the linguistic viewpoint, the Indian languages (Sanskrit and its descendants in North India and Sri Lanka) are studied as closely related to the Iranian languages (Ibid.:6). Archaeologists such as John Marshall, R.E. Mortimer-Wheeler, Ramprasad Chanda, S.K. Chatterjee and R.D. Banerji have argued that in struggles/wars with the Dravidians, the Aryan invaders destroyed the Indus valley civilisation (Ramaswamy, 2001: 105-145). Such references in ancient Indian literature establish the fact that the Aryans entered the northwest of India around

1500 B.C. According to the Vedic scholar, Malati Shendge, the Aryan invaders entered through the northwest crossing the Indus and its tributaries..... met with continuous opposition from the Asuras and the Raksasas (Shendge, 1977:181). Prior to the Aryan emigrants, amongst the non-Aryan aborigines were the Dasyus, the Nishadas and the Dravidians. Among the Dravidians were the Tamilians, the Tulus, the Koorgs, the Gonds, the Oraons, the Khonds, the Todas, the Kols, the Juangs, the Santals, the Mundas, and the Hos.

During the *Rig Vedic* times, there were wars between the Aryan invaders (nomads) and their opponent non-Aryans, viz., the Asuras (agriculturists), the Raksasas (demons/warriors), the Yaksas (fearful beings), the Pisacas (architects/carvers), the Dasas (fishermen/sailors), the Dasyus (village folk), etc. After several attempts, Indra and Vishnu defeated the Asuras. Indra was the leader of the Aryans, the killer of the Dasas/Dasyus. In the *Rig Veda*, there are references to the forts of the Dasas (Jaiswal, 1998:146). The Dasas and the Dasyus had armies of women warriors (Shendge, 1977:145). Indra killed the non-Aryan enemies, Sambara, Pipru, Arsasanas, Sushna and Namuci, who are described as black and short-nosed (Kosambi, 1964:78-79). Indra defeated and killed 30,000 Dasas, the dark skinned, who were settled in the land of the seven rivers, using a cunning strategy (Shendge, 1996:29). Another Aryan hero, Vishnu, had battles with the Asuras, the Dasas, etc. After the defeat and looting of the wealth of the Dasas by the *Rig Vedic* Aryans, they were made slaves (Jaiswal, 1998:146, 157). The lower classes of Hindus consist of ..... aboriginal inhabitants (Trautmann, 1997:175). The aborigine Dasyus/Dasas are described as the Raksasas/Mlechhas, the barbarians (Ibid.:197). They had no practice of sacrifices or performing rites and they were phallus worshippers (Ibid.:208-9).

For obtaining victory over the Asuras, the Devas appropriated the rites of sacrifice, i.e. fire worship, from the Asuras (Shendge, 1977:92-94). After the victory of the Aryans over their enemies, certain events of transformation took place.

One, the practice of fire rites was created. Two, the heroes, namely, Indra and Vishnu, of the Aryans became gods, and the enemies, viz., the Asuras, the Raksasas and others, became demons. And Vishnu was placed as the highest of the gods. Third, the defeated enemies were given the lowest status in the Aryan social structure by forbidding their participation in *yajnas,* the newly created religion of fire (Ibid.:283). Krishna, the dark-skinned hero of the Yadu tribe, a protector of cattle, who never invoked at a fire sacrifice where animals were offered, is a demon, an enemy of Indra in the *Rig Veda*. (Kosambi, 1964:115). Thus, the Dasas/Dasyus and the Panis suffered loss of social status because of their resistance (Shendge, 1977:284). The historicity of Dipavali, the festival of lights, is that it was introduced by the Aryans as a mark of victory over the destruction of Asura Bali and Naraka, the non-Aryan leaders. But, unfortunately, the non-Aryans also joined the celebration because of their ignorance.

We find the appearance of the word 'Aryans' in the *Rig Veda* text (1400 B.C.). They were divided into three social classes, viz., the warriors, the priests and the commoners (Thapar, 1966:37). They composed the hymns of the *Rig Veda*. In the *Rig Veda*, the word 'Brahman' is used as one of the seven priests and it evolved gradually as a class of priests in the *Rig Vedic* period itself (Misra, 1978). The Brahmans are "the repositories both of the divine word, and of the spirit of devotion or prayer" (Monier-Williams, 1877:12). In the second division of the *Veda,* called *Brahmanas* (1000 B.C.), we find the idea of sacrifice and rituals. The Vedic divisions of the *Brahmanas* have the *Aitareya*, the *Taittiriya*, the *Satapatha*, and the *Gopatha*, etc. The Brahmans developed ritualism when they settled in the northwestern part of India (Ibid.:24). For attaining immortality, three objectives of sacrifices were agreed upon: (i) to nourish the gods as a necessity of their being, (ii) to expiate for sins committed, and (iii) to acquire superhuman power. Initially, humans were offered in sacrifices. Later, animals—horses, oxen, cows, sheep and goats—substituted for them.

Sacrifices of all kinds increased in the *Brahmana* period (probably from 800 to 500 B.C.) (Monier-Williams, 1877: chap. III). D.D. Kosambi adds one more object—of getting victory in war (Kosambi, 1964:87). King Janamejaya III performed a great sacrifice for the total destruction of the Nagas (Ibid.:92). King Dasarath performed an Aswamedha (horse sacrifice) for obtaining a son (Wheeler, 1973:10). The sacrifices were enclosed between the two upper castes, viz., Brahman and Kshatriya. The Raksasas alluded to the different tribes of aborigines which had opposed the Brahmans and their sacrifices (Ibid.:38). J. Wheeler cites that the Raksasas once rushed to defile the Brahmans' sacrificial altar with bones and blood, but it was prevented by Rama (Ibid.:44). Perhaps this could be the reason for excluding Shudras in the Brahmanic sacrifices in Vedic India.

The Rise of Buddhism and Jainism

The above stray mention shows that there was opposition to the practices of Brahmanic sacrifices. The revolt against the Vedic religion of sacrifices (*yajnas*) by Gautama Buddha, the Shakya (532-487 B.C.), and Vardhamana Mahaveera, the Licchavi (539-467 B.C.), and their teachings, developed later as independent religions, in the form of Buddhism and Jainism, respectively. Both religions uphold non-violence and ethical practices in personal as well as social life. Buddha prohibited Bhikkus from holding private property and from remaining householders, contrary to the practices of the Brahman priests of the Vedic religion. Upali, a barber, Sunit and Svapak, scavengers, were admitted as monks to the Bhikku Sangha. Women were also admitted to the Sangha. Mahaveer did the same, but with strict rules of austerity and non-violence. The Licchavis and the Mallas did not follow the Vedic practices (Monier-Williams, 1877:130).

According to B.R. Ambedkar, "The history of India is nothing but a history of a mortal conflict between Buddhism and Brahmanism" (Ambedkar, 1987: 267). Ambedkar defines Brahmanism in terms of the spirit: "the idea of high caste and low caste—which implanted the idea of pollution from human beings and implanted social privileges and inequality" (Keer, 1971:89) and "the negation of the spirit of liberty, equality and fraternity" (Ibid., 303). Also, the effects of Brahmanism have been elaborated further mentioning "not confining only to social rights such as interdining and intermarrying. It denied them also the civic rights. So omniscient is Brahmanism that it even affects the field of economic opportunities" (Ibid.:304). He notes certain facts of the triumph of Brahmanism in the history of India. Sisunag, the aboriginal Nag, founded the kingdom of Magadha in Bihar in 642 B.C. Nanda, who ruled the Magadha Empire upto 322 B.C., replaced the Sisunag dynasty. Chandragupta Maurya, who was related to the Sisunag dynasty, and restored the Naga empire of Magadha, dethroned the last Nanda king. The Mauryan empire extended its boundaries by a number of conquests. Ashok Maurya succeeded in 270 B.C. After large-scale killings of animals and men in the war of Kalinga, Emperor Ashok realised the horror of what he had done and converted to Buddhism. We find the Buddha's *Dhamma*, which Ashok promulgated on his rock edicts, is as follows:

1. No animal should be slaughtered for sacrifice.
2. Performing rites or ceremonies for luck on the occasion of sickness, weddings, and childbirth, or starting a journey, are worthless.
3. Honour should be paid to all belonging to other sects.
4. The *Dhamma* is doing benefits to others; compassion; liberty; truth; purity.

Since Ashok made Buddhism the official religion of his great empire, the Brahmins lost their chief source of living, performing sacrifices. This lasted for nearly 140 years during the Maurya period, which, according to Ambedkar, was the greatest blow to Brahmanism (Ibid.:268). Therefore, Pushyamitra Sung (180-151 B.C.), the Sam Vedic Brahman, the believer in animal sacrifices, took up the cause of destroying the Buddhist state and reinstating the Brahmanic religion. After ascending the throne, Pushyamitra not only performed the horse sacrifice, but also launched a violent persecution of the Buddhists. He proclaimed a price of 100 gold pieces on the head of every Buddhist monk (Ibid.:269). The *Smritis* and *Puranas* were written during Gupta period (2nd c. B.C. 4th c. A.D.), after triumphing over Buddhism.

The point of conflict between the Brahmins and the Shudras or between the Brahmanic followers/protectors and the Buddhists is reflected in the epic, *Ramayana*. During the *Ramayana* times (400 B.C.-400 A.D.), great stress was laid upon caste distinctions (Wheeler, 1973:8). The conflict between Rama and Ravana is interpreted as "local conflicts between the agriculturists of the Ganges valley and the more primitive hunting and food-gathering societies of the Vindhyan region" (Thapar, 1966:33). The character of Rama is depicted as a protector of the Brahmans and an opponent of Buddhism. The known example is that Rama beheaded Shambuka, who did penance for the acquisition of merit. Rama had the purpose of destroying Ravana, who was a Buddhist sovereign (Wheeler, 1973:347) and Buddhists (Ibid.:233). Ravana is also believed to be a Dravidian king, the chief of the Raksasas, the aborigines, and the protector of his subjects. In the conflict, although Brahmins conquered the Buddhists, there is evidence of revering Ravana. Ravana is still worshipped in the Dravidian country and in a few villages in the North. On Vijayadashmi, the festival symbolising the victory of good over evil, the villagers in Ravana, a village named after Ravana in Netaran taluka of Vidisha district in Madhya Pradesh, worship the nine foot tall stone idol of Ravana installed there in the 12th century. People from the villages around Ravana assemble for the celebration (*The Times of India,* October 27, 1993, and *Loksatta*, Pune, October 25, 2001). An idol of Ravana is also worshipped in Mandsor of Madhya Pradesh, in Devadha near

Sultanganj of Bihar and in Fattehapur district of Uttar Pradesh (*Maharashtra Times*, Mumbai, October 22, 1985).

For the emergence of Buddha, Ambedkar draws attention to a few of the social evils of the Aryan community of the pre-Buddhism days. He mentions drinking Soma and Sura, gambling of honour and dignity, the drinking and dancing of the Aryan women, sexual immorality (e.g. Vashishta and Manu who married their own daughters, Shatrupa and Ila, respectively), the Yajna Bhumi (place of sacrifice) becoming an open ground for cohabitation and sexual intercourse, the practice of renting out women to others for a time (e.g. King Yayati gave his daughter, Madhvi, to his teacher, Galav, and thereafter to the kings), and, allowing women to have sexual intercourse with the Devas and Aryans of superior status and prowess for good breeding (Ambedkar, 1987: Vol.3, Chap.6). These social practices of the Aryans reveal that the Aryan religion was never concerned with a righteous life (Ibid.:176). Buddha, therefore, emerged as a reformer. He laid down five precepts for the laity: (i) not to kill, (ii) not to steal, (iii) not to lie, (iv) not to be unchaste, and (v) not to consume intoxicants. He denounced the *yajna* as a form of religion as well as the caste system and admitted low-caste men to the rank of Bhikku (priest).

Buddhism spread across several parts of India, but disappeared gradually. Ambedkar offered two main reasons for the fall of Buddhism. One was the invasion of the Muslims, who used their swords to massacre the Buddhist priests, and the other was the persecution of the Buddhist laity by the Brahmanic rulers, namely, Lalliya who founded the Brahmin Shahi dynasty (880-1021 c. A.D.) in Punjab, Jayapala (960-980 c. A.D.), Anandpal (980-1000 c. A.D.) and Trilochanpal (1000-1021 c. A.D.), who belonged to the Brahmanic faith (Ibid.:229-31). He cited the source of Vincent Smith for instances of persecution of the Jains in southern India in the 7th century and in Gujarat in the 12th century by Ajayadeva, a Saiva King (Ibid.:238).

The Revival of Brahmanism

The downfall of Buddhism is seen to coincide with the revival of Brahmanism in the post-Mauryan period. If Emperor Ashok promoted Buddhism as the religion of the state, Pushyamitra Sung (180-151 B.C.) ended the degradation of the Brahmans by destroying the Buddhist state (Ibid.:268). During the reign of Pushyamitra, the *Manusmriti* was promulgated, stated Ambedkar. Ambedkar regarded the *Manusmriti* as the institution of Brahmanism (Ibid.:271). He held Manu responsible for upholding the principle of gradation and rank in the caste system (Ibid.:25). It is through the prescriptions in *Manusmriti* that the religious, ritualistic and social life of all castes was governed.

In Ambedkar's view, Brahmanism brought about the following changes:

1. It established the right of the Brahman to rule and commit regicide.
2. It made the Brahmans a class of privileged persons.
3. It converted the *varna* into caste by making status and occupation hereditary.
4. It brought about a conflict and anti-social feeling between the different castes.
5. It degraded the Shudras and women.
6. It forged the system of graded inequality.
7. It made legal and rigid the social system, which was conventional and flexible.

Interestingly, Ambedkar stated facts contrary to the view that the Hindu civilisation is *sanatan* (unchanging). Brahmans have always changed things to suit their interests. The Vedic gods—Indra, Vishnu, Varuna, Mitra, Brahma—whom they worshipped in the Vedic times were abandoned when they started worshipping non-Vedic gods, including the Muslim Pirs (Ambedkar, 1987: Vol. 4, 5-6). Brahmans became temple priests, household ritual performers, etc., because they received offerings/gifts. He described this characteristic as faithless. This is why the Brahmans made priesthood their privilege. Hinduism is polytheistic unlike Islam, Judaism and Christianity, all monotheistic religions, "because the Hindu society has been formed by the conglomeration of many tribes and many communities each of whom had their own separate Gods" (Ibid.:79). Absorption has been a characteristic of Hinduism. The protest traditions of Buddhism, Jainism, the Bhakti movement, etc., and the traditions of little communities have been absorbed into it. For that, the idea of incarnation was also evolved, making Buddha, Krishna, etc., incarnations of Vishnu. According to Indologist, R.G. Bhandarkar, the *avataar*, incarnation, has always been assumed for destroying all the demons (Bhandarkar, 1982:50).

In his paper, Castes in India: Their Mechanism, Genesis and Development (1917), Ambedkar stated the thesis of the *superimposition of endogamy on exogamy* towards the creation of caste and observed the role of customs, viz., (i) *sati*, the burning of the widow on the funeral pyre of her husband, (ii) enforced widowhood, and (iii) child marriage, in preserving the caste endogamy. Ambedkar noted two socio-psychological characteristics of the hierarchical organisation of the caste system, which produced (i) a spirit of rivalry among the different castes for dignity, and (ii) an ascending scale of hatred and descending scale of contempt (Ambedkar, 1987: Vol. 4, p. 48). The segmentation of Indian society into castes has been brought about with a view to prevent united action by non-Brahmans to overthrow Brahmanism (Ibid.:304).

Ambedkar classifies Hindu society into four classes. The broader division he classifies into two, i.e. (i) caste Hindus and (ii) non-caste Hindus. Class I constitutes the privileged castes of Dvijas (i.e. Brahmins, Kshatriyas and Vaishyas), Class II, the low castes of the Shudras (i.e. peasants and artisans), Class III, the primitive as well as criminal tribes/castes and Class IV, the segregated untouchable castes (Ambedkar, 1989:167). In *The Untouchables* (1948/1990) Ambedkar advanced the Broken Men theory, tracing two roots of untouchability: (i) contempt and hatred of the Broken Men as of Buddhists by the Brahmans, and (ii) continuation of the eating of beef by the Broken Men after it had been given up by others. In support of his argument, he cited the source in *Mricchakatika*, a Sanskrit drama written in the 4th century A.D., and evidence of Chandragupta II (412 c. A.D.) who made cow killing a *Mahapataka*, a mortal sin. But his theory lies outside the consideration of the mainstream historians. For more details, in this volume, consult the chapter, The Broken Men Theory of Untouchability.

Besides religion and caste as categories of grouping in Indian society, gender is also an important category. Gender discrimination has been one of the distinctive features of Hindu society. In the later Vedic period, i.e. 900-500 B.C., women were not allowed to recite or listen to Vedic hymns. In the Buddha's time, the status of women was elevated by admitting them in the community of Bhikkus (priests) and allowing them to gain and impart religious knowledge. In ancient Hindu society, the injunctions of devotion, virtuousness and subordination to her husband were imposed on the wife, especially during the *Sriti* and *Smriti* periods. In the *smriti* period, they had no right to make offerings in a *yajna*. Also, they had no life as an ascetic. A woman was treated as untouchable due to her menstrual cycle. *Manusmriti* denied her the right to property. A woman was put in subservience to a man. For marriage, a woman had to be a virgin and, after marriage, she had to be loyal to her husband. In the notion of *kanyadaan*, giving a away daughter as a gift in a Hindu marriage, a woman is conceived of as an object, like property. In the traditional Hindu order, a woman is not viewed to be independent because she is protected in her childhood by her parents, after marriage by her husband and in her old age by her son. In Ambedkar's view, women have been seen as a means to preserve caste endogamy and, so, the Brahmans have introduced the practices of child marriage, *sati* and enforced widowhood. These practices are the characteristic features of a Brahmanic society.

The rules of endogamy, hereditary occupations and commensality within the social group are universal characteristics of any traditional society. As regards the Hindu society, the question is that of understanding the basis of social distinctions and the privileges enjoyed by the high castes and the number of social disabilities imposed on the lower castes. Indologist G.S. Ghurye attributes the idea of ceremonial purity to an exclusive social stratification (Ghurye, 1969:171). According to him, the first regulations began with the exclusion of the Shudras, the aborigines, from the religious worship developed by the Aryans. They forbade their presence in their sacrificial hall (Ibid.:172). To preserve their fair skin and cultural integrity, the Brahmans regulated endogamy (Ibid.:173). As Ghurye says: "Caste in India is a Brahmanic child of the Indo-Aryan culture, cradled in the land of the Ganges and the Jamna and thence transferred to other parts of the country" (Ibid.:176). Thus, the rules of purity and impurity were not only applied to treat the social groups of different physical, cultural and vocational traits hierarchically, but also to put restrictions on marital, social, occupational and other such relations also. In the *Rig Veda*, three classes, viz., Brahma, Kshatra and Visha, are mentioned. In Vedic times, there were no restrictions of commensality, marriage and following/adopting a vocation. We, therefore, find a number of mentions in pre-Buddhist literature of sages, namely, Vyas, Vasishtha and Valmiki, who were born in the lower classes. In Buddhist India, people could change their vocations. A Kshatriya could work as a potter, basket-maker, reed-worker, garland-maker or cook (Rhy-Davids, 1903:54-55). A Jain source informs that Sovaga, a Chandala by birth, visited the sacrificial enclosure of a Brahman teacher and lectured to him on certain values of life (Sharma, 1958:134).

In the *Manusmriti*, which came only in 200 A.D., the clear distinctions of the caste and regulation of the caste system are found manifested. But, ancient history scholar, Suvira Jaiswal pushes it to a much later period. According to her, "The emergence of endogamous subcastes within the brahman varna is a post-Vedic, presumably early medieval phenomenon" (i.e. 600 A.D.) (Jaiswal, 1998:157-8). Besides priestly activities as a source of the Brahmans' livelihood, many provisions were made in the *Manusmriti* for strengthening their economic position. Brahmans were exempted from taxes (X. 79), taking away property by the king was made impossible (IX. 189) and they were given the right of recovering their fees (X. 85). Being the lawgiver class, they recommended the gift of land to Brahmans as being a Mahadana, a great gift, for attaining spiritual merit and they became a class of landowners (Nath, 2001:23-24). And so they were landlords till the implementation of the land reform laws in post-Independent India.

Ambedkar perceived Hinduism as the modified form of ancient Brahmanism. He said that in Hinduism, there was no difference between law and ethics. Both are concerned with "regulating the conduct of the low class Hindus to *subserve* the ends of high-caste Hindus" (Ambedkar 1987, Vol.3:84). In this way, Ambedkar summarised Hinduism as serving the interests of the Brahman class at the centre. In the interest of the untouchables, he denounced Hinduism, which stood for inequality and oppression, and embraced Buddhism, which promoted knowledge, love, compassion, equality and morality. In the historical background, he justified conversion for the "self-respect and honour of the untouchables" (Ambedkar, 1989:412). For the emancipation of the untouchables, he did not see conversion as the only remedy and so he launched a struggle for obtaining for them social rights, educational attainment, and places in government administration and political power.

Movements against Brahmanism

To counter the dominance of Brahmanism, some religious and social traditions were developed in India. We have seen the emergence of Buddhism and Jainism as protest movements against the Vedic religion and practices of sacrifice. According to M. Monier-Williams, in the post-Buddha period, the founders of Vaishnavism and Shaivism and their followers imitated Buddha in requiring their followers to drop caste distinctions (Monier-Williams, 1877:57). Interestingly, the Rudra-Shiva is assumed to be the great God of the pre-Aryan settlers of the Indus Valley (Daweewarn, 1982:6). The Shaivites worship both the bull and the phallus. The tradition of worshipping both is non-Aryan and inherited from the Harappans (Wheeler, 1968:109). It is seen even today in South India. The revolt of the Brahman prime minister of Bijjala against Brahmanism in 1160 A.D. in the north Karnataka and south Maharashtra region is prominent. Basava (1131-67 A.D.) founded Veershaivaism, which rejects the authority of the *Vedas* and the doctrine of rebirth, objects to child marriage, approves of the remarriage of widows, and nurses an intense aversion to the Brahmans (Ibid., 1982:17). Basava not only preached equality of caste and sex, but also brought it into practice. He treated equally all Shaivaite untouchables. He did not believe in the Brahmanic notion of impurities. Veershaivaites, therefore, do not accept the impurities of birth, caste, menstrual cycle, death and remnant food. Basava considered women fit for entering the temple and worshipping the 'linga'. The 'linga' is not regarded as an idol. Basava criticised idol worship. He helped in bringing about an intercaste marriage between the daughter of a Brahman and the son of a cobbler. Basava gave dignity to labour and offered the freedom to follow any occupation to all individuals (including women). This is why, the Veershaivaites have taken up enterprising activities, rather than spiritual ones. Veershaivaism emphasised non-violence. The followers, therefore, are vegetarian. Basava approved of widow remarriage and he organised such marriages. A Lingayat widow could participate in all religious as well as social ceremonies and festivities. In his time, Basava gave women the freedom to form an association for spreading education and awakening political interest. Under his leadership, Nagalambika and Gangambika started a political movement. Veershaivaite women are also given the freedom to contribute earning to the household income by taking up any productive/industrial activity. Basava founded an association of individuals of different occupations (including untouchables' jobs) and professions. All these practices show how Veershaivaism developed distinctly from the Brahmanic religion of believing in caste based on birth, gender inequality, sacrifices (*yajna*), ritual purity, predetermined action (*karma*), etc. (Ghugare, 1995). On the whole, Basava was a social revolutionary of his times.

A long tradition of the Bhakti movement advocating social equality is widespread both in South and North India. The Bhakti concept is found in the *Bhagavad Gita* (about 467 A.D.) and is a movement of saints who emphasised the equality of all devotees, irrespective of caste and gender. The movement originated especially as a popular movement of protest against Brahmanism and the rigours of the caste system (Jaiswal, 2000:14). The Tamil Alvar saints belonged to the 6th century A.D. (Ibid.:15). They had non-Brahmanic origins, namely from the Appar, the Vellala and the peasant caste, and one amongst them was a Nandanar, a Parayan/Panar, an outcaste (Ibid.:18). It is noteworthy that most of the saints of the medieval and modern times belong to the Bhakti movement. They emerged from non-Brahman communities. Namdeo (14th c. A.D.) was a tailor from Maharashtra. Kabir (1440-1518 A.D.), the son of a Brahman widow, was nurtured and brought up by a Mohameddan weaver family. Kabir condemned the rites, ceremonies and other practices of the Brahmans (Bhandarkar, 1982:101). He is known for rejecting the caste system. He did not believe in the concepts of god, soul, reincarnation and rebirth. While comparing a donkey and a dog with a Brahman, a donkey carries a load and a dog serves its master honestly, but a Brahman does nothing, says Kabir in a couplet. There are references to Buddha, Mahaveera and Charvak in his couplets. Kabir had followers from all castes. In 1463, Kabir's disciple,

Dharam Das, a Bania, distributed eighteen lakh rupees in charity (Prakasam, 1998:60). Meerabai (15th c. A.D.), a Sisodia Rajput rebel, accepted Saint Ravidas, a cobbler, as her guru (teacher). She intermingled with male devotees and associated with lower caste people. Besides Namdeo, Kabir and Meerabai, the other non-Brahman saints were Dhana (a Jat peasant), Sena (a barber), Tukaram (a Maratha), Savata Mali (a gardener) and Chokhamela (a Mahar or untouchable). Among the saints, there were women too, viz., Andal in the Tamil country, Akkamahadevi in the Kannada country, Janabai and Soyarabai in Maharashtra, and Meerabai in Rajasthan. In the words of M.N. Srinivas: "The Bhakti movement of medieval India was really pan-Indian attracting a large number of men and women from the lower orders and it even crossed the religious divide between Hindus and Muslims as with Kabir and, much later, Shirdi Sai Baba" (Srinivas, 2003:459).

Guru Nanak, the founder of Sikhism, had come under the influence of the egalitarian philosophy of the 16 Hindu and Muslim saints and he incorporated their couplets in his *Guru Granth Sahib.* Guru Nanak was against idol worship, Brahmanic rites and caste distinctions. Brahmanic ideology undermines manual labour. Guru Nanak encouraged his followers to take up enterprising activities. The Sikh movement in the 16th century was initiated to bring about changes in the Brahmanic values. A tradition of *langar* (free community meals) and *pankit* (a line without caste distinction) at the Golden Temple in Amritsar is an example of practising equality. The temple is open to all, irrespective of caste, religion and gender. In Sikhism, there is absence of a priestly caste and the performers mostly belong to the middle castes. Women can also become priests. Guru Amar Das trained 146 persons to go out as priests and missionaries and of those, 52 were women. Sikhism facilitated a change in the character of caste structure, for instance, the Jats started practising intercaste marriages by accepting girls from lower castes (Judge, 2002:180-181).

Various religious movements continued their struggle against social inequality from the ancient times of the Buddha through the medieval and modern times of saints such as Kabir and Gadge Baba of Maharashtra, respectively. The leaders of these movements reacted against the notion of caste and gender hierarchy at the ideological level and tried to be equalitarian in practice at the individual level. But they faced the limitations of their times. The saints of the Bhakti movement, while rejecting Brahmanism, emphasised humanitarian and egalitarian values in their preachings, but they appealed to god. Since they had no action programme, it did not help much in bringing about a social change.

About the egalitarian order of Hindu society, the Hindus believed that it was ordained and so, unalterable. It was in the British regime that some non-Brahmans could have modern education, especially in the Christian missionary schools, and under the impact of rational thinking, a few rebels emerged to question birth-based inequality, offering the opinion that it was man-made, particularly by the Brahman priestly class in their self-interest. The non-Brahman leaders of the social reform movement, therefore, started not only attacking the Brahmans' authority and their *Shastras* in public meetings, but also adopted the action programme of breaking several rules of caste and gender customs.

The 19th and 20th centuries witnessed social protest/ reform movements in various parts of India. The movements of Ghasi Das in Chattisgarh, the Mahima Dharma in Orissa, Sri Narayan Guru in Kerala, Jotiba Phule and B.R. Ambedkar in Maharashtra, the Ad Dharam in Punjab, and the Namshudra in Bengal and the Adi Dravida and Periyar in Tamil Nad are some examples. These movements in the real sense have helped in elevating the social status of the non-Brahmans, especially intermediate and depressed castes. So it is necessary to take an overview of protest and reform movements launched by the leaders/revolutionaries of the times in their regions.

To improve the social status of the Chamars (cobblers), Ghasi Das, an ex-untouchable, initiated a movement between 1820 and 1830 in the Chattisgarh region. He was against idol worship. He threw away the idols of Hindu gods and goddesses. His followers gave up their traditional caste jobs, rejected the authority of the Brahmans, ignored Hindu festivals and resisted high-caste domination (Prakasam 1998:69-70). Ghasi's son, Balak Das, challenged the privilege of the high caste by travelling on elephants and horses (Ibid.:72). The Mahima Dharma (1826-76) in Orissa resisted the *varna* order and was developed as a counter to the Hinduisation of the upper-caste domination (Pati, 2001:4207). The Chamars in Punjab launched the Ad Dharm movement in the 1920s, rejecting their Hindu roots, and as many as 4,18,789 persons reported themselves as Ad Dharmis in the 1931 Census of Punjab. The conversion to Buddhism by B.R. Ambedkar and a million of his followers in Nagpur on 14th October, 1956, is an epoch making event in the history of the conversion movement. The conversions of a large number of ex-untouchables to Christianity and Sikhism are other examples of rejection of Hinduism. Religious conversions are described as redemptive (Omvedt, 2002:294). These conversions helped not only in registering a protest against Hinduism, but also in the formation of a distinct identity for obtaining freedom for development. However, it did not help end the age-old discrimination or assist the converts in entering the government administration and positions of power.

Jotirao Phule (1827-1890) was regarded a revolutionary thinker/activist who propounded non-Brahmanic thinking in the modern period. He viewed Brahmanism as a powerful system of oppression of the Shtrishudratishudra, i.e. women-peasants-untouchables. He reacted vehemently against the ordination of caste and the performance of rituals by Brahman priests, labelling it an occupation of mendacity, and their devised system of Hindu mythology. Prior to the spread of the Aryan culture of sacrifice, patriarchy and gradation of

Hindu society on the basis of the purity-impurity notion, there were the cults of worshipping Jotiba, Khandoba, Mhasoba and such other idols, which Phule calls the Assyrian culture of the earlier natives. He, therefore, expressed a desire for the reign of Mahabali, the Asura king, who ruled over the Malayala Nadu. Mahbali is revered as an icon of social justice and equality in Kerala even today. Thiru Onam, the festival of flowers, is celebrated in the spirit of Mahabali's reign of justice. Phule offered Sarvajanik Satyadharma, the universal religion of truth, a proclamation of equality of all men and women, as an alternative to Brahmanism. Besides, Phule saw education as the key to solve many socio-economic ills and adopted a programme of imparting education, especially to women and untouchables in the 1850s.

Chhatrapati Shahu (1874-1922) of the Karveer (Kolhapur in the southwest of Maharashtra) state is known as a great social revolutionary who spearheaded the struggle against Brahman bureaucracy. He was denied his claim as a Kshatriya for a Vedic recitation and was treated as a Shudra by his royal priest in October 1899. The incident shocked him. He decided to fight against the domination of Brahmans in education, administration and politics. He is known for his anti-untouchability crusade and regarded as the originator of the reservation policy for backward classes (including Muslims and native Christians), introduced on his birthday, 26th July, 1902, in his state services. In 1913, to end the monopoly of the Brahman priests, Shahu encouraged the Satyashodhak ideology of Phule by founding a Satyashodhak school to train non-Brahman priests in performing religious rituals. As a result, in the Karveer state, as many as 5,161 religious events were performed by non-Brahman priests in 1913 itself (Suryawanshi, 1984:473). Shahu abolished several ill practices, viz., untouchability, slavery, and the daily appearance of persons of criminal castes before the village police officer, bonded labour and dedicating girls to god. The caste system is characterised by the restrictions of marriage, occupational mobility and commensality. He took steps to remove all these. For social and national integration, in February 1918, he issued the order for intermarriages and took the initiative in bringing about intermarriages. He issued the notification permitting widows to remarry in July 1917. To end the exploitation of the peasants, he abolished the monopoly of the Kulkarnis, who were Brahmans and the village revenue officers. Shahu realised the importance of education and so he made primary education compulsory in his state. For girls' education, he founded separate schools for them. He encouraged girls in medical education as well. In the Karveer state, the number of educational institutions increased from 224 in 1894 to 559 in 1922 and the number of non-Brahman students both in college and high school increased five-fold (Pawar (ed.), 2001:597-8).

To demolish the domination of Brahmans in politics, Chhatrapati Shahu gave support to the non-Brahman movement and encouraged it in the Deccan in the early 1920s. A similar movement was started in southern India around 1892. There was not a single non-Brahman legislator in the Madras Legislative Council. In Madras, the Justice Party was founded on 20th November, 1916. Although the political representation to non-Brahman communities, including women, was the main item on the agenda of a non-Brahman movement conference held about then, other issues of education, including of women, intermarriage, forging a fraternity between non-Brahman communities, including Muslims, Christians, Adi Dravidas and other depressed classes, for both political and social purposes, were also discussed.

E.V. Ramasamy Periyar separately launched the Self-Respect Movement in 1925. He was an atheist, an upholder of Buddhism and a critic of Brahmanism. The Self-Respecters launched a movement against the sacred texts of Brahmanism, especially the *Ramayana*, an Aryan text because it signified the Aryan conquest over Ravana and the *Raksasas*, who were the earlier natives. Periyar and the Self-Respecters considered atheism, Buddhism and Islam as alternatives to Brahmanism.

They conceived of a new community, which they described as a Samadharmic society, where rights, claims and responsibilities would be equal. To devalue the status of Brahman priests, they called for a boycott at non-Brahman weddings and evolved a simple ritual to be performed either by a community elder or a Self-Respecter or a distinguished non-Brahman. They deliberately conducted marriages on days considered unholy by Hindus and at inauspicious hours. They also conducted intercaste marriages. For instance, a landlord married a woman from a *devadasi* family. To fight Brahmanism, Periyar emphasised a new relationship of mutuality and reciprocity of the Shudra non-Brahmins and the Adi Dravidas. The Self-Respecters redefined their gender concern. Penn-ina-nallar wrote an article, *Women's Depressed Status*, in the *Kudi Arasu* of April 22 and 29, 1928. In 1929, Periyar started an informal organisation for women in his house in Erode and ran a sort of home for deserted wives. In his article, *Masculinity Must Be Destroyed*, Periyar stated that the term 'masculinity' degraded women. He considered marriage a symbol of womanhood and the burden of motherhood, which made woman a property, a slave. He perceived the liberation of woman from the Brahmanic patriarchal dominance, in equal rights to property and authority in the household and outside, in motherhood as a choice and in granting divorce. He advocated birth control and opposed abortion. Periyar was critical of the wasteful expenditure on rituals, festivals and pilgrimages. Regarding the temple priest, the Brahmans had their hereditary claims. The practice of appointing a temple priest on a hereditary basis was done away with by passing an amendment to the Hindu Religious Act in 1970 by the Dravida Munnetra Kazhagam under chief minister K. Karunanidhi, the inheritor of Periyar's ideology (for details, see Geetha and Rajadurai, 1998).

In the non-Brahmanic religious traditions, viz., Buddhism, Jainism, Veershaivaism, Sikhism, etc., gender equality was not only normatively advocated, but also practised in certain spheres of life and relations. Some instances of the practised equality between men and women have already been given earlier. In the social reform tradition of the 19th century, reformers such as Raja Ram Mohan Roy, Justice M.G. Ranade, Maharshi Karve and Gopal Ganesh Agarkar took up the issues of the abolition of sati, allowing widow remarriage and banning child marriage. But in practice, Justice Ranade married a young girl and Maharshi Karve did not give admission to the sister of social reformer Maharshi Vitthal Ramji Shinde in his home for widows at Hingne near Pune because she belonged to the Maratha caste, lower than Brahmans. These instances show how their programmes of reform were narrowed down for their caste group (i.e. Brahmans). Justice Ranade had not become free from the impact of conservatism. But Mahatma Phule observed the roots of evil customs as the impact of Brahmanism and so he gave the call of unity of the Shtrishudratishudra, in which women, as a class of Shudras, were included, and appealed to the oppressed to reject Brahmanism. Like Phule, E.V. Ramasamy Periyar also deplored saw women's oppression in the Brahmanic society. Thus, both Phule and Periyar rejected Brahmanism and its practices.

In Maharashtra, some activist scholars who were influenced by the ideologies of Phule and Ambedkar developed the non-Brahmanic feminist perspective. It rejects the rule of caste, class and patriarchal domination and believes in the independent status of women. The perspective is developed to reinterpret the history of the institutions of caste, marriage, family and property. From this perspective, the bipolar notions of purity-impurity and superiority-inferiority have been seen as Brahmanic (Bhagwat and Pardeshi, 1998).

After independence, the intermediate/peasant castes dominated the state and other institutional power. This new elites started playing the role of Brahmanism in their areas by doing injustice, inflicting atrocities and observing discrimination in distributing the benefits of government policies and programmes to the members of SCs, STs, OBCs, nomadic tribes and Muslim minority. This experience has caused the rise and growth of the Bahujan Samaj Party in Uttar Pradesh and other states (see Pai, 2002).

Issues of Identity and Conversions

The notion of identity is important for several reasons. One, it involves the sense of belongingness of people to a territory/ country and, hence, it becomes a matter of right over means/ resources. Two, it relates to the culture which a group represents. Three, a group may have a linguistic identity. In this way, identity is associated to several things. So far as India is concerned, her identity is seen changed a number of times in the past. India in the past was known as Vedic India, Buddhist India, Hindu India and, today, Secular India. It shows that the identity of India was/is known by the religion/culture of her people. Thus, we do not find continuity of any one identity. The point is that social groups, which were 'given' a particular identity by others, were/are in quest of their identity. Since the identity of the people has changed, it calls for re-examining their history. Thus, the issue of identity is not important to those who belong to the dominant religion/society, but it is important to those who are 'broken' in their struggle. Ambedkar called untouchables 'broken men'. There are several such social groups in India, e.g. the denotified tribes in post-Independent India, who were/are branded the 'criminal tribes'. A brief account of both rejecting the identity given by the upper-caste Hindus and constructing/inventing an identity by the oppressed/suppressed/depressed is given below.

The people living in India have been called Hindus since the middle of the 6th century B.C. (Chaudhuri *et al*, 2003:xii). It is both in social and religious senses. For Hindus, Muslims and Christians are other. But, amongst the Hindus, since the Hindu religion has not created a feeling of brotherhood, caste is considered important for identification. Each caste group has its distinct identity and a distinct way of life determined by the

Brahmanic system. Since the members of several thousand castes were called Hindus, they were supposed to be entitled to the right to worship Hindu gods and goddesses in temples, the right to recitation of hymns, the right to Vedic performances, etc., and several civil rights besides. Although the members of the underprivileged castes were called Hindus, they were not allowed to enjoy religious and civil rights and they had to suffer from their caste disabilities, including such prominent figures as Shivaji Chhatrapati and Shahu Chhatrapati, who were denied their Kshatriya claims to the Vedic rites. The issue of caste identity was triggered for discovering the roots of those who were denied their rights and the rights of those earlier inhabitants, especially untouchable and Adivasi communities.

The earlier attempts of Shudra-Atishudra castes were to find their place within the Hindu social order. For that, there have been attempts for upward mobility by asserting claims to get the status of Kshatriya. Also, the untouchables had to fight for temple entry as well as for civil rights both in pre- and post-Independent India. In post-Independent India, the Shudra castes gave up the idea of assertion of Kshatriya daim since those have become the ruling castes in their regions. And the powerless castes and Adivasi communities sought the path of conversion. Lancy Lobo, in his paper (see in this volume), *Brahmanical Social Order and Christianity in India*, attributes the large-scale conversion of untouchables and Adivasis to the ill treatment that they received at the hands of the upper castes. When they met with failure in their attempts, they had to seek a solution in conversion to other religions, namely, Christianity, Islam and Buddhism. For instance, Ambedkar took the path of conversion because he saw no opportunity for liberation within Hinduism. Through his conversion to Buddhism on 14th October, 1956, the revival of Buddhism was seen as a protest to Hinduism. Interestingly, Ambrose Pinto describes 'conversion as subversion of hierarchy' and so he views the attacks on egalitarian religions from insecurity and imagined threats to the economic and sociai interests of the Hindutvavadis (see his essay in this volume). After conversion, naturally, they adopted a new religious identity. The self-respecting untouchables objected then to being called Harijans and Dalits. Those who embraced Buddhism were proud of being identified/recognised as Buddhists.

But the Hindutva activists, rejecting their aboriginal status, call the Adivasis as Vanwasis, forest dwellers. The tribals adopted the identity of Adivasi with the formation of the militant Adivasi Mahasabha in 1938. In this identity, there is an assertion that they are the original inhabitants of the country.

Apart from the attempts at developing alternatives to Hinduism, the development of independent religious ideologies helped many others find a religious identity of their own. The followers of Jainism held the Jain identity. The development of Sikhism culminated in Kahn Singh Nabha declaring in 1899 that "we are not Hindus" and formed the identity of the Sikhs as distinct from the Hindus. There are status groups among the Sikhs, but Sikhism does not grant those by birth. To undermine caste distinctions, between 1880 and 1920, the leaders of the Singh Sabha movement encouraged the people to replace clan names with village names.

Thus, when the identity given to them by others within the Hindu framework is not seen as acceptable, self-respecting members of the non-Hindu communities have developed a self-constructed identity for themselves. The new identity held by the members of caste/tribe/religion group represents a new spirit of egalitarian values.

The above discussion on the course of history since pre-Vedic times reveals that there have been conflicts in intermittent or in silent form between the proponents and the opponents of Brahmanism. The Vedic religion is characterised by sacrificing animals to the fire to maintain the purity of the altar, the chanting of Vedic hymns by the Brahman priests and the perpetuation of graded classes. In the Vedic times, the earlier inhabitant Raksasas, the Licchavi Mahaveer and the Shakya Gautama opposed the sacrifices. During Ashok's time, Brahmanism was paralysed. But Pushyamitra Sung revived Brahmanism and a lot of literature was produced to rule over the Shudratishudra classes. We have a long tradition of the Bhakti movement preaching equality till yesterday. Today, the role of social reform movements in social transformation has been recognised. And, since Phule's time, the resistance has taken a shape and the representation of lower castes in national politics, especially the rise of the Bahujan Samaj Party of the Bahujans in the northern states, has been described as 'India's silent revolution' (Jaffrelot, 2003). This struggle is continued with the adoption of new identities such as Dalit, Buddhist and Adivasi, which contain both a sense of egalitarian values and a spirit of assertion. In the essay, *Decoding Dalitism: Reflections on Dalit Literature in Maharashtra*, S.P. Punalekar perceives the Dalit as a category 'to dismantle hegemony of the ruling ideas of the socially entrenched groups and classes'.

Prominent in the movements of Phule, Shahu, Periyar and Ambedkar against Brahmanism were the issues of caste and gender discrimination as well as the issue of representation in government. From the early decades of the 20th century, as the non-Brahman movement viewed power politics as being on top of its agenda, the real issue of fighting against Brahmanism was relegated to the background, resulting in the disunity of non-Brahmans. Consequently, the dominant castes gradually joined the Hindutva politics in post-Independent India and the sole section of untouchable castes were left fighting against the discriminatory practices adopted by both the upper as well as intermediate castes in social life, politics and administration. The problem is that the peasant, artisan, untouchable and Adivasi communities belong to the oral tradition and they have become the victims of the written tradition.

The Relevance of the Non-Brahmanic Perspective

The present knowledge of history, religion, culture and society, which has been produced and disseminated, is quite one-sided. In this respect, some observations can be mentioned here. S.M. Michael's paper, *Conversion, Empowerment and Social Transformation*, draws attention to the Brahmanic/Sanskritic world-view of G.S. Ghurye, N.K. Bose and RSS historians, who captured the diversity of cults, deities and practices of the Shudratishudras and Adivasis under the rubric of Hinduism and termed them the Sanskritic Hindus and the biggest converters in India. Surinder Jodhka, in his paper, *Nation, Anthropology and the Village* (in this volume), has undertaken a review of 'mainstream Indian sociology', which, produced by the Brahmans, offers a biased view emphasising the unity and solidarity of all social groups within a village, and adds Ambedkar's realistic view of a village as the site of caste oppression. Some social scientists broadly categorised Indian traditions as great and little. For example, the mother goddess, which is worshipped by all in every village, has been regarded a part of little tradition. It means the scholars of Indian religions and social history perceived the development of Buddhism and such other sects, the Bhakti traditions and local traditions of the masses as parts of the broader Hinduism and ignored the dimension of opposition in a variety of forms and a history of value conflict. It shows that what is practised by the upper castes becomes a matter of great tradition and the rest, of little tradition. Padma Velaskar, in her paper, *Educational Stratification, Dominant Ideology and the Reproduction of Disadvantage in India*, argues that the dominant ideology of the upper castes and classes have restricted the hopes of equal opportunity of the socially oppressed people and maintained the heights of elitism in education. In his paper, *Confronting Caste Inequality*, Satish Deshpande is critical of joining the anti-Mandal stance by sociologists and the failure of Indian sociology to address the issue of caste inequality in terms of policy perspectives. And based on the data of the NSSO 55th Round and Santosh Goyal's study (1992) on social inequality, Deshpande argues that the sharp caste inequalities have continued in contemporary India. Thus, the hegemony of the upper and the dominant caste Hindus is a challenge to both scholars and socio-political activists of radical ideas to thwart the mainstream ideology.

The distinctive features of the non-Brahmanic perspective can be summed up as under:

1. The perspective has a basis in the philosophy of humanitarian and egalitarian religions such as Buddhism, in the preachings of the saints of the Bhakti movement, Phule's Sarvajanik Satyadharma (universal religion of truth) and the like.
2. It helps in understanding social forces in the struggle against Brahmanism.
3. It focusses on the examination and analysis of social inequalities and the impact of practices on the continuity/ marginalisation of social groups in other fields of life.
4. It is useful to identify the oppressed/depressed sections of society as the result of the creation and maintenance of hierarchical order based on caste and gender.
5. It seeks the binary domains of knowledge of the Brahman and the non-Brahmanic traditions.
6. It provides the framework for understanding the participation of actors across caste, religion, gender in an action and the programme of anti-caste, the programme against gender discrimination, etc.
7. It assumes the continuity of relatively non-discriminatory/egalitarian practices.
8. It believes in the truth of age-old myths, oral traditions also as sources for interpreting history.
9. It believes in the unity of oppressed untouchables, Adivasis, Muslims, Christians, denotified and nomadic communities.

References

Ambedkar, B.R., 1987, *Dr. Babasaheb Ambedkar, Writings and Speeches*, Vol. 3, Mumbai: Government of Maharashtra.

—, 1987, *Dr. Babasaheb Ambedkar, Writings and Speeches*, Vol. 5, Mumbai: Government of Maharashtra.

—, 1989, *Dr. Babasaheb Ambedkar, Writings and Speeches*, Vol. 4, Mumbai: Government of Maharashtra.

—, 1990, *Dr. Babasaheb Ambedkar, Writings and Speeches*, Vol. 7, Mumbai: Government of Maharashtra.

Bhagwat, Vidyut, and Pardeshi, Pratima (eds.), 1998, *Abrahmani Strivadi Itihaslekhanachya Dishene* (Marathi), Pune: Women's Studies Centre, University of Pune.

Bhandarkar, R.G., 1982, *Vaisnavism, Saivism and Minor Religious Systems*, Pune: Bhandarkar Oriental Research Institute.

Chaudhuri, Nirad C., Biardeau, Madeleine, Pocock, D.F., and Madan, T.N., 2003, *The Hinduism Omnibus*, New Delhi: Oxford University Press.

Daweewarn, Dawee, 1982, *Brahmanism in South-East Asia (From the Earliest Time to 1445 A.D.)*, New Delhi: Sterling Publishers Pvt. Ltd.

Geetha, V., and Rajadurai, S.V., 1998, *Towards a Non-Brahmin Millennium: From Iyothee Thass to Periyar*, Kolkata: Samya.

Geetha, V., 1999, 'Gender and the Logic of Brahminism: Periyar and the Politics of the Female Body' in Sangari, Kumkum, and Chakravarty, Uma (eds.), *From Myths to Markets: Essays on Gender*, New Delhi: Manohar Publications.

Ghugare, S.B., 1969, *Veerashaivaism in India*, Gadhinglaj (Kolhapur district): Veerabasappa Balasaheb Ghugare.

Ghurye, G.S., 1969, *Caste and Race in India*, Mumbai: Popular Prakashan.

Jaiswal, Suvira, 1998, *Caste*, New Delhi: Manohar Publications.

—, 2000, 'Change and Continuity in Brahmanical Religion with Particular Reference to Vaisnava Bhakti', *Social Scientist*, Vol. 29, May-June.

Jaffrelot, Christophe, 2003, *India's Silent Revolution*, Delhi: Permanent Black.

Judge, Paramjit, 2002, 'Religion, Caste, and Communalism in Punjab', *Sociological Bulletin*, 51 (2), September.

Keer, Dhananjay, 1971, Dr. Ambedkar: Life and Mission, Mumbai: Popular Prakashan (Reprint 1991).

Kosambi, D.D., 1964, The Culture and Civilisation of Ancient India in Historical Outline, New Delhi: Vikas Publishing House Pvt. Ltd. (Reprint 2001).

Misra, Padma, 1978, Evolution of the Brahman Class, Banaras Hindu University, Sanskrit Series, Vol. VIII.

Monier-Williams, M., 1877, *Hinduism*, Kolkata: Susil Gupta (India) Ltd. (Reprint 1951).

Nath, Vijay, 2001, 'From Brahmanism to Hinduism: Negotiating the Myth of the Great Tradition', *Social Scientist*, Vol. 29, March-April.

Omvedt, Gail, 2002, 'Ambedkar and After: The Dalit Movement in India' in Shah, Ghanshyam (ed.), *Social Movements and the State*, New Delhi: Sage Publications.

Pai, Sudha, 2002, *Dalit Assertion and the Unfinished Democratic Revolution: The Bahujan Samaj Party in Uttar Pradesh*, New Delhi: Sage Publications.

Pati, Biswamoy, 2001, 'Identity, Hegemony, Resistance: Conversions in Orissa, 1800-2000', *Economic and Political Weekly*, November 3.

Pawar, Jayasingrao (ed.), 2001, Rajarshi Shahu Smarak Grantha (Marathi), Kolhapur: Maharashtra Itihas Prabhodhini.

Prakasam, Gnana, 1998, Social Separatism—Scheduled Castes and the Caste System, Jaipur: Rawat Publications.

Ramaswamy, Sumathi, 2001, 'Remains of the Race: Archaeology, Nationalism, and the Yearning for Civilisation in the Indus Valley', *The Indian Economic and Social History Review*, 38(2).

Rhy-Davis, T.W., 1903, *Buddhist India*, Delhi: Motilal Banarasidas (Indian Reprint 1997).

Sharma, R.S., 1903, *Sudras in Ancient India*, New Delhi: Allied Publishers Pvt. Ltd.

Shendge, Malati J., 1977, *The Civilized Demons: The Harappans in Rigveda*, New Delhi: Abhinav Publications.

—, 1996, *The Aryans: Facts without Fancy and Fiction*, New Delhi: Abhinav Publications.

Srinivas, M.N., 2003, 'An Obituary on Caste as a System', *Economic and Political Weekly*, February 1-7.

Suryawanshi, K.G., 1984, *Rajarshi Shahu Raja va Manus* (Marathi), Pune: Thokal Prakashan.

Thapar, Romila, 1966, *A History of India*, Vol.1, New Delhi: Penguin Books (Reprint 1990).

Tilak, B.G., 1903, *The Arctic Home in the Vedas* (Reprint 1956), Pune: Tilak Bros.

Trautmann, Thomas R., 1997, *The Aryans and British India*, New Delhi: Vistaar Publications.

Wheeler, J. Talboys, 1973, India of the Brahmanic Age: With Reference to the Ramayana, Vol. II of the *History of India*, Part-I, New Delhi: Cosmos Publications.

Wheeler, Sir Mortimer, 1968, *The Indus Civilization*, London: Cambridge University Press.

2

Understanding Indian Society

The Relevance of the Perspective from Below

T.K. Oommen

Indian society is the product of a long and complex historical process. The seven major events that contributed to the formation of this process are the Aryan advent, the emergence of the Indian 'protest' religions—Jainism, Buddhism, and Sikhism, the entry of non-Indic religions into the sub-continent as immigrant religions, the Muslim conquests, western colonialism, the anti-colonial freedom struggle and the partition of the Indian sub-continent in 1947 on the eve of the British exit (Oommen, 1998:229-40). The product of this long process is a four-in-one society.

Like all societies, Indian society too is stratified based on age, gender, rural-urban differences and class, but unlike many of them, Indian society is marked by considerable cultural heterogeneity, too, particularly because of a large number of speech communities, counting more than 1,500, including some 680 tribal communities. But India's religious plurality, complicated by the uneasy co-existence of religions of Indic and non-Indic origin, is a rare phenomenon in most contemporary societies. However, what is unique to India is the all pervasive caste hierarchy, legitimised through the Hindu doctrine of *karma* and reincarnation.

As one observes the complex structure called Indian society at the turn of the century, four major trends of social transformation are in evidence (Oommen, 1998:229-40). First, a transitional trend from *cumulative to dispersed dominance.* If status, wealth and power were earlier concentrated in the hands of the twice-born caste Hindus—Brahmin, Kshatriya and Vaishya—accounting for a mere 15 to 20 percent of the population, now there is an incipient trend towards dispersal of political power to the Other Backward Classes (OBCs), Scheduled Castes (SCs) and Scheduled Tribes (STs), together constituting the vast majority of the Indian population. This is the result of the universal adult franchise introduced in India with the arrival of independence.

In addition to the dispersal of political power there is also a limited dispersal of wealth among the above categories, heralding the birth of a middle class among them. But the reasons for the emergence of this middle class vary across these categories. The policy of protective discrimination as in reserving seats in educational institutions and government service are primarily responsible for the emergence of a bourgeoisie among the SCs and STs. The Kulaks among the OBCs are a product of agrarian reforms, which abolished absentee landlords and transferred land to the tenants and sharecroppers drawn from among them, and the Green Revolution, which provided subsidised inputs and assured minimum prices for agricultural products to owner cultivators.

The changes in power and wealth are not matched by a change in status, that is weakening of the importance of the ritual dimension. Inter-dining, inter-marriage and social interaction between the twice-born and the SCs are still rare, particularly in rural areas. This results in status incongruence, that is their upward mobility in wealth and power is not matched by mobility in status. In the case of the OBCs, status incongruence results from their low representation in the higher echelons of bureaucracy and professions even as they become politically powerful.

The second major trend in social transformation manifests in the gradual movement from *hierarchy to equality*, resulting in the decline of traditional collectivism and the emergence of individualism. With the emergence of individualism, the salience of traditional collectivities manifested through joint family, *jati*, village, etc., are relegated to the background. While there is no neat and tidy displacement of collectivism by individualism, the birth of the Indian individual is clearly in evidence. I am stressing this point because conventional wisdom upheld the view that individuals do not exist in Indian society unless one becomes an ascetic (Dumont, 1970). This is not true any more.

The third important trend in social transformation in India is the *simultaneous demands for equality and the assertion of collective identity*. The Indian Constitution unambiguously assured equality and, concomitantly, social justice to all individuals, irrespective of caste, creed or class. Initially, most of the traditionally disadvantaged groups believed that the implementation of the constitutional promise would follow automatically and the maintenance of their group identity would become irrelevant. At any rate, the stigma associated with their identity prompted them to abandon it and plumb for assimilation, as the process of sanskritisation implied. But gradually it dawned on them that individual equality *per se* would not emancipate them and they needed to re-invent dignity in their collective identity. Expressions such as Dalits and Adivasis in the place of Scheduled Castes and Scheduled Tribes clearly point to this trend.

While the Constitution does not clearly recognise identities based on religion, caste, language and tribe, it does not completely overlook these identities either, if these are disadvantageous to the collectivities concerned. This ambiguity is evident both from the constitutional provisions and the administrative measures as exemplified in the special rights conceded to religious minorities (e.g. upholding their civil codes), the policy of reservation in the case of SCs and STs, the recent steps taken to provide representation to OBCs and women in selected contexts, the special treatment extended to tribal communities and the linguistic reorganisation of Indian states as administrative units. All these steps have inevitably given fillip to the relevant collectivities to assert their identity when it pays off.

The fourth transition that I am referring to is the movement from a *plural society to pluralism* (Oommen, 1997(a):259-71). A plural society, as initially conceptualised by J.S. Furnivall (1948), alludes to an arrangement in which different social and cultural segments uneasily co-exist, interacting in the economic context, but prohibiting legitimate transfusion of blood (inter-marriages) or transmission of culture. This arrangement prevailed within the Hindu society through the operation of the jajmani system for centuries. Latterly, the twice-born castes interact with the OBCs and SCs both in the political and economic contexts, but have very limited interaction in the socio-cultural contexts. This description also fits in with the mode of interaction which prevails between Hindus, particularly the upper castes, and those who profess the non-Indic religions in the rural areas.

I suggest that the four trends of change that I have listed, namely the movement from cumulative to dispersed dominance; from hierarchy to equality and the consequent birth of individualism; the simultaneous demand for equality and identity and the gradual transition from a plural society to pluralism (the dignified co-existence of different socio-cultural segments as equals in the polity) have tremendous methodological implications for the study of Indian society. However, I do not propose to discuss all these dimensions, but shall confine my attention to those which are relevant for the present theme, namely the perspective from below.

The 'view from below' is an old and persisting issue in social science, particularly in sociology and social anthropology. But concomitant to the emergence of the traditionally oppressed and stigmatised collectivities as partially emancipated and empowered ones, their conventional silence is being replaced by audible new voices. In turn, the need for their representation in the process of knowledge production is grudgingly being recognised. That is, the very framing of the issues and terms of discourse have changed over time. The demand for a perspective from below is an indication of this massive change in society. If earlier, those who occupied the bottom of society were invisible due to the cognitive blackout perpetuated by upper caste, middle class, urban, male researchers, today, they are in full view and demand their legitimate share of representation in the production and representation of knowledge.

All societies have their bottoms. Thus, the bottoms of societies which are homogenous and merely stratified are occupied by women, youth and the proletariat. These categories have questioned the knowledge produced by their counterparts—men, adults and the bourgeoisie. Over a period of time, the specific role of each of these disadvantaged categories has come to be recognised in the production of knowledge.

In the case of culturally heterogeneous societies, if the constituted segments are unequal, either because they are numerically small or economically weak or culturally 'backward' or all of these, the tendency is to ignore them in the representations of reality. There are numerous instances when these ignored or marginalised communities demand to be represented in the process of knowledge production. A familiar example in India is the neglect of the numerous less developed linguistic communities. Their emerging identity assertions are also indicative of the clamour for their representation in the context of knowledge production.

In plural societies, the unrepresented bottom categories are invariably viewed as outsiders to the society, as in the case of followers of the non-Indic religions in India. Voices of protest from them have gradually led to the provision of space for their experience in the context of knowledge production. For example, the distinctiveness of religious minorities is increasingly recognised in studies of sociology and social anthropology in India.

The bottom layer in hierarchical societies is constituted by the cumulatively deprived sections of society. Unlike women, youth, proletariat, culturally backward or alien segments, which are deprived in one of the contexts, the cumulatively deprived are subjected to multiple deprivations. They are found only in hierarchical societies. The ex-untouchables of India afford an ideal example of this category of bottom.

For the reasons listed above, I shall confine my attention to the most 'oppressed bottom' found in hierarchical societies. It is also necessary to indicate here what the perspective from below is not. First, the view from below should not be confused for the study of other cultures, the conventional avocation of anthropologists (Beteille, 1964). Anthropologists did not consider other cultures, at least by definition, as inferior, but only as different. It is another matter, however, that the colonial context in which anthropology was practised did create an inferior-superior dichotomy between native tribes and western anthropologists. However, once the native anthropologists started investigating their co-citizens, who were tribals, this dichotomy became irrelevant. At any rate, the rise of anthropologists from the tribal communities rendered redundant the original distinctiveness of anthropology as a discipline which studied other cultures.

The specificity of anthropological 'method' is the distinction between the etic and emic approaches, both of which entailed the technique of participant observation, which is often mystified (Oommen, 1969:809-15). But the demystification of participant observation was bound to happen when anthropologists started investigating their own societies. The point of interest for the present is that in hierarchical societies, anthropologists drawn from the upper castes were invariably reluctant to 'participate' at the bottom rung of the society, given the norms and values associated with the practice of untouchability. Should an effort to participate in the life-world of the untouchables be made by a *savarna* anthropologist, it will be disapproved, not only by his own *jati* peers, but also by the untouchables themselves given the grip of the doctrine of *karma* and reincarnation on them.

Even the distinction between the etic and emic approaches remained problematic. The etic approach identified and studied social reality independently of the natives' cultural judgements. The emic view, in contrast, is an insider's view. However, there can also be different emic views in so far as different cultural segments within a society have their own constructions of social reality and value orientations about them. The researcher should not appropriate the monopoly of defining the people, nor can he uncritically endorse the self-definitions advanced by the people. Having said this, I should insist that self-conceptualisations such as Dalits are emancipatory as contrasted with terms such as exterior castes, *panchamas*, Harijans, scheduled castes, etc. We need to use double hermeneutics to incorporate both the emic and the etic perspectives.

The different cultural segments in heterogenous societies may have differing insiders' views. Further, the lack of co-terminality between political boundaries and cultural boundaries creates problems. This is exemplified in the difference between an Indian Bengali anthropologist studying the Bengali society spread across India and Bangladesh and his investigating the Tamil society, spread across India and Sri Lanka. While in West Bengal, he is both a political and cultural insider (that is a citizen and a national), in Bangladesh, he is a cultural insider (national), but a political outsider (non-citizen). In Tamil Nadu, he is a political insider (citizen), but a cultural outsider (non-national), and in Sri Lanka, he is both a political and a cultural outsider (non-citizen and non-national) (for an exemplification of these concepts, see Oommen, 1997(b)). It is difficult to believe that these differing identities of the investigator will not affect the process of investigation. But yet, it is important to insist that the etic-emic distinction be an insider-outsider distinction and *not* an inferior-superior distinction.

Second, the perspective from below should not be confused for the much-heralded subalternist perspective. Subalternists focussed their attention on the circles of elite politics and have emphasised the insurrectionary activities and potential of the subaltern classes (artisans, poor peasants and landless labourers, which are essentially economic categories), who, according to them, possessed self-conscious and coherent conceptions of resistance that were directed against rich peasants, urban traders/merchants or the colonial revenue administrators. Subalternists claim to have unfolded the incapacity of nationalist historiography to incorporate the voices of the weak into the project of history writing (Guha and Spivak (eds.), 1988).

The setting for subaltern history was provided by colonial India and the freedom struggle. If nationalist historians were macro-holists who ignored the 'voices from below', subalternists are micro-individualists who missed the view from above (Oommen, 1985). But both confined their attention to different dimensions of and the actors involved in the freedom struggle. The perspective from below goes much beyond this. It focusses on the implications of the nature of social structure and the location of the researcher in the process of production of knowledge. Hierarchy, as a feature of Indian society, existed much before colonialism arrived and the freedom struggle started.

Third, the view from below is different from the proletarian, feminist or generational perspective. Class in the sense of social gradations exist in all societies and there are no immutable boundaries between classes. Both embourgeoisement and proletarianisation are perennial possibilities. Indeed, de-classing has been advocated and successfully attempted by many investigators. There was a time, say in the 1960s, when the widespread belief prevailed that the youth alone had the capacity to cognise truth; those above 30 were adjudged to be incapable of perceiving truth (Feuer, 1969).

The extremists among feminists seem to take the view that only women can understand and analyse issues concerning women. The corollary of this is that only men can understand their problems. Even as one concedes the existence of differences between men and women, those who belong to the same class within a society and share the same culture have many things in common, irrespective of gender differences. But as I have noted, the above differences based on class, age groups and gender exist in all societies, including homogeneous societies. And, both age groups and sex groups are distributed across classes. To a large extent, the method *verstehen* advocated by Max Weber will help one to cope with the problem.

Fourth, in plural societies, the segments, even when they are equals, remain cultural strangers. That is, even as they interact in the economic and political contexts which result in interdependence, culturally, they are insulated. To the extent socio-cultural insulation persists, hostility could develop between them. But they could be, and they often are, equals. What strangers suffer from is stigmatisation. Following Simmels' (1950) notion, one can even accept the advantages of doing research among strangers. The point I want to make for the present is that the perspective from below is the specific need of hierarchical societies, such as that of India, wherein the society is so tightly compartmentalised that one segment cannot penetrate into the other.

Having said the above, I need to add a caveat here. If one were to take a position that there is no possibility of an outsider ever investigating a segment of society to which he does not belong, then each segment will have to produce its own set of researchers. This will leave some segments uninvestigated for ever. For example, who will study children, invalids, imbeciles or insane people? At any rate, there is an advantage for those segments which can be studied by its own representatives and by outsiders also. None of these preclude the need to have a perspective from below.

The need for a perspective from below is inextricably interlinked with the hierarchical nature of societies such as those of India. All the available evidence suggests that Indian sociologists and social anthropologists, predominantly drawn from the twice-born caste Hindus, at least until recently, have largely neglected the social realities of the lowly placed and oppressed—the OBCs and the SCs. This is not simply a matter of praxiological aberration, but also that of a theoretical blackout.

I propose to pursue this argument invoking the first presidential address to the All India Sociological Conference held in 1955 delivered by D.P. Mukherji. There are several reasons why this address is used as a case in point. First of all, it happens to be the first presidential address. Secondly, D.P. Mukherji was not aligned with or sympathetic to the Hindutva ideology. Thirdly, many thought that he was a Marxist, although he preferred to call himself a Marxiologist. Fourthly, there was no doubt that he was a 'modernist' and a 'progressive'.

In his address, which was pregnant with fertile ideas, Mukherji insisted that it was not enough that an Indian sociologist be a sociologist, but that he be an Indian first. And how do sociologists acquire Indianness? By situating himself in Indian lore, both high and low. But, "unless sociological training in India is grounded in Sanskrit, or any such language in which the traditions have been embodied as symbols, social research in India will be a pale imitation of what others are doing" (Mukherji, in Saksena, 1961:23). Although Mukherji wanted sociologists to be familiar with Indian lore, both high and low, he thought that our traditions were embodied in Sanskrit. There are several problems with this advocacy.

First, only the twice-born caste Hindus were allowed any access to Sanskrit, in which the traditional texts of knowledge were written. By insisting that Sanskrit be the route through which Indian sociologists could cultivate originality, Mukherji was narrowing the recruitment base of Indian sociologists. Second, by the time education became a constitutional possibility for the vast majority of Indians, Sanskrit ceased to be a live language. Which is to say, if one is not traditionally privileged to learn Sanskrit, he can scarcely have the opportunity to learn it. Third, the reference to 'such other languages' may be an allusion to Pali and Tamil, but does it include Persian, too? If indeed all the four languages—Sanskrit, Pali, Tamil and Persian—are under reference, one cannot talk of tradition in the singular, for indeed, there is a multiplicity of traditions in India.

Fourth, even if one takes such an accommodative view, still all the traditions under reference are Great Traditions. And, the traditions of the vast majority of the people of India are Little Traditions, confined to folk regions. No sociologist can afford to neglect this rich variety of traditions if he wishes to be called authentic. In fact, there is greater possibility of cultivating sociological originality by familiarising oneself with these grassroot and ground realities. Fifth, it is difficult to comprehend why training in sociology grounded in Sanskrit and/or other such languages can inform sociology of originality. By Mukherji's prescription, an overwhelming majority of Indian sociologists are pale imitators. On the other hand, those handful of Sanskrit-knowing sociologists hardly demonstrated any originality; they invariably indulged in exegetical analyses. In turn, this blurs the distinction between Indology and sociology.

Mukherji, in his presidential address entitled, *Indian Sociology and Tradition*, made another curious observation pertinent to the present discussion. He said: "All our *Shastras* are sociological." There is an interesting link between the need to anchor a sociologist's training in knowledge of Sanskrit and the observation that the *Shastras* are sociological because the latter are in Sanskrit. But, a few uncomfortable facts may be noted here.

First, *our* in the observation stands for Hindus. But Indian sociology cannot be equated with Hindu sociology for the simple reason that one out of every eight Indians is a non-Hindu. Second, Hindu sociology necessarily implies Muslim sociology, Buddhist sociology and the like, the very antithesis of sociology as a humanistic and encapsulating enterprise.

Third, *our* does not stand even for all Hindus, the majority of the Hindu population (the OBCs and SCs) have no role in the making of these *Shastras* and they are treated as congenital inferiors by twice-born Hindus. In fact, the *panchamas*, those of the fifth order (the untouchables) are not even accounted for in the 'Chaturvarna' theory which deals with the Hindu doctrine of creation. Not only that, the *Shastras* also assign a marginal position to the women of even the twice-born Varnas. To put it pithily, the *Shastras* privilege upper-caste males and treat the vast majority of Hindus as inferiors. Can they be sociological? Sociology cannot ignore the experiences of any segment in society much less treat them as inferior. The mission of sociology is all embracing and ought to be humanistic.

While the *Shastras* are theological, they cannot be sociological. Theology deals with the issues of 'ought'. The concern of sociology is primarily with 'is'. That is, the *Shastras* are prescriptive and normative. True, sociology cannot ignore the normative and it should take into account the 'ought', but its primary concern is with reality as it exists and operates in society. To anchor Indian sociology to the Hindu *Shastras* is to undermine sociology's secular and humane foundations. Finally, I may recall here that Dr. B.R. Ambedkar, in his debates with M.K. Gandhi in the 1930s, insisted that only if the *Puranas* and *Shastras* and all scriptures that supported caste (i.e. inequality and injustice) were disowned, could he call himself a Hindu. As is well known, the challenge was not admissible to caste Hindus and Ambedkar embraced Buddhism in 1956.

Indeed the 'book-view' of sociology in India was/is excessively in favour of projecting the view from above. To counter this, the field-view would have been greatly helpful if executed with care. But that was not to be. Almost all field studies in sociology and social anthropology until recently were undertaken from the perspective of twice-born middle class Hindus. For example, there is hardly any study of a village, a much celebrated theme in Indian sociology, which views the village reality from the perspective of a Cheri, Maharwada or Chamar Mohalla. And, in field studies as in texts those below the pollution line are designated as Chandals, Mlecchas, exterior castes, untouchables etc., if they are referred to at all. Even designations such as Scheduled Castes preferred by the state and Harijan coined by Narasinh Mehta and propagated by M.K. Gandhi are not acceptable to them. That is, the very labelling of these categories has been debilitating and stigmatising. The compelling need for a view from below will have to be situated in this context.

But let it be noted here that the bottom layer of Indian society itself is no more uniform and homogenous. The upwardly mobile, urban educated Dalit elite are qualitatively different from the cumulatively dominated rural, illiterate, economically stagnant Dalits. While it is the rise of the former which eventuated in the plea for giving proper space to the voice of the latter, the embourgeoisement of the urban Dalit elite should not be allowed to endanger the cause and interests of the cumulatively oppressed rural Dalits. That is, the perspective from below is the epistemological privilege of the cumulatively oppressed. Those who are incorporated into the establishment often get disembeded from their roots.

It is time that I indicated the theoretical foundation of the approach designated as the 'perspective from below'. If experience and knowledge are inextricably interlinked in social science, then the location of the knowledge producer, the researcher, in social structure is crucial from the perspective of production of knowledge. That is, the perspective from below is necessitated by to the politics of location. The process of production of knowledge and the advantages and disadvantages emanating out of one's location in the social structure are inevitably linked. One can dismiss this formulation as excessively ideological, indeed political, and hence harmful to the generation of 'objective' knowledge, only at the cost of ignoring the quality of knowledge produced. And the proof of the quality of knowledge is in its content and orientation.

There has been a cognitive black-out in Indian social science, at least until recently, as far as knowledge regarding the life-world experiences of Dalit-bahujans is concerned. The fact that the lifestyles of upper castes and Dalit-bahujans vary dramatically in terms of food habits, worship patterns or gender relations is tacitly acknowledged. But instead of squarely recognising these variations and explaining why they exist, the dominant tendency in Indian sociology has been to suggest that the Dalit-bahujans are abandoning their way of life in favour of the lifestyle of caste Hindus. This is what sanskritisation is all about. In this perspective, not only are the norms and values of caste Hindus privileged, but they are also christened as norm setters and value givers for society as a whole. Conversely, the norms and values of Dalit-bahujans are knocked out, ignored, stigmatised and de-legitimised. Indeed, the field-view has made Indian sociology more authentic as compared with the book-view, but its authenticity has been largely partial. To correct this imbalance, we need the perspective from below.

If the white anthropologist indulged in the 'invention of primitive society', to invoke the felicitous phrase of Adam Kuper (1988), the twice-born sociologist of India projected an idealised picture of Hindu society mainly based on classical texts. Even the field view has not covered this deficit entirely. That is why, we need a counter-view even if it is an idealised version of the Dalit-bahujans. I shall attempt to present such a view based on the recent ones of Dalit intellectuals (Ilaiah, 1996). What is important about this view is not its factual content but its promise. Such a view was non-existent and considered to be inadmissible in the lexicon of the *savarna* social scientist of India.

First, the Dalit-bahujans do not subscribe to the notion of an all-India or pan-Indian Hinduism, not even regional Hinduism, ideas widely accepted in Indian sociology (Srinivas, 1952). In fact, the Dalit-bahujan identity is essentially a localised caste identity and a series of mini-traditions, not even a Little Tradition. Their religion does not admit patriarchal Hindu gods and absence of professional priesthood is a pronounced feature. In the Hindu pantheon, as and when the Dalit-bahujan gods are acknowledged, they are assigned a low status matching the status of their worshippers in the social structure.

Second, the Dalit-bahujan women enjoy considerable economic independence and sexual freedom. Absence of sharp sexual division of labour is a prominent feature of the Dalit society. These traditional values of Dalit-bahujans are actually much acclaimed values of modernity and even post-modernity. But they tend to lose these values as and when they get Sanskritised.

Third, in the Dalit-bahujan society, gender relations are largely open and egalitarian; the parent-child interactions, including father-child interactions, are intimate; widows are respected and not stigmatised; widow remarriages are practised. The incorporation of patriarchal values into their society is changing these norms and values.

Fourth, while there is an over-evaluation of the occupations of caste Hindus (priesthood, administration, trading) there is a studied lack of respect for the occupations of Dalit-bahujans such as agriculture, arts and crafts. In turn, the knowledge associated with production of wealth is undervalued. Generally speaking, only knowledge relating to the occupations of caste Hindus is given importance. There is a conspiracy of silence regarding the knowledge associated with Dalit-bahujan occupations.

Fifth, the language used by Dalit-bahujans in their everyday life is different from that used by caste Hindus. Their language is not only non-Sanskritic, but not even standard vernacular languages such as Hindi, Tamil or Bengali. Not only is their language not recognised by the state, but it is stigmatised by the people of caste Hindu society, both of which undermine Dalit-bahujan identity. The Dalit-bahujan names are quite different from those of caste Hindus, but as they are disparaged, they are inclined to shift either to Sanskritised or Anglicised names.

Sixth, the ideas generated by the organic intellectuals of Dalit-bahujans are hardly recognised, let alone communicated to the new generations. Even when Dalit-bahujan intellectuals are recognised reluctantly (e.g. Dr. B.R. Ambedkar), the politics of knowledge transmission invariably renders their contribution insignificant. Given the localisation of Dalit-bahujan castes to their respective linguistic regions, their leaders rarely become all-India figures even when they have made signal contributions as illustrated by the cases of Mahatma Phule in Maharashtra, Basava in Karnataka, Narayana Guru in Kerala or Narla in Andhra Pradesh. Consequently, the basic cleavages and differences between caste Hindus and Dalit-bahujans remain unnoticed.

Seventh, generally speaking, the exclusive political voice of Dalit-bahujans remains muted and submerged due to the absence of political parties to champion their cause. As and when such parties emerge and operate, their influence is confined to certain pockets. For example, the Republican Party of India founded by Ambedkar is virtually confined to Maharashtra. And the recently established Bahujan Samaj Party's influence is confined largely to Uttar Pradesh. Consequently, the political voices of Dalit-bahujans are being articulated through mainstream parties wherein they remain subordinated.

Eighth, given the numerical importance of Dalit-bahujans, universal adult franchise did make them politically salient. But this is not adequately matched by their upward economic mobility in spite of the numerous development programmes initiated by the government to improve their economic condition. The change in the ritual context is the least which continues to bestow on them low social prestige. Consequently, the existential condition of Dalit-bahujans is characterised by status incongruence. Their efforts to interrogate the entrenched castes often result in atrocities against them.

Ninth, although rebels challenged the Hindu caste system periodically in the last 25 centuries and tried to establish separate religions or sects, they did not succeed; they were silenced by incorporation into the Hindu system, usually assigning a low status. Gautama Buddha was a Kshatriya who revolted against the Brahmanic order. But he was gradually incorporated into the Hindu pantheon as an avatar of Vishnu and rendered powerless as a reformer. This has happened to the rebels of Bhakti movement, too, which erupted between the 8th and 18th centuries in different parts of the Indian sub-continent. This clearly points to the near impossibility of reforming the Hindu caste system so as to provide a respectable position to the Dalit-bahujans. That is, in so far as caste hierarchy exists, the perspective from below will remain relevant.

Finally, it is necessary to recognise that knowledge has two uses: oppression and perpetuation of hegemony and institutionalisation of equality and justice. The view from above sometimes directly and almost always indirectly aids and abets oppression and hegemonisation. The view from below can and should provide the much-needed antidote to this, facilitating the institutionalisation of equality and social justice. This is the rationale and justification for the perspective from below, which can contribute to the nurturing of a robust civil society.

References

Bettie, J., 1964, *Other Cultures*, London: Cohen and West.

Dumont, Louis, 1970, *Homo Hierarchicus: The Caste System and Its Implications*, Chicago: Chicago University Press.

Feuer, Lewis S., 1969, *The Conflict of Generations*, London: Hinemann.

Furnivall, J.S., 1948, *Colonial Policy and Practice*, Cambridge: Cambridge University Press.

Guha, Ranajit, and Gayatri Chakravorty Spivak (eds.), 1988, *Selected Subaltern Studies*, New York: Oxford University Press.

Ilaiah, Kancha, 1996, *Why I am not a Hindu*, Kolkata: Samya.

Kuper, A., 1988, *The Invention of Primitive Society: Transformation of an Illusion*, London: Routledge.

Mukherji, D.P., 1961, 'Indian Sociology and Tradition' in R.N. Saksena (ed.), *Sociology, Social Research and Social Problems in India*, Mumbai: Asia Publishing House.

Oommen, T.K., 1969, 'Data Collection Techniques: The Case of Sociology and Social Anthropology', *Economic and Political Weekly*, Vol. IV (19), 809-15.

—, 1985, *From Mobilisation to Institutionalisation: The Dynamics of Agrarian Movement in Twentieth Century Kerala*, Mumbai: Popular Prakashan.

—, 1997(a), 'From Plural Society to Pluralism: Towards a Just and Humane Social Order in India', *Social Action*, Vol. 47, July-September, 259-71.

—, 1997(b), *Citizenship, Nationality and Ethnicity: Reconciling Competing Identities*, Cambridge: Polity Press.

—, 1998, 'Society: Tradition and Autonomy', in Hiranmay Karlekar (ed.), *Independent India: The First Fifty Years*, New Delhi: Oxford University Press.

Simmel, Georg, 1950, 'The Stranger' in Kurt. H. Wolf (ed.) *The Sociology of Georg Simmel*, Illinois: The Free Press of Glencoe.

Srinivas, M.N., 1952, *Religion and Society among the Coorgs of South India*, New Delhi: Oxford University Press.

3

Nation, Anthropology and the Village

Surinder S. Jodhka

The study of the 'village community' has undoubtedly been the single most important preoccupation of sociologists and social anthropologists working on/in India. Though it was during the British colonial rule that India was first imagined as a land of 'village republics', sociologists and social anthropologists who carried out 'village studies' during the 1950s and 1960s also saw the essence of India being located in the village. There was something obvious about the 'village' being the primary unit of Indian civilisation. For a long time, the village was regarded as a natural entry point to the understanding of traditional Indian society and for documenting the patterns of its social organisation. It was the ultimate signifier to the authentic native life, a place where one could see or observe the 'real' India and develop an understanding of the way local people organised their social relationships and belief systems. The institutional patterns and cultural values of the village society were assumed to be typical examples of traditional Indian society. As Beteille argued, "The village was not merely a place where people lived;

it had a design in which were reflected the basic values of Indian civilization" (Beteille, 1980:108).

Though the village has been a popular subject of research in all social sciences in India, it is the disciplines of sociology and social anthropology that did the most 'village studies' in different parts of India during the 1950s and 1960s. The publication of these studies also marked the beginning of a new phase in the history of Indian social sciences. They, for the first time, showed the relevance of fieldwork-based understanding of Indian society. Apart from popularising the method of qualitative fieldwork of modern social anthropology, the village studies played a crucial role in institutionalising the twin disciplines in the Indian university system.

Basing their accounts on "participant observations", mostly carried out by the social anthropologists themselves while staying with the community over a long period of time in a single village, they offered what has come to be known as the 'field-view' of India. Undertaking a village study and providing an account of village social life was not just an exercise to be carried out by a university undergraduate in a remote village for the award of a doctoral degree. For most of them, particularly for the social anthropologists of Indian origin, doing a village study meant much more. These studies were carried out almost immediately after India's independence from colonial rule, when post-independence India was trying to develop the new self-identity of a nation state. Modernisation of the traditional India was the major preoccupation of the new elite.

The field-view of India was constructed through the use of scientific method and, therefore, offered a more authentic picture of Indian social reality than the one provided by the book-view of Indian society constructed by Indologists using classical Hindu scriptures. The book-view was partial because it was constructed from sources that were mostly produced by the Brahmans and thus reflected a biased, upper-caste notion of Indian civilisation. Such a biased view of India obviously needed to be revised in post-independence democratic India!

I would like to argue in this paper that through the village studies, sociologists and social anthropologists acquired a sense of relevance for themselves and for their disciplines by participating in the national project. Using more or less similar kinds of theoretical frameworks and methods of data collection, social anthropologists studied villages in different parts of the sub-continent and produced a picture that had many similarities in the way social life was organised in a 'typical Indian village'. I shall try to show that since in the village was reflected India in microcosm and the social structure of the villages was more or less similar everywhere, the village studies tried to establish the fact, intentionally or unintentionally, that the socio-cultural identity of India was an indisputable empirical fact. By underlining the 'unity' of the village, social anthropologists of this genre also underscored the civilisational unity of India. More explicitly, the village studies were to construct a picture of the traditional India on the basis of which the new Indian state and its planners were to work towards its development and modernisation.

Locating Village Studies

While Indian sociologists and social anthropologists saw themselves as undertaking an important task for the nation by carrying out empirical studies of village social life, there were other important developments too, in the global academy that made village studies a popular theme of research during the 1950s.

The emergence of the 'new states' following de-colonisation during the post-war period influenced dramatically the research priorities in social sciences. The most significant feature of the newly emerged Third World countries was the dependence of large proportions of their populations on a stagnant agrarian sector. The struggle for freedom from colonial rule had also developed new aspirations among the masses and the elite of these societies. In some of these struggles, the peasants had played an important role. Thus, the primary agenda for the new political regimes was the transformation of their backward and stagnant economies. Though the strategies and priorities differed, modernisation and development became common programmes in most Third World countries. It was in this historical context that 'development studies' emerged as one of the most important areas of academic interest in the global academy. Development studies were supposed to provide relevant data and prescriptive knowledge for socio-economic transformations. The western powers also had a great deal of political interest in the paths of development being pursued by different developing countries in the Third World. Much of this concern emanated from their anxiety about the possibility of these countries choosing a socialistic pattern of development and their consequent tilt towards the then existing Soviet block.

Since a large majority of the populations in the Third World countries were directly dependent on agriculture, understanding the prevailing structures of agrarian relations and working out ways and means of transforming them were recognised as being priorities in development studies. Western political interest in the rural inhabitants of the Third World and the growing influence of modernisation and development theories also brought with them a great deal of funding for the study of peasant economies and societies (Silverman, 1987:11). It was in this context that the concept of 'peasantry' found currency in the discipline of social anthropology.

At a time when primitive tribes were either in the process of disappearing or had already disappeared, the 'discovery' of the peasantry provided a new lease of life to the discipline of social anthropology (Beteille, 1974b). Krober defined peasants as 'part societies with part cultures' (Krober in Redfield, 1965:20). The peasantry was seen as a universal human type having "something generic about it, a kind of arrangement of humanity with some similarities all over the world". They were attached to land through bonds of sentimentality and emotions.

Agriculture, for them, was "a livelihood and a way of life, not a business for profit" (Redfield, 1965:17-18; Shanin, 1987).

This notion of peasant society fitted well with the new evolutionist mode of thinking being made popular by 'modernisation theory' around the same time. Peasantry, in this framework, invariably referred to what Europe had been before the industrial revolution and what the Third World still was. Thus, the notion of traditional society conceptualised by the modernisation theory as the opposite of modern society, resembled very closely the notion of peasantry in the new discipline of 'peasant studies'.

The village community was identified as the social foundation of the peasant economy in Asia (Breman, 1987:1). Beteille argues that this conceptual identity of village with peasant community "is rooted in European ideology and European scholarship" (Beteille, 1974b:47). It is rather easy to see the connection between the Redfieldian notion of peasant studies and the Indian village studies. Among the first works on the subject, *Village India: Studies in the Little Community* (edited by M. Marriot, 1955) was brought out under the direct supervision of Robert Redfield. He even wrote a preface to this book. His concept of 'little community' has also been quite popular among the social anthropologists in India.

Apart from these, there was also what could be called a received common sense about Indian society. From colonial bureaucracy to the nationalist freedom struggle, everybody had emphasised on the village being the essence of India. It was perhaps this historical context that made sociologists and social anthropologists treat the village as the obvious and natural entry point to the study of India.

History and the Method[I]

Having found a relevant subject in the village, the social anthropologists (many of whom were either from the West or were

Indian scholars trained in western universities) initiated field studies in the early 1950s. A number of short essays providing brief accounts of individual villages were published by them in the newly launched Indian journal called *The Economic Weekly* (which later came to be known as the *Economic and Political Weekly*) during October 1951 and May 1954. These essays were put together by M.N. Srinivas in the form of a book with the title, *India's Villages*, in 1955. In the same year, M. Marriot published another collection by the name of *Village India*. Interestingly, the first volume of *Rural Profiles* by D.N. Majumdar also appeared in 1955. All three were edited volumes and many of the contributors were common. Srinivas, for example, had a paper in each of the three volumes. The first full-length study of a village near Hyderabad in the Telangana region, *Indian Village*, by S.C. Dube also appeared in the same year.

There was a virtual explosion of village studies in the 1960s and 1970s. "Although social anthropologists were the first in the field which they dominated throughout, scholars from other disciplines—political science, history, economics, and so on—were also attracted to it" (Beteille, 1996:235). Though most of the studies provided a more general account of the social, economic and cultural life of the rural people, some of the later studies also focussed on specific aspects of the rural social structure, such as stratification, kinship and religion.

An anthropologist typically selected a single 'middle'-sized village where he carried out intensive fieldwork, generally by staying with the 'community' for a fairly long period of time, ranging from one to two years. At the end of the stay, he was supposed to come out with a 'holistic' account of the social and cultural life of the village people. The most important feature that qualified these studies to be called anthropological was the fieldwork component and the use of participant-observation, a method of data collection that anthropologists in the West had developed while doing studies of tribal communities. The method of intensive fieldwork came to be seen as the defining characteristic of the discipline of social anthropology and there was a fairly standardised pattern that had to be followed by the practitioners.

> A typical piece of intensive fieldwork was one in which the worker lived for a year or more among a community of perhaps four or five hundred people and studied every detail of their life and culture; in which he came to know every member of the community personally; in which he was not content with generalised information, but studied every feature of life and custom in concrete detail and by means of the vernacular language (River in Beteille and Madan, 1975:2).

The rules and regularities of the native customs were not merely to be recorded by the ethnographer with camera, notebook and pencil, but more fruitfully observed by himself as a participant in the happenings around him. "Intensive fieldwork experience was of critical importance in the career of an anthropologist. It formed the basis of his comprehension of all other societies, including societies differing greatly from the one of which he had first-hand knowledge. No amount of book-knowledge was a substitute for field experience" (Srinivas, 1955a:88). The participant-observation method was seen as a method that 'understood social life from within, in terms of the values and meanings attributed to it by the people themselves' (Beteille, 1996:10).

Majumdar, too, contended that after the isolated tribal communities, the village came to be seen as the right kind of subject matter for anthropologists. The genuine field of study for anthropologists, he argued, was the *Gemeinschaft*, the 'closed community' and it was "in the context of 'evaporation' of tribal societies due to assimilation and (or) extinction, that they were compelled to turn their attention to the rural community which continues to retain the essential face-to-face *Gemeinschaft* character". The anthropologist's love for rural studies was a natural extension of his interest in tribal studies. A typical anthropologist lived with the people he studied, established a rapport with them, participated in their day to day life, spoke their language, and recorded his observations of the ways of life of the people (Majumdar, 1956:138). Participant observation also provided continuity between the earlier tradition of anthropology when it studied the tribal communities and its later preoccupation with the village. As Beteille writes:

> In moving from tribal to village studies, social anthropologists retained one very important feature of their craft, the method of intensive fieldwork.... Those standards were first established by Malinowski and his pupils at the London School of Economics in the twenties, thirties and forties, and by the fifties, they had come to be adopted by professional anthropologists the world over (Beteille, 1996:233-4).

However, despite this continuity with the earlier tradition of anthropology, the historical context of the village studies was very different from the tribal studies.

Perceived Significance of the Village

Interestingly, a good number of scholars who carried out village studies have also written about their field experience and on what motivated them to undertake such studies.

The discovery of peasantry had rejuvenated the discipline of social anthropology. In the emerging intellectual and political environment during the post-war period, anthropologists saw themselves as playing an important role in providing an authentic and scientific account of the 'traditional social order', the transformation of which had become a global concern. Many village monographs emerged directly from projects carried out by sociologists and social anthropologists for development agencies. These included studies by Dube (1955), Majumdar (1958) and Lewis (1958). Lewis, who studied a Delhi village, for example, writes:

> Our work was problem oriented from the start. Among the problems we studied intensively were what the villagers felt they needed in housing, in education, in health; land consolidation programme; and the newly created government-sponsored panchyats (Lewis, 1958:ix).

Lewis was appointed by the Ford Foundation in India to work with the Programme Evaluation Organization of the Planning Commission to help in developing a scheme for an objective evaluation of the rural reconstruction programme.

A typical anthropologist, unlike his economist counterpart, saw the village "in the context of the cultural life lived by the people" and the way "rural life was interlocked and interdependent" which "baffled social engineers as it could not be geared to planned economy. It was here that the economists needed the assistance of sociologists and anthropologists" (Majumdar, 1955:iv). Though they were intended to only assist the 'big brother' economists in the planning process, the anthropologists saw their perspective as being 'superior'. "He alone studied village community as a whole, and his knowledge and approach provided an indispensable background for the proper interpretation of data on any single aspect of rural life. His approach provided a much-needed corrective to the partial approach of the economist, political scientist and social worker, he tried to keep his value judgements to himself, and this gave him the necessary sympathy to grasp the rural or tribal situation" (Srinivas 1955b:90). The importance of the village studies lay in their ability to sensitise planners about the felt needs of the people. In absence of a serious fieldwork tradition in the social sciences, "planners and government tended to treat people like dough in their hands. The fact that people had resources of their own, physical, intellectual and moral, and that they could use them to their advantage, was not recognised by those in power" (Srinivas, 1978:34). While economists used quantitative techniques and their method was 'more scientific', the anthropological approach had its own advantages.

Anthropological studies provided qualitative analyses. The method of anthropology required that its practitioners select "a small universe which could be studied intensively for a long period of time to analyse its intricate system of social relations" (Epstein, 1962:2).

However, not all of them were directly involved with development agencies. In fact, most of them saw the relevance of their works more in professional terms. Taking a position against the close involvement of anthropologists with the development process, Srinivas argued that "the anthropologist has intimate and first-hand knowledge of one or two societies and he can place his understanding at the disposal of the planner. He may in some cases even be able to anticipate the kind of reception a particular administrative measure may have. But he cannot lay down policy because it is a result of certain decisions about right and wrong. From the point of view of the growth of social anthropology, concentration on the merely useful or practical is not altogether healthy" (Srinivas, 1960:13). Maintaining a 'safe' distance from the state and the development agencies was seen to be necessary because sociology and social anthropology, unlike the discipline of economics, did not have a theoretical grounding that could help them become applied sciences. The need for value neutrality and objectivity emphasised so strongly by the classical founders of the two disciplines and the 'self-regulating' notion of society being central to the functionalist perspective obviously discouraged sociologists and social anthropologists from being identified too closely with the state.

The relevance of studying the village was mostly seen in terms of it being a medium through which a scientific understanding of Indian society could be developed. "Villages were close to people, their life, livelihood and culture" and they were "a focal point of reference for individual prestige and identification". As "an important administrative and social unit, the village profoundly influenced the behaviour pattern of its inhabitants". Villages were supposed to have been around for "hundreds of years, having survived years of wars, making and breaking up of empires, famines, floods and other natural disasters". They were the "principal social and administrative unit" in the region. This perceived "historical continuity and stability of villages" strengthened the case for village studies (Dasgupta, 1978:1).

Though village studies did not celebrate the peasant way of life, they did have a 'subalternist' element in their perspective. It was not merely because of the method of participant observation. Village studies were also seen as one way of contesting popular elitist notions about rural people. It will be useful to quote Srinivas here once again:

> The educated Indian elite commonly regards the peasant as ignorant, tradition-bound, and resistant to progress. His action and motivation appear anything but rational to the elite... and he lacks the sense to take advantage of the many benefits offered by a benevolent government working through a plethora of institutions and specialists.
>
> Rationality does not exist in a vacuum but in a cultural context, and human satisfactions are themselves frequently culturally determined. The elite are annoyed with the peasant for not making choices which they want him to make, but they seem to be ignorant of the fact that choices are linked to structural economic and cultural factors (Srinivas, 1978:33).

While agreeing that the Indian peasants indeed were conservative, Srinivas offered a sympathetic explanation for their attitude towards change, one that only an anthropologist could appreciate:

> The anthropologist who has made an intensive study of a village community is unable to subscribe to the current views regarding the peasant. The conservatism of the peasant is not without reason. His agricultural techniques are a prized possession embodying as they do the experience of centuries. His social and cultural institutions give him a sense of security and

permanence and he is naturally loath to change them (Srinivas, 1955b:92-94).

Most importantly, for the anthropologists, the village was not just an area of specialised interest. Specialising on India meant studying 'village' or 'caste'. The village and its hamlets represented 'India in microcosm' (Hoebel in Hiebert, 1971:vii). The two were seen as the defining features of Indian society. The people of India lived in villages and their social organisation could be understood by referring to the structure and ideology of caste hierarchy. This is perhaps best articulated by Beteille in the introductory pages of his study of a Tamil Nadu village, as he wrote:

> ...it is possible to study within the framework of a single village many forms of social relations which are of general occurrence throughout the area. Such, for instance are the relations between Brahmins, non-Brahmins and Adi-Dravidas (untouchables) and between landowners, tenants and agricultural labourers.
>
> These relations are governed by norms and values which have a certain generality... much can be learnt about the relationships between principle and practice by making detailed observations in a single village.
>
> The village... may be viewed as a point at which social, economic, and political forces operating over a much wider field meet and intersect (Beteille, 1996:1-2).

Srinivas, too, thought and argued in a similar vein. Villages, for an anthropologist, were

> invaluable *observation-centres* where he can study in detail social processes and problems to be found occurring in great parts of India, if not in a great part of the world. An anthropologist goes to live in a village... not because he wants to collect information about curious and dying customs and beliefs, but to study a theoretical sociological problem, and his most important aim is to contribute to the growing body of theoretical knowledge

about the nature of human societies (Srinivas, 1955b:99, emphasis added).

It was seen to be particularly critical to carry out village studies during the 1950s and the 1960s because that was the time when Indian society was seen to be experiencing fundamental changes and the anthropologist needed to record details of the 'traditional social order' before it was too late. Srinivas underscored this urgency when he wrote: "We have, at the most, another ten years in which to record facts about a type of society which is changing fundamentally and with great rapidity" (Srinivas, 1955b:99).

Unity and Diversity: General Features of the Village

Unlike tribal communities, Indian villages had a considerable degree of diversity. This diversity was both internal as well as external. The village was internally differentiated in diverse groupings and had a complex structure of social relationships and institutional arrangements. There were also different kinds of villages in different parts of the country. Even within a particular region of the country, not all villages were alike. By definition, peasants, unlike tribal people, were not isolated communities. "The peasants," Redfield argued, "had firm relations with townsmen; not only economic, but also social and cultural." It was this feature that distinguished "the peasantry from its counterparts, the tribal communities. When Krober remarked that a peasant community was a half society and a half culture, he was referring to this fact. The community was completed by its other parts: the society and culture of gentry or townsmen. The priest, Brahman, and city-bred elite carried into the village a superior authority, explicit models of manners and conduct, and communicated to it something of the more reflective dimension of the civilised culture. Whether these representative of the great tradition were present in the village as residents, or came to the village occasionally, or were encountered as the peasant went to the town, in one way or another, this cultural dependence on the outside and superior world characterised peasant society" (Redfield, 1956:63). This fact was repeatedly underlined by the anthropologists who carried out field studies of villages in different parts of India. The stereotypical image of the Indian village as a self-sufficient community, Beteille argues, has been contested by anthropological studies. As regards Sripuram, his study village, "at least as far back in time as living memory went, there was no reason to believe that the village was fully self-sufficient in the economic sphere" (Beteille, 1996:136-7). M.W. Smith wrote in his paper on a Punjab village:

> In terms of economic and social specialization, marital ties, and religious and political organization, the structural unit is larger than the village. These are not contacts in which the villager may indulge, they are imposed upon him by the habits of his existence.... Important as these village studies may be, therefore... it does not seem to me that my complete picture of Punjab life can be obtained from them alone (Smith, 1960: 178-179).

In his introduction to the celebrated collection, *India's Villages*, M.N. Srinivas, too, contested the colonial notion of the Indian village being a completely self-sufficient republic. This, Srinivas argued, was a myth. The village "was always a part of a wider entity. Only villages in pre-British India were less dependent economically on the town than villages are today" (Srinivas, 1960:10; also see Srinivas and Beteille, 1964).

However, despite this contention about the village having links with the outside world and explicating the diversities that marked the rural society of India, it was the 'unity' of the village that was underlined by most anthropologists. The fact that the village interacted with the outside world did not mean it did not have a design of its own or could not be studied as a representative unit of Indian social life. While villages had horizontal ties, it was the vertical ties within the village that governed much of the life of an average person in the village. Among those who stressed this aspect the most were Dube and Srinivas. Village was represented as providing an important source of identity to its residents. Different scholars placed different emphasis on how significant the village identity was when compared to other sources of identification, such as those of caste, class or locality. Srinivas argued that individuals in his village had a sense of identification with their village and an insult to one's village had to be avenged like an insult to oneself, one's life, or one's family (Srinivas, 1976:270).

Similarly, while Dube recognised the obvious fact that "Indian villages varied greatly in their internal structure and organisation, in their ethos and world-view, and in their life-ways and thought-ways, on account of a variety of factors", nevertheless, he argued that:

> Village communities all over the Indian sub-continent have a number of common features. The village settlement, as a unit of social organization, represents a solidarity different from that of the kin, the caste, and the class... Each village is a distinct entity, has some individual mores and usages, and possesses a corporate unity. Different castes and communities inhabiting the village are integrated in its economic, social, and ritual pattern by ties of mutual and reciprocal obligations sanctioned and sustained by generally accepted conventions. Inside the village, community life is characterised by economic, social, and ritual co-operation existing between different castes... Notwithstanding the existence of groups and factions inside the settlement, people of the village can, and do, face the outside world as an organized, compact whole (Dube, 1960:202).

In his monograph on the Telangana village also, Dube constructed the village in cooperative and communitarian terms and underlined its interdependence and unity. He wrote:

> Within the village community there is an appreciable degree of inter-caste and inter-family co-operation... (T)he social system enjoys co-operation between a number of castes in the field of economics and ritual. Several aspects of community life depend for their smooth running on the traditional system of mutual give and take. Apart from conventional ties which are a constituent part of the social structure, several relationships involving voluntary co-operation can be observed (Dube, 1955:199).

Working in the same kind of a framework, Opter and Singh argued:

> Not only does everyone have some place within the Hindu system, but it is significant that every group, from Brahman to the Chamar caste, has been somehow integrated into the social and ceremonial order of the community and has been given some opportunity to feel indispensable and proud (Opter and Singh, 1948:496).

It was W.H. Wiser, who, much before the village studies took off had, in his classic study of *The Hindu Jajmani System* (first published in 1936), conceptualised the social relationships among caste groups in a north Indian village in the framework of 'reciprocity'. The framework of reciprocity implied that though village social organisation was hierarchical, it was the interdependence among the different caste groups that characterised the underlying spirit of the Indian village. There were differences, but the interdependence united the village community. Reciprocity implied, explicitly or implicitly, an exchange of equal services and non-exploitative relations. Mutual gratification was supposed to be the outcome of reciprocal exchange. Wiser emphasised the equality of reciprocal exchange when he wrote:

> Each serves the other. Each in turn is master. Each in turn is servant (Wiser 1969:10).

Though later studies were much more elaborate and contained long descriptions of different forms of social inequalities and differences in rural society, many of them continued to use the framework of reciprocity, particularly while conceptualising the unity of the village social life. Foremost amongst these were the writings of Srinivas. He is so much in agreement with Wiser's notion of reciprocity as the characteristic feature of the village social structure that he went to the extent of generalising it for all of India. Regarding Wiser's study of Karimnagar as being the first proper anthropological work on an Indian village, Srinivas writes:

> The method adopted by the Wisers in their study of Karimnagar was quite different from that of the economists. They spent years in the village, talked to the local inhabitants in Hindi, participated in their activities, and did their utmost to help the needy and alleviate the suffering of fellow villagers. The quality of information gathered by the Wisers was superior to anything collected before, and when this was put in a holistic framework... *the result was a memorable picture not only of Karimnagar, but of village life in the sub-continent, microcosm reflecting the macrocosm* (Srinivas 1996:181-2, emphasis added).

Even when Srinivas recognised the existence of 'vertical ties' between "landlord and tenants, between master and servants, and between creditors and debtors" (Srinivas, 1955a) as structural features of village social life, he did not see these relations as being necessarily conflictual or exploitative in nature. On the contrary, it was the interdependence of the caste groups resulting from such ties that defined the village. As he wrote:

> When caste is viewed as hierarchy, it is the distinctiveness of each group and its separateness and distance from the others that receive emphasis. But distinctiveness and distance go along with the interdependence of the different castes living in a village or

group of neighbouring villages. The two are parts of a single system (Srinivas, 1976:185).

Srinivas' position is stated most explicitly in his response to Dumont and Pocock's critique of village studies in their review of the two abovementioned volumes on Indian villages published in 1955, which were edited by Marriot and Srinivas. Dumont and Pocock, in a review article in the then newly launched journal, *Contributions to Indian Sociology*, had contested the relevance of treating the village as a representative unit for understanding Indian society. Villages, they argued, were not 'communities' in the classical sense of the term because the caste system hierarchised India. Further, they argued, caste ties went much beyond the village and therefore, to explain the structure of Indian society, the sociology of India should focus on the caste system and not on the village (Dumont and Pocock, 1957; Pocock, 1960).

Arguing against Dumont, Srinivas insisted that unequal groups living in small face to face collectivities could have common interests binding them together and, therefore, they could qualify to be treated as 'communities'. It may be worthwhile to quote him at length on this.

> The tendency to stress intra-caste solidarity and to forget inter-caste complementarity is to ignore the social framework of agricultural production in pre-British India. Castewise division of labour forced different castes living in a local area to come together in the work of growing and harvesting crops. Landowners forged inter-caste ties not only with artisan and servicing castes but also with castes providing agricultural labour. These last mentioned ties involved daily and close contact between masters from the powerful dominant castes and servants from the untouchable or other castes just above the polluting line. Again, in context of a non-monetized or minimally monetized economy, and very little spatial mobility, relationships between households tended to be enduring.

> *Enduringness itself was a value, and hereditary rights and duties acquired ethical overtones* (Srinivas, 1994:43, emphasis added).

Elsewhere, he writes:

> ... it must be remembered that in pre-British India there was a general acceptance of caste, and of the idiom of caste in governing relationships between individuals and between groups. Given such a framework of acceptance of hierarchy, it ought not to be difficult to conceive of communities which are non-egalitarian, their people playing interdependent roles and all of them having a common interest in survival (Srinivas 1987:57).

However, not everyone emphasised the unity of the village the way Srinivas and Dube or earlier Wiser did. Some anthropologists explicitly contested the unity thesis, while others qualified their arguments by recognising the conflicts within the village and the ties that villagers had with the outside world. For instance, Paul Hiebert, in his study of a south Indian village, although arguing that the caste system provided a source of stability to the village, also underlined the fact that "deep seated cleavages underline the apparent unity of the village and fragmented it into numerous social groups" (Hiebert, 1971:13). Similarly, Majumdar pointed out that the assumption about the village being an "integrated whole, a way of living, thinking and feeling has its limitations in the Indian conditions". Kinship ties integrated the village "at different levels with the total social system of the country" (Majumdar, 1958:325). However, the more important fact that divided the village was its settlement pattern.

> The caste-wards that we find in most of our villages, the 'purer' settlements which are inhabited by the higher castes, and the 'polluted' quarters owned by the lower and scheduled castes are so widely dissimilar that even within the village, we may have little in common, in idea, beliefs and practices, in education, income and levels of living in the matter of inter-caste relations,

> life and living habits are different, and these are gaps which have remained so, in spite of centuries of joint living, and co-operation within the village (Ibid.:325-6).

However, unlike Dumont and Pocock, Majumdar did recognise the relevance of studying villages. "A village was not merely a way of life, it was also a concept—it was a constellation of values and so long as our value system did not change or changed slowly and not abruptly, the village would retain its identity" (Ibid.:329). He also underlined the fact that there were occasions when different sections of the village came together. This process was clearly illustrated in the religious life of the village "in which there was a perfect give-and-take and reciprocity of relationship". And, he argued, that "despite economic competition and continued exploitation of the lower by higher caste groups, there existed common problems and common interests" (Ibid.:326).

> Andre Beteille too had argued that his study village "Sripuram as a whole constituted a unit in a physical sense and, to a much lesser extent, in the social sense" (Beteille, 1996:39).

> the primary cleavages within this unit subdivide it into the three more or less well-defined communities of Brahmins, non-Brahmins, and Adi-Dravidas;...each of these subdivisions, particularly the first and the last, is a unit in a much more fundamental sense than the village as a whole (Ibid.:39).

However, like Majumdar, Beteille, too, recognised that there were spheres of life where the village exhibited a semblance of unity, most importantly in the sphere of economy and religion.

> In the economic sphere the Brahmins of Sripuram...enter into relations with the non-Brahmins and Adi-Dravids. A large number of them are landowners, dependent upon the services of non-Brahmins and Adi-Dravidas as tenants and agricultural labourers...(T)he ideology of caste itself forces Brahmin

> Mirsadars to enter into economic relations with non-Brahmins by forbidding to them the use of the plough.
>
> .... A complex set of ties thus binds together the Brahmins, Non-Brahmins, and Adi-Dravidas of the village in a web of economic interdependence (Ibid.:100).

He further argued:

> The productive process, by bringing into existence social relations between different classes of people, gives a kind of vertical unity to the village, making landowners, tenants, and agricultural labourers dependent upon one another. People having a diversity of backgrounds and interests are brought into relationship with each other by virtue of their complementary roles in the system of production (Ibid.:128-9).

However, though the process of production created vertical ties among different social groups, this did not necessarily imply a unity of the village as "these relations of production easily overflowed the boundary of the village. About half of the landowners of Sripuram lived outside the village" (Ibid.:129).

Answers to the question of unity and the relevant unit of social organisation also depended on what was being discussed. A.C. Mayer, who focussed on kinship in a central Indian village, argued that "the social universe of the people of his village, Ramkheri, comprised a region of a few hundred villages" (Mayer, 1960:270). However, for him, the village as a concept was also critical and he insisted that "it would be a mistake to think of the village and provided village-wide participation in some events. And differences of custom and caste composition in other villages added to a feeling of separateness which quickly turned into *village patriotism*" (Ibid.:132, emphasis in original).

Among those anthropologists who nearly rejected the idea of the communitarian unity of the Indian village were Lewis and Bailey. Comparing the Indian 'village community' with the American neighbourhood, Lewis argued:

> ...in Rampura...the community in the sense of a cohesive and united village community or in the sense of the American neighbourhood, village... hardly exists. Caste and kinship still form the core of village social organization and this splits the village into separate communities which have their close affiliation across village lines...(Lewis, 1958:148-9).

> ...caste system divides the village and weakens the sense of village solidarity. The caste generally represents a distinct ethnic group with its own history, tradition, and identification, and each caste lives in more or less separate quarters of the village...each caste forms a separate little community (Ibid.:314).

Even the so-called 'village common land' was not the common property of everyone. Far from working as a "source of village unity, it had often been a source of dissension". Rights to use the common lands were confined to the landowning dominant castes and were "based upon the amount of private land each Jat held" (Ibid.:94).

However, it was F.G. Bailey who provided a radical critique of the 'unity-reciprocity' thesis and offered an alternative perspective. Stressing on the coercive aspects of caste relations, he writes:

> ...those who find the caste system to their taste have exaggerated the harmony with which the system works, by stressing the degree of interdependence which means that everyone depends on everyone else: it means reciprocity. From this it is easy to slip into ideas of equality: because men are equally dependent on one another, they are assumed to be equal in other ways. Equality of rank is so manifestly false when applied to a caste system that the final step in the argument is seldom taken, and exposition rests upon a representation of mutual interdependence, and the hint that one caste could bring the system to a standstill by refusing to play its part, because castes do not in fact use this

> sanction to maintain their rights against the rest. In fact, of course, the system is held together not so much by ties of reciprocity, but by the concentration in one of its parts. The system works the way it does because the coercive sanctions are all in the hands of a dominant caste. There is a tie of reciprocity, but it is not a sanction of which the dependent castes can make easy use (Bailey, 1960:258).

However, this kind of a perspective did not become popular among the anthropologists doing village studies. It was the agrarian studies that later took up these issues. The village studies largely continued with the unity-reciprocity thesis, though different studies varied in their emphasis on interdependence and harmony characterising these relationships.

Field-View and Fieldwork

More than anything else, it was the method of participant observation that distinguished the village studies and the anthropological constructions of rural social life from the rural surveys being conducted by economists and demographers. And it was this method of qualitative fieldwork that helped social anthropology gain a measure of respectability in Indian academia. As Beteille and Madan write in their celebrated volume on fieldwork, *Encounter and Experience: Personal Accounts of Fieldwork*, "Fieldwork, more than anything else perhaps, is what today characterises social anthropology as a mode of inquiry into society and culture... The sociology of India would not be what it is today but for the insights fed into it by intensive fieldwork" (Beteille and Madan, 1975:1). As mentioned above, the field-view of the village was a superior way (when compared to the book-view) of understanding contemporary Indian society because the anthropologist used a scientific method of inquiry and provided a holistic picture of village social life.

However, despite this self-image of a scientist and a repeated emphasis on value neutrality towards the subjects being studied, a close reading of what these students of the Indian village have written about their experiences in their village during fieldwork provides a completely different picture. Apart from pointing to the kind of problems they faced in getting information about village social life, they provide vivid descriptions of how their own location and social background influenced their observations of the village society and conditioned their access to different sections of the villagers. The place they chose to live in the village during the fieldwork, the friends they made for regular information, the social class they themselves came from, their gender, the caste status bestowed upon them by the village, all played important roles in the kind of data they could access.

The manner in which an individual anthropologist negotiated his relationship with the village determined who was going to be his informant. One of the first questions asked of a visitor was regarding his caste. Accordingly, the village placed the visitor in its own structure and allocated him a place and status. The anthropologist was not only expected to respect this allocation of status bestowed on him by the village, he was also asked to conform to the normative patterns of the caste society. The anthropologist had to come to terms with the village social structure because the method of participant observation required that he go and stay in the village personally for a fairly long period of time. The easiest way of developing rapport with the village was through the village leaders or the head of the panchayat who invariably came from the dominant upper caste. Since most of the anthropologists themselves came from upper or middle class backgrounds, it was easier for them to approach these leaders. This also helped them execute their studies with fewer problems. Majumdar is explicit about this:

> The ex-zamindar family provided accommodation and occasionally acted as the host, and this contact helped...to work with understanding and confidence; little effort was needed to establish *rapport* (Majumdar, 1958:5).

Moreover, in an Indian village during the 1950s and 1960s, only the richer upper-caste landowners could have provided accommodation to the visiting anthropologist. The low-caste rural poor rarely had enough housing even for their own requirements. However, finding a place to live was not merely a matter of convenience. It identified the investigator with certain groups in the village and this identification had its advantages as well as disadvantages. While it gave them access to the life-ways of the upper castes, it also made them suspect in the eyes of the lower castes. Recognising the significance of this, Shah, who did a study of the household dimensions of family in rural Gujarat, writes:

> ...the village headman arranged a house for our stay during our first visit to the village. We could not exercise our choice in this matter. When we had to vacate this house and find another, again we could not exercise our choice. The latter house was also located in the same ward as the former...This ward was populated mostly by three upper castes, Brahmins, Rajputs and Patidars, and most of the village leaders, including the headman, lived there. Our living in this ward gave us certain advantages as well as disadvantages. The main advantage was that we could observe the village leaders more closely...The main disadvantage was that we could not observe as closely the untouchables (Shah, 1979:35).

Others also had similar experiences. The Tamil village that Beteille studied was divided into three clearly demarcated residential areas on the basis of caste. He was 'permitted' to live in a Brahman house in the *agraharam* (the Brahman locality), 'a privilege', he was told, "never extended to an outsider and a non-Brahman before". However, his acceptance in the *agraharam* as a co-resident was on certain implicit conditions.

> I could live in the agraharam only on certain terms, by accepting some of the duties and obligations of a member of the community....The villagers of Sripuram had also assigned me a

> role; and they would consider it most unnatural if I decided suddenly to act in ways that were quite contrary to what was expected (Beteille, 1975:104).

This, Beteille himself recognised, had serious implications for his fieldwork. The residents of the *agraharam* had their own perspectives on the village. For them, Sripuram was primarily their own locality. The village had over three hundred houses, while those who lived in the *agraharam* counted only about a hundred. For them, the village meant only the *agraharam*. This process of exclusion operated not merely in the counting of heads, but also in other, more subtle, ways "which often go unnoticed by the fieldworker who stayed only for a short while in the village" (Beteille, 1996:277).

Living in the *agraharam* also gave him the identity of a Brahman in the village. "I was identified with Brahmans by my dress, my appearance, and the fact that I lived in one of their houses" (Ibid.:9). For the non-Brahmans and Adi Dravidas, he was just another Brahman from North India. This meant that his "access to these groups was, therefore, far more limited than to the Brahmans" (Ibid.:9). His visits to the Harijan locality received loud disapproval from his Brahman hosts and he was also suspected by the Harijans. To put it in his own words:

> My first visit to the Harijan *cheri* taught me that such a visit was not only frowned upon by the Brahmins but also viewed by the Harijans with suspicion. I went there in the company of a Brahmin, and until the end most Harijans had no way of knowing that I myself could be anything but a Brahmin. The Harijans regard a visit to their homes by a Brahmin as unnatural, and some believe that it brings them ill luck (Ibid.:278).

The village was not only caste conscious, it was also class and gender conscious.[2] To quote Beteille again:

> If I asked the tenant questions about tenancy in the presence of the landlord, he did not always feel free to speak frankly. If I arranged to meet the tenant separately to ask these questions,

> the landlord felt suspicious and displeased... It is only by facing such problems in practical terms that the fieldworker learns what each party has at stake in these common arrangements (Ibid.:284).

Underlining the role gender played in fieldwork, Leela Dube, one of the few Indian women anthropologists who has worked in a village, writes, "I was a Brahman and a woman, and this the village people could never forget" (Dube, 1975:165).

Srinivas tells a similar story about his experiences in the field. Since his family originally came from the region where he did his field study, it was easier for the villagers to place him. For the villagers, he "was primarily a Brahman whose joint family owned land in a neighbouring village" (Srinivas, 1976:33). The older villagers gave him the role of a Brahman and a landowner. By doing this, they were able to make him behave towards them in certain predictable ways, and they in turn were able to regulate their behaviour towards him.

As a 'successful' participant observer, he could get himself accepted in the village to such an extent that on social occasions, almost everyone in the village treated him as a Brahman. He tells us: "However poor the host, I was given a green coconut and a cash-gift (*dakshina*) of eight annas or a rupee" (Ibid.:35). He also participated as a 'learned Brahmin' whenever the village had its *puja* (ritual cermonies). Almost all his friends in the village were from the dominant social groups.

More significant here perhaps is the fact that he very consciously confirmed to the normative patterns and the local values as he came to understand them.

> It did not *even occur to me* to do anything which might get me into trouble with the village establishment. I accepted the limitations and tried to work within them (Ibid.:47, emphasis added).

A similar kind of anxiety is expressed by Leela Dube when she writes:

> If I had to gain a measure of acceptance in the community, I must follow the norms of behavior which the people associated with my sex, age, and caste (Dube, 1975:165).

This conformist attitude towards the village social structure and its normative patterns as received through the dominant sections had such an important effect on their fieldwork that some of them quite consciously chose not to spend much time with the low-caste groups. Srinivas, for example, admits that while he was collecting genealogies and a household census, he "deliberately excluded the Harijan ward". He thought that he "should approach the Harijans only through the headman". The consequence was that his account of the village was biased in favour of the upper-caste Hindus. This was so obvious a fact that he himself recognises this as a shortcoming of his study.

> My shortcomings as a field-worker are brought home to me poignantly when I contemplate the Harijans and Muslims. I realise only too clearly that mine was a high caste view of village society. I stayed in a high caste area, and my friends and companions were all peasants or Lingayats (Srinivas, 1976:197-8).

It was not merely the 'insider' Indian scholars who, while doing "participant observation", had to negotiate with the social structure of the village. The scholars from the West, too, had to come to terms with the status that the village gave them and caste group with which they came to be identified. The British scholar, Adrian Mayer, who studied a village in Central India writes:

> I was caught up in the village's caste situation, ...It was impossible for me merely to "observe" the caste system. I had to participate in it, by the fact of my living in Ramkheir.
>
> ...I could not avoid being "placed" in the commensal hierarchy, with all the implications that this entailed... the village stated

> that I should be regarded as a person of undesignated upper caste status and that my links with Harijans should be consistent with this. And this is what they turned out to be. The Harijans never asked me for a meal from one of their hearths (Mayer, 1975:30-31).

By the time he left the village, Mayer was mostly closely identified with the Rajputs, the locally dominant caste.

Nation and the Village

In much of the writings, either by the social anthropologists themselves, who carried out the village studies (as shown in the previous section), or by those who have critically commented on these studies[3], the dominant tendency has been to attribute the weaknesses of the village studies mostly to the limitations of their methods or the theoretical perspectives. The admission of an upper-caste bias in their picture of the village social life, in most cases, was a post facto 'confession' by the social anthropologists, rather than a limitation stated in the preface of the book. The implicit suggestion being that had they been careful enough and aware of these problems beforehand, they could have followed a different fieldwork strategy and the bias could have been corrected!

Similarly, there seems to have been little anxiety about the historical and geographical limitations of the categories like caste, tribe, village, *jajmani* relations, tradition or civilisation. Not only was the village treated as a natural entry point to the study of India, its Indianness was also taken for granted. There were villages in India everywhere and they were all more or less alike. From Kerala to Punjab and even the Himalayas, from Rajasthan to Bengal and Orissa, village life had many similarities. (The collection of small essays edited by Srinivas in 1955 had studies from different parts of India—Punjab, the Himalayas, Nilgiris, Tamil Nadu, Mysore, Kerala, Uttar Pradesh, Rajasthan, the Deccan, Orissa, and Bengal).

The point that I wish to make here is that apart from the strengths and weaknesses of the village studies in terms of their relevance in understanding the rural social structure, one also needs to locate them historically. Intentionally or unintentionally, the social anthropological enterprise, particularly through the village studies, was actively participating in the national project by affirming the structural unity of India.

India, for the social anthropologists of this genre, was not the India of the 1950s and 1960s. Theirs was a search for the traditional India, an India that had been around since ages. The very naming of the project as a field-view of India that was to replace the book-view, assumed that parallels could be drawn between the India constructed from the classical Hindu texts and that which was being constructed by the social anthropologists through their observation. The field-view was superior not because the book-view was ancient and therefore no more relevant, but because the classical Indian (not Hindu!) texts were mostly written by upper-caste Brahmans.

Similarly, when the social anthropologists questioned the assumptions of the colonial ethnographers that the Indian village was isolated, they did not invoke a historical method of explanation. The integration of the village in the regional economy was not a historical fact that could be attributed to the colonial policies of administration. The village, i.e. the traditional Indian village, was 'never' isolated.[4] The functionalist theoretical framework saw the process of social change in dichotomous universal evolutionary patterns. The societies changed from traditional to modern.

However, despite such a universal frame of reference, the Indianness of the Indian village was also an important fact. The Indian village had to be different if India's claim of being a distinct nation had to be ascertained. The Indian village communities were different from the European peasant communities. The distinctive character of India, above anything else, lay in its caste system. The caste system was a feature of the entire sub-continent. The core social institution that the village studies looked at was the caste system. Not only could caste be found in the entire sub-continent, it was also practised by everyone—Hindus, Muslims, Christians and Sikhs, none could escape from this essentially Indian practice.

However, caste was not something for which we needed to be ashamed. Untouchability was rarely seen as the defining feature of caste. Caste, as mentioned above, was not looked at in the framework of power and domination. If the villages were to qualify to be communities, caste could only be seen in the framework of reciprocity, a framework that also confirmed the unity of India as a people.

There are interesting similarities in the ways caste and rurality were constructed in the nationalist discourses and the manners in which social anthropologists conceptualised the two. One can identify three distinct notions of rurality in the nationalist discourse attributable to the three leaders of the freedom struggle, Gandhi, Nehru and Ambedkar. Gandhi saw the village community as a site of authenticity, the recovery of which was a pre-condition for true *swaraj*. Nehru and the left wing of the nationalist movement looked at the village and its social organisations, particularly the institution of caste, in terms of backwardness. The modernisation of India was to transform the village and its social organisation into an open system of stratification (Chatterjee, 1995:173-175). There was also a third but less influential stream in the nationalist thought, which was represented by Ambedkar. The village, for Ambedkar, was a site of oppression. There was no escape from caste oppression in the village.

While one can see the elements of the Gandhian village in the notion of the village community in the village studies and, similarly, that of backwardness in the notion of traditionality as a characteristic feature of the Indian village, there is virtually no reference to the idea of the village being a site of oppression in the village studies. It was only in the 1970s, and more importantly in the 1980s, that caste began to be looked at from a Dalit perspective. This was also the time when the nation began to get redefined by the powerful 'new social movements' that became increasing visible during the 1980s.

Notes

1. This and the following section are based on a earlier paper of mine (see Jodhka, 1998).
2. For a detailed discussion of the manner in which gender relations were constructed by anthropologists conducting these studies, see Jodhka, 1999.
3. See, for example, Dumont and Pocock, 1957; Pocock, 1960; Inden, 1990; Breman, 1997; Patel, 1998; *Contributions to Indian Sociology* (new series), Volume 12 (1) (special issue on M.N. Srinivas' *Remembered Village*).
4. Cohn has interestingly argued that the colonial construction of the Indian village communities as being 'isolated' and independent from the centralised authority had helped the British rulers to legitimise the colonisation of the sub-continent. Since the village, the basic unit of the Indian society, was anyway unchanging, isolated and an autonomous social reality, it did not really matter who actually ruled India. The Hindus, the Mughals, or the Sikhs were mere rulers and the British could legitimately replace them without touching the order of the 'village republics'. The indigenous rulers had no specific claims over their British counterparts to rule India. Rulers, natives or outsiders anyway had very little in common with the lifestyles of the 'village communities' (Cohn, 1990:200-23).

   Viewed in this context, the questioning of the autonomy of the village thesis by the social anthropological village studies also implied that India had a legitimate and historical right to be recognised as a nation state, a cultural community with a long and shared history of its people.

References

Bailey, F.G., 1960, *Tribe, Caste and Nation*, Mumbai: Oxford University Press.

Beteille, A., 1996, *Caste, Class and Power: Changing Patterns of Stratification in a Tanjore Village*, Delhi, Oxford University Press (first published in 1965).

—, 1974, *Six Essays in Comparative Sociology*, Delhi: Oxford University Press.

—, 1980, 'The Indian Village: Past and Present' in E.J. Hobsbawm et al. (eds.), *Peasants in History: Essays in Honour of Daniel Thorner*, Kolkata: Oxford University Press.

—, 1975, 'The Tribulations of Fieldwork' in A. Beteille and T.N. Madan (eds.) *Encounters and Experience: Personal Accounts of Fieldwork*, Delhi: Vikas.

Beteille, A. and T.N. Madan (eds.), 1975, *Encounters and Experience: Personal Accounts of Fieldwork*, Delhi: Vikas.

Breman, J., 1987, *The Shattered Image: Construction and Deconstruction of the Village in Colonial Asia*, Amsterdam: Comparative Asian Studies.

—, 1997, The Village in Focus in J. Breman, P. Kloos and A. Saith (eds.), *The Village in Asia Revisited*. Delhi: Oxford University Press.

Chatterjee, P., 1995, The Nation and its Fragments: Colonial and Postcolonial Histories, Delhi: Oxford University Press.

Cohn, B.S., 1990, *An Anthropologist among Historians and other Essays,* Delhi: Oxford University Press.

Contributions of Indian Sociology (new series) (January-June 1978), Volume 12 (1) (special issue on M.N. Srinivas' *Remembered Village*).

Dasgupta, B. (ed.), 1978, *Village Studies in the Third World*, Delhi: Hindustan.

Dube, L., 1975, 'Woman's World—Three Encounters' in A. Beteille and T.N. Madan (ed.), *Encounters and Experience: Personal Accounts of Fieldwork*, Delhi, Vikas.

Dube, S.C., 1955, *Indian Village*, London: Routledge and Kegan Paul.

—, 1960, 'A Deccan Village' in M.N. Srinivas (ed.), *India's Village*, London: Asia Publishing House (first published in 1955).

Dumont, L., and D.F. Pocock, 1957, 'Village Studies', *Contributions to Indian Sociology*, 1(23-41).

Epstein, T.S., 1962, *Economic Development and Social Change in South India*, Manchester: Manchester University Press.

Hiebert, Paul G., 1971, *Konduru: Structure and Integration in a South Indian Village*, Minneapolis: University of Minnesota Press.

Inden, R., 1990, *Imagining India*, Cambridge: Blackwell.

Ishwaran, K., 1968, *Shivapur: A South Indian Village*, London: Routledge and Kegan Paul.

Jodhka, S.S., 1998, 'From "Book-view" to "Field-View", Social Anthropological Constructions of the Indian Village', *Oxford Development Studies*, Vol. 26, No. 3.

—, 1999, 'Patriarchy as a 'Natural Order': Constructions of Caste and Gender in the Indian 'Village Studies',' *Studies in Humanities and Social Sciences*, Vol. VI(2), Winter 1999.

Lewis, O., 1965, *Village Life in Northern India: Studies in a Delhi Village*, Urbana: University of Illinios.

Majumdar, D.N. (ed.), 1955, *Rural Profiles* (1), Lucknow: Ethnographic and Folk Culture Society.

Majumdar, D.N., 1956, 'Rural Analysis: Problems and Prospects' in A. Aiyyappan and L.K. Balaratnam (eds.), *Society in India*, Chennai: Book Centre.

—, 1958, *Caste and Communication in an Indian Village*, Mumbai: Asia Publishing House.

Marriott, McKim (ed.), 1955, *Village India: Studies in the Little Community*, Chicago: The University of Chicago Press.

Mayer, A.C., 1960, *Caste and Kinship in Central India: A Village and its Regions,* London: Routledge and Kegan Paul.

—, 1975, 'On Becoming a Participant Observer' in A. Beteille and T.N. Madan (eds.), *Encounters and Experience: Personal Accounts of Fieldwork*, Delhi: Vikas.

Opter, M.E. and R.D. Singh, 1948, 'The Division of Labour in an Indian Village' in C.S. Coon (ed.), *A Reader in General Anthropology*, New York: Henry Halt and Co.

Patel, S., 1998, 'The Nostalgia for the Village: M.N. Srinivas and the Making of Indian Social Anthropology', *South Asia* (new series) Vol. 21, No. 1.

Pocock, D.F., 1960, 'Sociologies: Urban and Rural', *Contributions to Indian Sociology,* Vol. IV (63-81).

Redfield, R., 1956, 'Primitive and Peasant: Simple and Compounded Society' in A. Aiyyappan and L.K. Balaratham, (ed.)

—, 1965, 'Peasants and Peasant Societies and Culture', Chicago: University of Chicago Press.

Shanin, T. (ed.), 1987, *Peasants and Peasant Societies*, London: Blackwell.

Shah, A.M., 1979, 'Studying the Present and the Past: A Village in Gujarat', in M.N. Srinivas, A.M. Shah and E.A. Ramaswamy (eds.), *The Field Worker and the Field: Problems and Challenges in Sociological Investigation,* Delhi: Oxford University Press.

Silverman, S., 1987, 'The Concept of Peasant and the Past: A Village in Gujarat', in M.N. Srinivas, A.M. Shah and E.A. Ramaswamy (eds.), *The Field Worker and the Field: Problems and Challenges in Sociological Investigation*, Delhi: Oxford University Press.

Smith, M.W., 1960, 'Social Structure in the Punjab' in M.N. Srinivas (ed.), *India's Village*, London: Asia Publishing House (first published in 1955).

Srinivas, M.N., 1955a, 'The Social Structure of a Mysore Village' in M. Marriott (ed.), *Village India: Studies in the Little Community*, Chicago: The University of Chicago Press.

—, 1955b, 'Village Studies and Their Significance', in D.N. Majumdar (ed.), *Rural Profiles* (1), Lucknow: Ethnographic and Folk Culture Society.

—, 1960, (ed.) *India's Village*, London: Asia Publishing House (first published in 1955).

—, 1976, *The Remembered Village,* Delhi: OUP.

—, 1978, 'Village Studies, Participant Observation and Social Science Research in India in B. Dasgupta (ed.), *Village Studies in the Third World*, Delhi: Hindustan.

—, 1987; 1994, *The Dominant Caste and Other Essays*, Delhi: OUP.

—, 1996, *Village, Caste, Gender and Method: Essays in Indian Social Anthropology*, Delhi: Oxford University Press.

Srinivas, M.N., and Andre Beteille, 1964, 'Networks in Indian Social Structure' in *Man*, Vol. 64 (Art. 212).

Wiser, W.H., 1969, *The Hindu Jajmani System*, Lucknow: Lucknow Publishing House (first published in 1936).

4

THE BROKEN MEN THEORY OF UNTOUCHABILITY

S.M. DAHIWALE

The Anthropological Survey of India studied 751 scheduled caste communities, i.e. former untouchable castes (Singh, 1998:XV). In the 1991 Census, their population (excluding Jammu & Kashmir) constituted 16.48 percent of the total population. If we consider the former untouchables among the converts to Islam, Christianity, Sikhism and Buddhism, their population could be estimated to be one-fourth of the total in India. They are generally found in every caste village. The author confines his discussion to examining the origin of untouchability, especially in the time of and after the Buddha. In this paper, five exclusive studies by V.R. Shinde (1933), B.R. Ambedkar (1948), S.N. Srivastava (1980), K.R. Hanumanthan (2004) and Vivekanand Jha (1975/2004) have been considered for examining the history of untouchability.

HISTORICAL BACKGROUND

Untouchability is a historical phenomenon. Here, therefore, an attempt is made to examine its origin and growth from a historical viewpoint. The growth of an institution of untouchability is seen as a process of several hundred years. The number of caste groups which are degraded to the status of untouchables has increased whenever and wherever the laws of untouchability are enforced. For instance, the Dhobi caste (washermen), which is regarded as untouchable in northern parts of India, is not regarded so in Maharashtra.

Vivekanand Jha traces the history of untouchables in four phases. According to him, in the later Vedic texts (circa the 6th century B.C.), the Chandalas (sweepers/removers of dead bodies of animals/cremators of corpses) and the Pulkasas/ Pukkasas (refuse cleaners from the temples and palaces/tanners) are mentioned as objects of *abhorrence*, but not as untouchables (Jha, 1975:14). Chandala, Pulkasa and Nishada (hunter) were tribes in the beginning (Ibid.). In the second phase, mentioning the source of the *Dharmasutras* (circa 400 B.C.), he states that infection was regarded transmitting from a Chandala through sight, speech and proximity, but shadow was not regarded as polluting (Ibid.:15). Jainism and Buddhism are contemporary religions. So it is necessary to check the source(s) of Jain texts. A story in the *Uttaradhyayana Sutra* reveals that a Sovaga (Svapaka/Chandala) who became a monk and sage, was possessed of the highest virtues and lectured to a Brahman teacher in his sacrificial enclosure... (cited in Jha, 2004:178). This example shows that the notion of untouchability towards the Chandalas was not institutionalised, but that the lowest social status was ascribed to them. We find rules such as not taking food from the house of Shudras, prohibiting them from listening to the recitation of Vedic hymns and coming in contact with Aryans on an equal footing, introduced first time in the *Dharmasutras*. In the Buddhist era, the Aryas'/Brahmans' priestly status/supremacy was challenged. In Panini's grammar, the term *nirvasita* is used. Patanjali defines it 'as a person whose contact was so forbidding that the pots in which he had dined could not be purified by any means whatsoever (Patil, 1982:280). According to Sharad Patil, 'the word literally means a person who lives not in a boycotted, but in a separate dwelling' (Ibid.:281). The Panini grammar is written in the 4th century B.C. It indicates that the untouchable castes were living in separate quarters. It is noted that before the writing of the *Manusmrti*, there is no mention of any untouchable castes other than the Chandala, the Pulkasa and the Nishada in the *Vedic Samhitas* (Jha, 1975:18).

In the third phase of the *Smrti* times (2nd c. A.D.) untouchability is *manifested*. Looking at various injunctions in the *Manusmrti*, the process of segregation of caste society in hierarchical order becomes nearly complete. In *Vishnusmrti* (3rd c. A.D.), the word *asprusya*, the untouchables, is used. The Svapaka is the other untouchable mentioned in it (Ibid.:24). *Yajnavalkyasmrti* (5th c. A.D.) lays down a fine for touching a person of higher caste (Ibid.:25). The above-mentioned groups appear as untouchables who are distinguished from the Shudras. These four phases have been distinguished without offering any explanation towards the growth of untouchability.

In his study, S.N. Srivastava also makes an attempt to discover the origin and growth of untouchability. He throws light on the aspect of '*conflict*' between the invader tribes and the aboriginals. In the early phase, his survey of ancient literature reveals the history of slavery of the defeated aboriginals in conflict with the Aryans, and in the later phase, the literature in the *Smrti* period (2nd c. A.D.-5th c. A.D.) shows the degradation of the Kshatriyas and the Shudras as well as groups belonging to the contemptuous occupations to the status of untouchables.

The history of the Vedic Age (14th–10th c. B.C.) reveals that there was antagonism between the Aryans and the Dasas-Dasyus. The Aryan invaders called the Dasas aboriginal enemies, viz., the Dasas-Dasyus and the Nishadas (Srivastava, 1980:3). The Dasas did not practise the Aryan rituals (Ibid.:4). In encounters, the Dasas and the Dasyus were slaughtered, their fortresses and walled settlements destroyed and they themselves defeated by the Aryans and made slaves with the function of serving others (Ibid.:9). The word 'Dasa' is used in the sense of slave in the later portion of the *Rig Veda* (Ibid.:14). There are a number of mentions of slaves in Vedic, Jain and Pali texts as well as on the inscriptions of Asoka (Ibid.:42,46). They were associated with the lands and dwelling places of the wealthy people. Srivastava mentions six classes of slaves, viz., (a) from birth, (b) from purchase, (c) from not paying of debts, (d) made during famine, (e) from non-payment of fines, and (f) war prisoners (Ibid.:45). All these sources reveal that there was slavery, but the literature does not indicate the existence of the notion of untouchability towards the slave population.

The Aryans were known for their institution of sacrifice. The celebration of the sacrificial rite was not open to the Shudras. *Taittiriya Brahmana* (10th c. B.C.) says that the Shudra had no right to touch milk at the sacred fire. It suggests that the notion of defilement by touch was confined to the sacrificial rite. Therefore, N.K. Dutt rightly notes that the Dasas or the Shudras were not considered impure (Dutt, 1968:20).

In the above-mentioned studies, both Jha and Srivastava have not accepted the theory of broken men offered by B.R. Ambedkar in his *Untouchables*, but neither has made any serious attempt to advance any theoretical or historical explanation on the phenomenon of untouchability.

Historical Roots

Louis Dumont is known for his fundamental conception, namely "the opposition of the pure and the impure" of the caste system (Dumont, 1988:43). In his analysis, three elements are shown: (a) the superiority of the pure over the impure, (b) the separation of the two, and (c) the division of labour of pure and impure occupations (Ibid.). Accordingly, those who are engaged in impure occupations are separated from the class of sacred objects. Ambedkar says the identification of untouchable castes by their engagement in impure jobs is an error because, according to him, the class of impure came into existence at the time of the *Dharmasutras* (4th c. B.C.), but the untouchables came into being much later than that. (Ambedkar, 1948:242). Thus, he refutes the occupational basis of the notion. The roots of the notion are in the religion of the Brahmans who brought marriage, family, caste and power relations under regulation—this is a known fact. Here, it is necessary to draw attention to Dumont's note, 24d, in which he says: "This ritual theory alone does not explain caste as seen in Indian society over the last thousand or two thousand years" (Ibid:356). Why did the Brahmans regulate social life in their favour and impose stringent codes on the lowest stratum of people? For explanation, in the present context of revivalism, it is necessary to advance certain historical aspects discussed by the non-Brahman scholars, Maharshi Vitthal Ramji Shinde and Dr. Babasaheb Ambedkar, in their work.

In the writings of some non-Brahman leaders of the social reform movements, we find statements/independent studies regarding Buddhism as the religion of untouchable communities. In the 1930s, Masilamani, a non-Paraiah but a Buddhist by conviction, and Iyothee Thass, a Buddhist by faith and a historiographer, both leaders of non-Brahmanism in Tamil Society, argued that the Paraiah's religion was Buddhism (Geetha and Rajadurai, 1998:96-97). Shinde (1976; first published 1933) collected data of about 30 years and published the book, *Bharatiya Asprushyatecha Prashna* (*The Problem of Indian Untouchability*) in Marathi in 1933. Ambedkar's work *The Untouchables*, appeared in 1948.

To trace the roots of untouchability, Shinde used ancient works such as the *Samhitas*, the *Bhagwad Gita*, Panini's grammar, *Upanishads*, Buddhist literature, some commentaries, empirical writings and his field observations in various parts of India and Myanmar. He adopted a multidimensional approach in dealing with the subject, viz., historical, anthropological, sociological, linguistical and comparative.

Shinde surveyed the ancient literature to look for mentions of untouchability. In his survey, the *Rig Veda*, the most ancient text (14th c. B.C.) does not indicate the names of outcastes. In the times of the Brahmans (10th c. B.C.), he notes that in the third chapter of *Krishnayajurvediya Taittiriya*, the Chandala and the Pulkasa are mentioned as *nations* (Shinde, 1976:23). In the *Brhadaranyaka* and *Chandogya Upanishads* (6th c. B.C.), there are contemptuous mentions of the Chandala and Pulkasa (Ibid.:22). In the times of the Buddha (born in 567 B.C.), untouchability was not manifested. Buddha is known for accepting Sunit, a scavenger, in his Bhikku Sangha (an association). Had there been a practice of untouchability, Sunit would not have dared to touch the feet of the Tathagata. In Shri Krishna's times (5th–6th c. B.C.), the Chandalas were chiefs of the nation and the incident which Shinde notes is that Krishna, a Kshatriya, was not only attracted to a Chandala girl, he even married her (Ibid.:27-30). But in the *Astadhyayi Panini* (4th c. B.C.), the Sutar, Lohar and Chandala are described as outcastes and their utensils termed not fit for use by upper-caste persons (Ibid.:21). Like other scholars, Shinde notes the manifestation of untouchability in the *Manusmrti*. But he is critical of it for making untouchable castes, the progeny of the mixture of castes. He also questioned the possibility of such untouchable castes in such a large population and condemned the *Smrtis* and *Puranas* as partisan books (Ibid.:44-48).

In Shinde's view, the Buddhist period (6th–1st c. B.C.) is important for certain remarkable changes in the pre-Buddhist culture of Aryan society. The early period of both Buddhists and Jains is known for the protests against the Arya practice of animal sacrifice and other Vedic practices. The noteworthy feature of the Buddhists is that they practised non-violence; the Jains were strictly vegetarian. Emperor Asoka (272-232 B.C.) is also known for stopping the killing of animals.

Brahmans' Vegetarianism

Because of the rise of Buddhism and Jainism against the practice of *yajna*, the institution of sacrifice, i.e. the killing of animals, especially cows and horses, the Brahmans, who were non-vegetarian in the Vedic Age, became vegetarian and teetotaller later (Dutta, 1931:204). And they maintained the strictly. They regarded vegetarianism and teetotalism as symbols of purity. These values adopted by the Brahmans helped them achieve higher status over the other non-vegetarian and alcohol imbibing castes. Jainism strictly forbids consumption of both meat and alcohol. The same is the case with Lingayatism (Veershaivism) after Basvesvara, i.e. the 12th century A.D. This is why Jains and Lingayats claim their superior status on par with the Brahmans. Since Buddha did not prohibit meat eating, the Buddhists did not give it up. And, the untouchable castes are known for their eating of beef, a forbidden food for other caste Hindus.

Some Untouchable Castes Were Rulers/Chieftains

Shinde defines untouchability as an extreme form of slavery (Shinde, 1976:15). According to him, when the defeated depressed castes were kept as servants by the conqueror castes, there was a possibility of the emergence of caste slavery, or untouchability (Ibid.). Since untouchability is associated with the filthy jobs of the untouchables, the statement confirms the verse in Chapter V of *Naradasmrti* (2nd c. A.D.) that impure work was done by the slaves. But there is no history of slaves who were made untouchables. On the basis of Sanskrit and Pali literature, he states that before the emergence of the Buddha, there were quarrels between the Brahmans and the Kshatriyas. And the Vaisyas and the Shudras had fallen into contempt in the eyes of the Brahmans. Further, he states that castes such as Chandala, Nishada, Vrushala and Pulkasa were at the outskirts of the village and outside the four-fold order of caste (Ibid.:19).

Some references are available about a few ex-untouchable castes as the original inhabitants of this land. We find mention in the *Mahabharata* and the *Ramayana* (4th c. B.C.–4th c. A.D.) that the Nishadas (the fishermen in the northern parts of India) were the rulers (Srivastava, 1980:49,53). Shinde states that

Maharashtra was the land of the Mahars and the Mangs. They were Patils (heads) of many villages before the advent of the Marathas, but once they were defeated, they became servants of the village/Marathas (Shinde, 1976:152-176). Even today, Mahars are sizeable landholders and Patils in some villages in the Nagpur region. It is interesting to note the etymology of Mahar as given by Mahatma Jyotiba Phule, who says it means a big enemy, and it is true that they were/are seen as enemies by the ruling castes, particularly the Brahmans and the Marathas. Similar is the case of the Malas in Andhra (Ibid.:104). Rajaramshastri Bhagwat described "Maharashtra as the nation of Mahars". Vamanrao Bhat said that the Mahars were the rulers of Maharashtra (Khairmode, 1978: Chapter 1).

The early social history of Tamil Nadu, especially during the Cankam age, the 1st–3rd centuries A.D., does not indicate any trace of untouchability. The social groups, viz., Kurava, Kurumpar, Pana, Paraiya and Valluvar, who were considered untouchables during the later period, were not segregated as untouchables in the Cankan age. The Kurumpars had their own kings and forts. The Panas served as minstrels of kings and chieftains. The Cola king, Killivalavan, had dinner with the Panas (Hanumanthan, 2004:128-131).

Talking about the Mangesh Temple in Goa, the Venkatesh of Tirupati (addressed as Mangalapati), the kingdom of Mangala destroyed by the Chalukyas, and the concentration of Mangs on a large scale in southern Maharashtra, the neighbouring border of Andhra and Karnataka, Shinde suggests that Mangs are also defeated people like the Paraiahs, Namsudras, Pulayas, Korwis and Bavuris (Shinde, 1976:78-79, 105-107).

Some studies observed that the Bhumij tribe, which had attained Rajput/Kshatriya status, and the Doms, who had founded their kingdoms in the Himalayan foothills in the 13th century, are reduced to the status of untouchables later (Jaiswal, 1998:88). But the history of their degradation is not ascertained.

Both Shinde and Ambedkar hold the view that the untouchable castes were rulers. In ancient times, many tribes entered the Indian territories and inhabitant groups were defeated in the ensuring fights (Srivastava, 1980:9). Although we do not have any available source of direct reference of the fights between invader tribes and untouchable castes, Ambedkar calls the untouchables the Broken Men in primitive society who were defeated in warfare (Ambedkar, 1948:275). The assumption is that some of the defeated had become Buddhists in the past.

Evidence of the Spread of Buddhism

We know that in ancient times, Buddhism was spread in India's neighbouring and the far eastern countries of the world, such as Myanmar, Sri Lanka, China, Korea, Thailand, Cambodia, Vietnam, Java and Japan. There is much archaeological and historical evidence to show that it was spread throughout India. The *stupas* at Sanchi in Madhya Pradesh, Sarnath in Uttar Pradesh, the Buddhist shrines in Bodh Gaya in Bihar, the Ajanta and Ellora caves in Maharashtra, the Buddhist universities at Nalanda and Taxashila are famous examples of the religion's spread. Little known Buddhist caves in Maharashtra are: Elephanta near Mumbai, the caves at Nashik and Kanheri, Karle, Bhaje and Naneghat in Pune district, and the Pandav caves at Panhala in Kolhapur district. In Andhra, Buddhist *stupas* and *viharas* were discovered during excavations at Nagarjunikonda in the 1930s. Buddhist inscriptions and sculptures that are nearly 2,000 years old were found close to the Jagannath Temple at Pauni in Bhandara district of Maharashtra in 1968. In May-June 2000, the Archaeological Survey of India found *stupas* of the Asokan era (273–232 B.C.) at Karsaria and at Lauriya-Nandangarh in Bihar. What happened to both ancient Buddhism and the Buddhists in India? The following is an excerpt that gives evidence of the destruction of Buddhism by the revival of Brahmanism:

> It is the humble opinion of the author of this thesis that if a thorough search is made in the ancient temples of Kerala, we will be able to bring to light many more Buddhist images and other vestiges. Till very recently, all the Buddhist images we have mentioned above have been lying unnoticed in temple tanks or in obscure sheds within the temple walls. Many Buddhist images must be now passing off as the images of Hindu deities. For example, the Killiroor and Bilamperoor images are even now being worshipped as images of Vishnu or Bhagavati (Alexander, 1949:74-75).

Is there a strategy among the Brahman priests of not allowing the common worshippers to enter the sanctum sanctorum or to touch the idol in the famous temples such as those of Balaji of Tirupati, Vithoba of Pandharpur and Mahalaxmi of Kolhapur? Is there a fear that the real image will be exposed to close observation?

To whatever extent, there is evidence of the destruction of Buddhism, but there is hardly any evidence of the present ex-untouchables' past as Buddhists. Nevertheless, in his Broken Men theory, Ambedkar states that the untouchables were Buddhists.

The Broken Men Theory

Ambedkar advanced the Broken Men theory of untouchability. It is very much along the lines of enquiry that Shinde considered in the 1930s. In the writing of *The Untouchables* (1948), Ambedkar did not acknowledge Shinde, but we have sufficient evidence to state that he must have read the writings of Shinde on the origins of untouchability, because four articles authored by Shinde on the untouchable class in Brhamadesh/ East Bengal have been published in four issues of the fortnightly periodical, *Bahishkrit Bharat*, edited by Ambedkar, on July 29, 1927; August 12, 1927; March 15, 1929; and March 29, 1929.

Adopting Shinde's perspective, Ambedkar developed the Broken Men theory for the origin and explanation of untouchability. According to him, "untouchability is the notion of defilement, pollution, contamination and the ways and means of getting rid of their defilement" (Ambedkar, 1948:249). He states the unique features of untouchability among the Hindus as follows:

(a) A case of permanent, hereditary stain, which nothing can cleanse,
(b) The isolation of a class—a class of territorial segregation in the ghetto, and
(c) Such people who are unfit to receive any religious service from a Brahman priest.

These features indicate that there is much antipathy towards the untouchables. Ambedkar offers an explanation, saying that the untouchables were the Broken Men and they were Buddhists (Ibid.). Since they were Buddhists, they did not revere the Brahmans, did not employ them as their priests and the Brahmans, on their part, preached contempt and hatred of the Buddhists (Ibid.).

Ambedkar traces two roots of untouchability:

(a) Contempt and hatred of the Broken Men as Buddhists by the Brahmans, and
(b) Continuation of beef-eating by the Broken Men after it had been given up by the others.

In the first place, in Ambedkar's view, the Brahmans created a feeling of hatred and contempt for the Buddhists in the minds of the Hindus (Ibid.). This statement is supported by some passages in *Manusmrti* and *Aparaksmrti*, which say that touching a Buddhist and entry into a Buddhist temple require a purificatory bath (Ibid.). Interestingly, P.V. Kane also mentions a kind of Chandala by conduct in his *History of Dharmasastras:* ".... persons were treated as untouchables simply through religious hatred and abhorrence because they belonged to a different sect or religion" (Kane, 1997:168). And further quoting verses from the *Sattrimsan-mata* and *Brahmandapurana* that "on touching Bauddhas, Pasupatas, Jainas, Lokayatikas, Kapilas (Samkhyas) and guilty of doing actions inconsistent with their caste, one should enter water with the clothes on and also on touching Saivas and atheists" (Ibid.:169). Thus, it is clearly revealed that persons of other religions/sects were looked down upon as Chandalas. Why did the notion of untouchability not develop against the non-Buddhists? Ambedkar answers that the Buddhists continued eating beef and since the Jainas, for example, were strict vegetarians, the question of abhorrence in practice did not arise. In *Mricchakatika* (4th c. A.D.), there is an incident of beating a Buddhist monk for no wrong done by him and another of shunning a monk travelling on the road. Both are the examples of hatred towards Buddhists (Ambedkar, 1948:316). The point is that of examining the religious background of the untouchables. In this regard, Ambedkar states that there is no direct evidence. But in other sources, there are some mentions of the Buddhist background of a few untouchable castes.

Buddhist Untouchables

Shinde elaborated the Buddhist background of a few of the present untouchable castes. Regarding the Pulayas in Kerala, based on Colonel Olcott's writing, *The Poor Pariah* (1901), mentioning the Pariahs' idol, Shasta, an another name of the Buddha found in *Amarkosh*, he states that they were Buddhists (Shinde, 1976:49-51). With reference to Mahamahopadhyaya Harprasad Shastri's *Modern Buddhism and its Followers in Orissa* (1911), he says that the outcastes in Orissa were Buddhists (Ibid.:54). He also gives another reference of Babu Nagendranath Basu who, during his tour of Orissa, found some Buddhist references in the Pana untouchables' folksongs and collected the idols of Mahayana Bouddha from the Bauri/Bathuri untouchables (Ibid.:55). Citing Harprasad Shastri's article in the monthly issue of *Deccan Review* (1921),

Shinde quotes: "As the saying goes, the depressed classes in Bengal were the descendants of Buddhists, who were the rulers in the past (Ibid.:59).

Regarding the second root of untouchability, it is a known fact that many of the untouchables eat beef, some caste persons remove the skin of the cow and other animals and numerous manufacture leather articles from it. Ambedkar discussed the beef-eating aspect and stated that the Brahmans who were beef eaters in Vedic times, gave it up because the Buddha rose against the Yajna and became vegetarian. The objective was to regain their supremacy. Manu prescribed penances for slaying a cow/bull (see *Manusmrti*, XI, 109,116,117). Since then, the Hindus have a taboo against beef-eating. Ambedkar quotes a verse from the *Vedavyasamrti*, which says that 'cow's flesh eaters are known as Antyajas' (Ambedkar, 1948:319). Another evidence is that Chandragupta II (412 A.D.) made cow-killing a *mahapataka*, a mortal sin or a capital offence. In such conditions, the law of interdictions does apply to the cow, the sacred object, and since the Broken Men continued eating beef, they were liable to be separated from the others (Ibid.:352-354). Thus, beef-eating was considered an additional ground for an offence to the Brahmans.

Taking into account the fact that beef-eating was a sin in Chandragupta's time, Ambedkar fixes an approximate time of about 400 A.D. for the appearance of untouchability (Ibid.:379). So let us have a look at Chandragupta's rule for the revival of Brahmanism.

Revival of Brahmanism

In the history of ancient India, the rules of both Pushyamitra Sunga and the Guptas are mainly responsible for combating Buddhism and reviving Brahmanism. Pushyamitra Sunga (180-151 B.C.) is known as a great persecutor of Buddhism. He had a combative attitude against Buddhism. He murdered the

Buddhist emperor, Brihadratha, of the Maurya dynasty. He performed two horse sacrifices as a mark of the revival of the Brahmanic religion when he ascended the throne of Patliputra. In his period, Brahmanic literature such as the *Ramayana*, and the *Mahabharata* were written. Sanskrit was made the court language.

The Brahmanic reaction was equally marked against Buddhism in the Gupta period (2nd c. B.C.–4th c. A.D.). This period is known for the revival of the Vedic religion and the predominance of Brahmanism. A.S. Altekar says that several sacrifices were performed during the period, 275-460 A.D. (Majumdar and Altekar, 1946:368-370). The *Puranas* and *Smrtis* (including *Manusmrti*) were written during this period. Two religious cults—Vaishnavism and Saivism—were developed as well. In the Gupta times to regain their lost status, the Brahmans declared cow a sacred animal and made cow-killing a sacrilegious act. The castes which were not the part of the Yajna culture did not give up beef-eating.

The Role of the Militant Saivites

It is interesting to note that in the early Saivite tradition, there was no feeling of caste and no notion of untouchability because the sixty-three statues of the lowest untouchable Saivites were erected in all the Siva temples (Hanumanthan, 2004:139). Who made the Buddhists untouchables and how? According to P.C. Alexander, the movement of the militant Saivites was mainly responsible for the Buddhists falling to the level of untouchables. For the consideration of readers, the following is the excerpt from his unnoticed historical study *Buddhism in Kerala* (1949):

> The Namboothiri Brahmans were the chief defenders of the Vedic faith and the chief opponents of the Buddhists in Kerala. Sankara's teaching had profound and far-reaching influences in Kerala. The Namboothiris constituted themselves into a militant band for establishing the supremacy of the Vedic faith

> and carried on a vigorous persecution of the Bauddhas. It was during this period that the word 'Bauddha' became a synonym for a contemptible man. The *viharas* of the Buddhists were converted into Hindu temples and the images of the Buddha were removed from all the prominent places. Social ostracism was the chief weapon which the Namboothiris used for destroying the influence of Buddhism. The Bauddhas were not allowed to enter Hindu houses and temples and to participate in social functions. They could not bathe in the public tanks or even touch the wells of the Hindus. The disabilities imposed on the Bauddhas were so great that they were compelled to change their religion (184-185).

Alexander does not state that the status of the present untouchable castes in India is the result of the Saivite movement. But his observation certainly helps us understand both the destruction of Buddhism in India and the downgradation of the earlier Buddhists to the low status of untouchables.

According to K.R. Hanumanthan, the notion of the caste system and untouchability occurred in the period of the Pallavas (575-900 A.D.), i.e. Brahmans of the Bharadvaja *gotra* (clan), who enacted laws of the Chaturvarna system. He discerns that the laws of taboo against the consumption of liquor prescribed in the *Dharmasastras* were applied to the toddy tapper Ezhavas and Tiyas in Kerala and the Shanars in Tamil Nadu. Also in Kerala, the Pulaiyas, who were killing, skinning and eating the flesh of both cow (the sacred animal) and bull (the vehicle of Siva) caused them to become outcastes (Hanumanthan, 2004:136-38).

To sum up, scholars adhering to the ancient works do not accept the Broken Men theory of untouchability without attributing it to any historical social condition. The mention of the Chandalas, the Pulkasas/Pukkusas, the Rathakaras, the Nisadas and the Nilakaras (basket makers), and the Venas (basket weavers) in Pali texts indicate their low and despised status. We have seen that these communities were the object of abhorrence, and not untouchables, as Vivekanand Jha perceived. This phenomenon remains unascertained. Despite their despicable status, Sunit and Svapak, for example, who belonged to the lowest caste, were admitted to the Bhikku Sangha. The *Uttaradhyayana*, a Jain source, reveals that a Sovaga, a Chandala by birth, visited the sacrificial enclosure of a Brahman teacher and lectured to him on certain values of life (cited in Sharma, 1958:134). Some questions are, therefore, pertinent to further enquiry. Despite the mention of many *theras* and *theris* from the lowest groups and the fact of the spread of Buddhism throughout India, how did it happen that the Buddhists in ancient India suddenly disappeared and that untouchable castes appeared in the *Smrti* period? The full growth of untouchability is traced to the early *Smrti* period, i.e. 2nd century A.D. the 4th century A.D., which Ambedkar pushed as the time for the appearance of untouchability, may not be accepted. But Buddhism, which had spread in various parts of India till the time of the rise of Pushyamitra Sunga (180 B.C.), was destroyed in the Gupta period. The destruction of Buddhism, especially in Gupta period, has hardly been made a matter of in-depth historical enquiry. The studies of Shinde, Ambedkar and Alexander indirectly attribute the growth of untouchability to the revival of Brahmanism in the Gupta period. The persecution movement of the Saivites against the Buddhists, as Alexander observes, could be considered a contributing factor. How could Alexander's observation regarding the ostracised status of the earlier Buddhists in Kerala be ignored? In addition, how can a source of P.V. Kane's *Dharmasastras*, which mentions Buddhists as Chandalas by conduct, be overlooked? Here, therefore, the attempt is not to generalise that all the present ex-untouchable castes were Buddhists. But it is difficult to reject the hypothesis that the resisting castes amongst the ex-untouchable sections belonged to the Buddhist faith. It requires more investigation to come up with sufficient evidence. How has the number of four despicable castes in ancient times increased to over seven hundred in later times? Could it be without the aggresive role of Brahmanism?

Note

The figures of centuries in parentheses are from the source: Ghatge, A.M. (ed.), 1978, *An Encyclopaedic Dictionary of Sanskrit on Historical Principles*, Vol. I, Part III, Pune: Deccan College Postgraduate & Research Institute.

References

Alexander, P.C., 1949, *Buddhism in Kerala*, Annamalainagar: Annamalai University.

Ambedkar, B.R., 1948, *The Untouchables* (Reprint in Dr. Babasaheb Ambedkar Writings and Speeches, Vol. 7, Mumbai: Government of Maharashtra,1990).

Dumont, Louis, 1988, *Homo Hierarchicus: The Caste System and its Implications,* New Delhi: Oxford University Press.

Dutt, N.K., 1968, *Origin and Growth of Caste in India*, Vol. I, Kolkata: Firma K.L. Mukhopadhyay.

Geetha, V. and S.V. Rajadurai, 1998, *Towards a Non-Brahmin Millennium: From Iyothee Thass to Periyar*, Kolkata: Samya.

Hanumanthan, K.R., 2004, 'Evolution of Untouchability in Tamil Nadu up to A.D. 1600' in Parasher-Sen, Aloka (ed.), *Subordinate and Marginal Groups in Early India*, New Delhi: Oxford University Press (Reprint from *Indian Historical Review*, July 1996-January 1997, pp. 41-65).

Jaiswal, Suvira, 1998, *Caste*, New Delhi: Manohar Publications (Reprint 2000).

Jha, Vivekanand, 1975, 'Stages in the History of Untouchables', *Indian Historical Review*, Vol. 2.

—, 2004, 'Candala and the Origin of Untouchability' in Parasher-Sen, Aloka (ed.), op. cit.

Kane, P.V., 1997, 'History of Dharmasastras, Vol. II, Part I, Pune: Bhandarkar Oriental Research Institute (3rd edition).

Khairmode, C.B., 1978, *Dr. Bhimrao Ramji Ambedkar* (Marathi), Vol. I. Mumbai: Pratap Prakashan (3rd edition).

Majumdar, R.C. and A.S. Altekar (eds.), 1946, *A New History of the Indian People*, Vol. VI, Lahore: Motilal Banarasidass.

Patil, Sharad, 1982, *Dasa-Sudra Slavery*, New Delhi: Allied Publishers Pvt. Ltd.

Sharma, R.S., 1958, *Sudras in Ancient India*, New Delhi: Motilal Banarasidass.

Shinde, Maharshi V.R., 1976, *Bharatiya Asprushyatecha Prashna* (Marathi), Mumbai: Government of Maharashtra (original edition 1933).

Singh, K.S., 1998, *India's Communities*, Volume VI, New Delhi: Oxford University Press.

Srivastava, S.N., 1980, *Harijans in Indian Society*, Lucknow: The Upper India Publishing House Pvt. Ltd.

5

Perspectives of the Anti-Caste Movements

Subaltern Sociological Visions

Gail Omvedt

The anti-caste movements, or Dalit-Bahujan movement, had a unique sociological vision. It contrasted with that of dominant social trends in its analysis of Indian national identity, religion, socio-economic development, indeed in all ways. More than Marxism (because Marxism has not been able to provide an analysis of caste, a major exploitative system), it provides a genuine subaltern "perspective from below" on Indian society. This paper will examine some of the elements of this perspective, contrasting it with the sociological perspective of the Indian elite.

Elite Sociological Perspectives

In a set of essays collected in *The Nation and Its Fragments*, Partha Chatterjee has taken up the question of the nation and the public as they concretely emerged in India in relation to colonialism. In industrialised, imperialist countries, though the market and factory production destroy old forms of community, the development of the nation and public sphere in the industrialised, imperialist countries takes place with a public sphere constituting the (bourgeois) equality of citizens and the nation serving as the (bourgeois) reconciliation of the community with the state. In the colonised world, however, Chatterjee argues there is a different process, precisely because there is no equality, not even bourgeois equality, in the political sphere. For this reason, the nation is not, and cannot be, simply created on the basis of the political and the public. Rather, it is created in a very different way, appealing to older forms of community, forms which can in some way be maintained outside the challenge of European power.

> The crucial break in the history of anticolonial nationalism comes when the colonized refuse to accept membership of this civil society of subjects. They construct their national identities within a different narrative, that of the community. They do not have the option of doing this within the domain of bourgeois civil-society institutions. They create, consequently, a very different domain—a cultural domain—marked by the distinctions of the material and the spiritual, the outer and the inner. This inner domain of culture is declared the sovereign territory of the nation, where the colonial state is not allowed entry, even as the outer domain remains surrendered to the colonial power. The rhetoric here (Gandhi is a particularly good example) is of love, kinship, austerity, sacrifice. The rhetoric is in fact antimodernist, antiindividualist, even anticapitalist. The attempt is, if I may stay with Gandhi for a while, to find, against the grand narrative of history itself, the cultural resources to negotiate the terms through which people, living in different, contextually defined, communities, can coexist peacefully, productively, and creatively within large political units (Chatterjee, 1992:237-9).

Thus, while the elite strove to extend the powers of Indians within the political sphere, in the nationalist movement against colonial rule, they simultaneously constructed a realm of national identity imagined in terms of spirituality and maintained primarily in the sphere of the home and the inner world. Thus, the 'nation' in a very major sense was seen as existing outside the state, and constructed in reference to the 'private' sphere of the inner life and the home.

However, this spiritual base of nationalism for the elite was constructed with reference to an updated Brahmanic tradition. It is worth stressing that all the elite social reformers as well as the orthodox nationalists, those who wanted to modify tradition and those who wanted to maintain it in its main form, agreed in seeing the *Vedas* as the fountainhead of Indian cultures, the Aryans as their forerunners, and the *Shastras* and *Smrtis* as constituting the important sacred texts providing the base for spirituality. Much of this was in reaction to colonial denigration of Indian tradition, but the elite seized the opportunity to defend this tradition as a whole. The term 'Hindu', with its originally geographical reference, was appropriated as the name for a religion, and the religion was identified as the national religion of the Indian people. Muslims and Christians were defined as following ideas and religions of 'foreign' origin, and while there was tremendous variation in ideas about what this meant—with the more reformist 'secular' elements stressing the need to form 'Hindu-Muslim unity'—there was not much disagreement about the idea that somehow the Brahmanic tradition was uniquely Indian and thus the source of nationalist inspiration.

Gandhi and Vivekananda provide vivid examples of this. When they argued that untouchables should not adopt a foreign religion, but rather try to reform 'their own' religion, what was precisely assumed was this national-religion of Hinduism as that of the people. There was really not much difference from the precise definition of Savarkar: "A Hindu is someone who considers India as his *patrubhumi* and *pitrubhumi*." They wanted to upgrade, change and develop this 'Hindu' tradition, but they wanted to maintain it.

This meant, as far as caste was concerned, that either two strategies were undertaken. For the more 'Hindu'-oriented nationalists there was an appeal to an idealised varna system, which had presumably fostered a harmonious society, in contrast to the degraded *jati* system of the modern era. This included the notion of *swardharma*, following the hereditary profession, so central to the new 'Bible' of Hinduism, the *Bhagwad Gita*. As Gandhi put it in his reply to Ambedkar's *Annihilation of Caste*:

> Caste has nothing to do with religion... it is harmful to both spiritual and national growth. Varna and Ashrama are institutions which have nothing to do with castes. The law of varna teaches us that we have each one of us to earn our bread by following the ancestral calling. It defines not our rights but our duties... it also follows that there is no calling too low and none too high. All are good, lawful and absolutely equal in status. The callings of a Brahman—spiritual teacher—and a scavenger are equal, and their due performance carries equal merit before God and at one time seems to have carried identical reward before man... Arrogance of a superior status by and of the varna over another is a denial of the law. And there is nothing in the law of varna to warrant a belief in untouchability. (The essence of Hinduism is contained in its enunciation of one and only God as Truth and its bold acceptance of Ahimsa as the law of the human family) (83).

The militant and more orthodox nationalists may have disagreed with the idea of ahimsa, but they did not challenge this notion of *varna*. Even Nehru, in *Discovery of India,* writes of the collective aspect of caste, which he considers more advanced than the 'individualism' of the modern West.

The other way of dealing with caste, however, was simply to ignore it. This was the main approach of the left nationalists, from the Communists to Nehru. It is worth remembering that Namboodripad's history of the freedom movement simply lamented the time being taken up with the 'mundane issue' of the uplift of the untouchables in Gandhi's Harijan movement. For the left, the central fact was economic, the relations of production and class struggle. Social issues, from caste to gender, could be relegated to the background because they were of little influence on class and nationalist struggle (except when the British could use them to divide and rule), and because they would be automatically solved with the socialist revolution. Marxism has been failing in India not simply because it did not provide the intellectual resources to deal with the concrete form of exploitation in Indian society, but even more than this, actively allowed its upper-caste proponents to ignore and sideline the question of caste. It also allowed a focus on 'nationalisation' or 'public ownership' (i.e. control by the bureaucracy, which has remained up to today upper-caste dominated) as the solution, by seeing exploitation primarily through private capital.

The 'spiritual' definition of the Indian nation, then (ignored and uncontested by the left secularists) allowed a reconciliation between the more orthodox and more reformist members of the nationalist elite, simply because it relegated concrete material issues of equality (not only interdining and intermarriage, but access to public resources and facilities, from use of public water facilities to government employment) to the background. Gandhians and Nehruvian leftists alike were in their own way 'Hindu nationalists' as much as Savarkarits and the increasingly belligerent RSS cadres.

What about the 'economic nationalism' of the elite? Today, we see a strange confluence in the arguments about *swadeshi*, with both the most right-wing Hindutva activists centred in the RSS and much of the left agreeing about the dangers of foreign capital and foreign cultural influence—a strange coming together on economic issues of the left and the Hindu right. This was also prefigured in the 19th century. *Swadeshi*—protectionism—was the solution offered by all sections of the Indian nationalists, and it was not for nothing that Phule wrote of "those stalwarts of purity (who) have been hiding their sword of religion under the guise of being great lovers of *swadeshi*, and telling the Shudras, Parsis and Muslims through their books, newspapers, Sabhas and similar methods that they should put aside all grumbling about the hierarchies and distinctions among those in the country and become united; and without becoming one, this unfortunate country will never make progress".

But *swadeshi* was not the only element of elite economic nationalism. At another level, we find an apparent contradiction, with two opposing trends—one, the dominant focus on heavy industry as the basis of development, and second, the Gandhian opposition to industrialisation and its praise of traditional village society and traditional industries (symbolised by the fostering of the *charkha* as a symbol of national identity). Here, Gandhism appears as a popular ideology, offering an alternative. After all, one might argue, what is the commonality between the fierce industrialism of most of the nationalists, who wanted heavy industry, a strong military, high technology and nuclear power so that India could become a 'leading nation' in the world, and the anti-industrial romanticism of Gandhism?

Yet the two coexisted very easily. The equation was simple: industrialism, bureaucracy and high technology for the elite; traditional industries and agriculture for the masses. Avoiding technology for mass-oriented consumption industries was (and continues to be) justified with the argument that since technology and automation presumably reduce employment, 'traditional' labour-using techniques were better. Hence, many consumption goods were 'reserved' for the small-scale sector and even for khadi industries; it was argued that these could produce for mass consumption. Similarly, 'basic education' for the masses (in fact, a neglect of primary education) and highly funded (but ultimately unsuccessful) universities for the elite. In fact, the policy followed in post-independent India, which united Gandhism and a heavy-industry focussed industrialisation, not only involved the exploitation of agriculture, but also the neglect and actual discouragement of much innovation in the production of consumption goods and simple tools, which were the main employment of most OBCs. In the process, agriculture remained backward (it has among the lowest production rates in the world today) and India's textile industry, which had once frightened British industrialists and which was a world leader even at the end of the colonial period, was to a large degree ruined: the western industrialised nations today get their clothes and many ordinary consumption goods, not from India, but from Latin American countries like Mexico and Asian countries like China.

What I would argue, in other words, was that an all-encompassing ideology, including the basic elements of 'Hindu nationalism' and 'economic nationalism', was formed by the upper-caste nationalist intellectuals in the 19th century. This provided the basic ideology for the Congress-led nationalist movements and the assumptions underlying the developmental policies followed after independence. The apparently different tendencies ranged from Hindutva to Gandhism, and also included Marxism in its Indian avatar, which accepted the 'Hindu' definition of Indian identity and the heavy-industry, state-oriented development. The true alternative, in contrast, was embodied in the Dalit and non-Brahman movements.

The Dalit-Bahujan Alternative

The nationalist movement has preoccupied the attention of scholars and intellectuals as the major movement in colonial Indian society. Yet there was another, equally powerful, but very different, movement, one with less access to resources, more dispersed, but with an equally strong vision. It is normally referred to as the 'social movement', yet this is a misnomer; it was equally national and political, though with very different assumptions and a very different social base.

I have referred to it as the anti-caste movement, though it can also be called the Dalit-Bahujan movement. Colonialism had not radically transformed the caste structure of traditional Indian society, rather it had consolidated it in a new form, with Brahmans dominating the bureaucracy as the centre of power and using new technologies of communication and organising to buttress their hegemony. Peasants became exploited by even heavier burdens of taxation than during pre-British times; artisans and traditional producers were affected by competition from the new British manufactured goods. The only bright spot was that a few from the masses of 'Shudras and Ati-Shudras' (in Phule's terminology) began to get education and emerge as intellectuals and leaders. Jotirao Phule in Maharashtra and Iyothee Thass in Tamil Nadu in the 19th century were followed by 20th century leaders such as Mukundrao Patil, Dinkarrao Javalkar, and, elsewhere in India, Mangoo Ram, Swami Acchutananad, Periyar and, of course, finally, B.R. Ambedkar. (It is worth remembering that Ambedkar referred to himself as a 'non-Brahman scholar' and affirmed his loyalty to the Satyashodhak movement even while criticising some of its trends.)

These intellectuals evolved an all-around theory, which has laid the basis for many of the social movements of recent decades. I will focus here on Phule, dealing with six major areas: caste, religion, nationalism, gender, imperialism and the economy, and environment and development.

Caste

The Dalit-Bahujan understanding of caste has its similarities with a Marxist approach: It views society as an amalgam of contradictions and exploitation—in contrast to the dominant elite depiction of a generally harmonious society and 'functionalist' interpretation of *varna*. However, the basis of exploitation was not 'class' as determined by relations to the economic means of production, but caste as historically constituted in Indian society. Bahujans and Dalits, or 'Shudras and

Ati-Shudras' in Phule's terminology, were the producing sections of society, but they were constituted historically and determined by heredity, i.e. by marriage and kinship along *jati* lines. The exploiting groups were the upper castes, but primarily the Brahmans in alliance with kings.

The intellectuals of the movement differed in their analysis of caste, with Phule and Periyar stressing the Aryan conquest of the original inhabitants of 'Balisthan' as crucial, and with Ambedkar denying this. However, they almost all saw a confluence of ideological/religious and political power as being the basis of exploitation and in this they differed from the Marxist emphasis on the means and relations of production.

Religion

The Dalit-Bahujan movement broke the tight link between religion and nation as constituted by elite nationalism, and denied the validity of Hinduism as the religion of the Indian people. Ambedkar himself gave one of the most trenchant criticisms of this in an early article on 'The Philosophy of Religion' when he made a distinction between 'ancient society' and 'modern society' and argued that in ancient society religion was constituted as a tribal religion, a religion of a people, while in modern society—and here he was not using the sociological identification, but seeing modernity as beginning with universal—religions were universal, seeing 'God' as the father of all and not just of a single ethnic group. In this case, Hinduism as defined by the Indian elite was a 'tribal religion'.

For Phule, 'Hinduism' was not a true religion; it was a creation of the 'Arya Bhat-Brahmans' to maintain their ideological hold over the masses; the words he used to describe it were *krutim, banavat, matlabi*—artificial, counterfeit, self-interested. Strikingly, when he described the ideal family as one in which people of different religious beliefs could live together, he mentioned the father as a Satyadharmist, the mother as a Buddhist, the son as a Muslim, the daughter as a Christian—Hinduism was not included.

All of the leading revolutionary intellectuals of the movement insisted that a true religion should be rationalist, based on truth (compatible with science), universalistic and promoting social justice. All of them rejected the Hinduism of their day, though the solutions they looked for were different—Phule in his version of deism, Periyar in atheism, Pandita Ramabai in Christianity and Iyothee Thass and Ambedkar in Buddhism.

NATIONALISM

While the emphasis on caste and the religious critique are well-known, the Dalit-Bahujan movement is rarely thought of as having a nationalistic vision. Phule and Ambedkar have been, in fact, consistently attacked as anti-national, the most recent being Arun Shourie's diatribe. This, however, is a crucially mistaken view of their approach. In fact, they had a very different vision of what constituted the nation.

Phule put the issue of nationalism very clearly in *Sarvajanik Satya Dharma Pustak:*

> Due to the false self-interested religion of the Aryans, the cunning Arya Bhat Brahmans consider the ignorant Shudras to be inferior; the ignorant Shudras consider the ignorant Mahars to be inferior; and the ignorant Mahars consider the ignorant Ati-Shudras inferior, but since marriage and social relations are forbidden among them all, naturally their various customs, eating habits, and rituals don't match each other. How can such a conglomerate of 18 grains be united to become a "nation" of integrated people?

This, of course, referred to the central role of equality in the Constitution of the modern nation that at a very important level, a nation had to be a community in which all were equals. This meant that the Indian nation was not, as with the elite, constituted in terms of the spiritual culture of the Indian people, but rather had to be realised at a material level. This did not necessarily require economic equality, but it did require the material exchange of marriage and social relations which could only exist among moral equals. This approach to the nation, needless to say, made it much easier to see people of different religious and philosophical beliefs (Muslims, Christians, Buddhists or whatever) as a genuine part of this belonging.

What this meant was specified even more starkly by Phule in the same work. In criticising the Sarvajanik Sabha, the dialogue went as follows:

> Govindrao: From the pure name of the Sarvajanik Sabha it would seem that Kunbis, Malis, Dhangars, Kolis, Bhils and other farmers must be its members, doesn't it?
>
> Jotirao: I think that there is no likelihood that Kunbis and others are its members.
>
> Govindrao: Then those Gujars, Marwaris and other shopkeepers who do business and the Salis, Koshtis, Khatris and others who sell cloth and other goods must be members, don't you think ?
>
> Jotirao: The Gujars, Marwaris and other shopkeepers and the Salis, Koshtis, Khatris and others are not even nominal members, as I have heard.
>
> Govindrao: Well, then, at least the Lohars, Sutars, Chambhars, Kumbhars, Nhavis, Parits and the Mangs, Bhats, Joshis and other village servants should be members of the sabha ?
>
> Jotirao: In that sabha! Don't even mention the name of the twelve village servants; among them the Brahman Joshis and Bhats are the only ones there; if any among them are government employees, then if they are not openly members ......Among these one or two may be independently rich while the rest live by doing law, clerical work, so on.
>
> Govindrao: What, in this Balisthan of all the 20 crores of population, only two crores are Arya Brahmans. If the Arya Brahmans of Pune have included only five or 20 people of other castes in the sabha, then how can anyone call this a Sarvajanik Sabha ?

This meant that the 'public' or 'national' community had to be a genuine, materially constituted one in the sense that all members of the various castes and communities should be represented in it. This not only led to the demand for 'reservations' in the bureaucracy, it also was in a sense a philosophical foundation for all the various struggles of the Dalit movement that were to come—struggles for water from public tanks, for the right to walk on public roads, for access to public facilities. Again, the existence of a national community had not simply to be proclaimed at the spiritual level, but actually constituted through the abolition of caste hierarchy, the developing of real social intercourse among all members of the nation, and the material access to public facilities and economic and political positions of power.

Gender

"My first salute is to Jotiba," is the beginning of a woman's liberation song of the new era of the women's movement. In fact, while the elite nationalists were constructing the image of the 'ideal Hindu woman', the Dalit-Bahujan movement was taking up the full-scale defence of women's rights. Pandita Ramabai, Tarabai Shinde and Savitribai Phule had been pioneers of the women's movement in India, even of autonomous women's organisations (the first being the Arya Mahila Samaj of Pandita Ramabai, founded in 1881 in Pune). With criticism mounting from even 'reformist' intellectuals against such efforts, Phule came strongly to the defence of women's rights in *Satkar,* arguing for women's superiority to men and for their right to full development of their personality. The marriage ceremony, he wrote for the *Satyashodhak Samaj,* showed its radicalism in the way in which husband and wife made vows to each other, with the husband admitting that women had been denied their rights, and promising to fight to establish them. The section on 'marriage' in the *Sarvajanik Satya Dharma Pustak* projected a system of free choice marriages, in which the girl and boy would however take the advice of their parents. This was as modern as could be imagined in the 19th century!

Imperialism and Economic Equality

While he generally approved of the cultural and philosophical impact of British rule, Phule's economic critique of British imperialism was as severe as any elite nationalist. It differed however in this: He saw the peasants as severely exploited through high taxes and constant cesses, but the 'drain of the surplus' went not simply to England and the English, but also to the Brahmans who constituted the bulk of the bureaucracy.

Phule also was quite aware of the degree to which the competition from British imported manufactured goods was ruining a good section of the Indian artisans. However, he forthrightly rejected the solution of *swadeshi*. This was for both philosophical and strategic reasons. At the philosophical level, Phule's image of humanity and its special characteristics differed both from the Marxist stress on man as a labouring being, and from the Gandhian notion of spirituality in which the ideal was represented by people content with the fulfillment of their limited needs in the traditional village society. Phule, instead, saw man as a being of intelligence and invention:

> Now, if we observe the process of nature, it will be seen that aside from knowledge, humans and all other animals are basically alike in their nature. Animals need food, sleep and sexual intercourse; they raise their young, protect themselves from their enemies and understand nothing aside from belching after they have eaten and since there is not a speck of change in this constant behaviour of theirs, there is no upheaval or basic change in their original condition. However, one marvellous specialty in the nature of human beings is intelligence. With its help, they have won superiority over all the fish, animals, birds, insects and other creatures; and with this intelligence they have invented the system of writing to put their thoughts down on paper. After this, since the people of the continents all around

> have kept note of all their experiences up to today, there has grown up a huge mass of experienced knowledge in the world, and with the help of this experiential knowledge and their intelligence, the Europeans send their important messages through telegraph wires thousands of miles to inform each other and bring lakhs of tons of grain by boat and train in the time of drought to save each other. And in the midst of such intelligent human beings, the Shudra Shivaji has brought to ruin the Muslim Badshah who worships one god and advised the farmers to take care of all the cows and the Brahmans and their self-interested religion! (*Shetkaryancha Asud*, Chapter 5).

Thus, it was, he argued, fundamentally, the gains in productivity—rather than imperialist profit—made possible by invention and innovation that made American and British manufactures so competitive. With its help, the British and captured the Laxmi of wealth and brought prosperity to their own country.

Similarly, Phule saw trade as basically progressive.

> In order that the domination won by their forefathers over the Shudras and Ati-Shudras by great exertion and fraud in ancient times should be indefinitely maintained, so that they would only serve them like horses, bullocks or other animals giving them happiness, or like lifeless land providing them with necessary and luxury foods, the Brahmans inserted into the Hindu religion that warning that no Hindu should go an inch beyond the *Atke* river, and if they went, they would become polluted. While the evil intention of the Brahmans was achieved by this, the rest of the people were greatly harmed. Since they could not get an idea of the customs of foreign people, they began to consider them as animals and not truly humans. With trade and commerce with people of other countries destroyed, they became destitute. (*Shetkaryancha Asud*, Chapter 2).

In other words, exchange of goods and ideas between people of different countries (globalisation) was fundamentally beneficial, and cutting off this exchange was one means that Brahmans had used historically to maintain their power.

What, then, was the solution to the problem of foreign competition? Here Phule's answer was clear—and it is very similar to that of people like Amartya Sen today. It could be summed up in two words, education and technology. The masses of people should be educated, with universal primary education being made compulsory and schools established with teachers drawn from the Shudras and Ati-Shudras, and it should be technologically oriented: Children should learn both literary skills and skills related to their occupation, whether agriculture or artisan crafts.

These emphases were continued in the later movement. Nearly all the regional sections of the Dalit-Bahujan movement opposed the nationalist *swadeshi* campaigns, including the Namashudras in Bengal, Iyothee Thass and his colleagues in Tamil Nadu and others. One of the earliest articles by Ambedkar in his first journal, *Mooknayak,* criticised *swadeshi* on economic grounds, arguing that if goods were being imported from foreign countries, it was because they were being produced more cheaply; barring them through protectionist measures might benefit domestic capitalists, but it would harm consumers. Similarly, the emphasis on education, and especially production-oriented education, was common to all the Dalit and non-Brahman movements—and the right to primary education was eventually written into the Ambedkar-drafted Constitution, though never enforced till today.

There was one more important aspect of the discussion of imperialism and exploitation that became lost with the later influence of Marxism: the emphasis on exploitation by the bureaucracy. Here, it is striking that Phule not only saw bureaucratic control as central and criticised the 'excessive pay and pensions' of its employees, he also asked for reservations for Dalits and Bahujans and for reduction of the bureaucracy (for example, of the Forest Department and Irrigation Department) and reduction in the pay scales of the higher-level employees. This had also been stressed in the earlier programmes of Periyar.

Environment and Development

With regard to the issue of environment and the path of development, the Dalit-Bahujan movement had its unique approach, one that can be found also in Phule. Phule looked at environmental issues from the perspective of farmers, criticising the 'gigantic Forest Department' which had monopolised every bit of common land and forest to the point where the farmers no longer had an inch of land to graze their cows, and attacking the Irrigation Department for giving immense money in interest to foreign moneylenders, but failing to provide water to the farmers' fields on time. His solution was a combined one of use of natural manures and composting with the development of all kinds of irrigation facilities, such as channels and 'small and big dams', along with technological precise delivery systems that could deliver the water to every farmer's field in the proper amount at the proper time.

In other words, Phule's approach was neither the Gandhian rejection of technologies, not the Nehruite orientation to high-tech industrialism; instead, it focussed on the upgrading of agriculture and related industries, and was a combination of indigenous 'natural' and modern technologies.

Thus, the Satyashodhak movement never opposed 'big dams'; indeed, reportedly when Senapati Bapat, a Brahman nationalist, organised the Mulshi Satyagraha, the Satyashodhak Samaj of the time took a position supporting the dam. Later, when Ambedkar was irrigation minister, he spoke of the need for just rehabilitation, but stressed the need for sufficient quantities of electricity for industrialisation, and multipurpose use of the dams being built—for hydropower, irrigation and transport (see Thorat). Similarly, when Shahu Maharaj of Kolhapur toured Europe looking for modern developments in animal husbandry and agriculture, he was expressing in practice the orientation to an agro-industrial development.

In conclusion, it can be said that the Dalit-Bahujan movements of 19th century India offered an all-encompassing alternative to elite nationalism. While there were differences, variations and historical development from the period of Phule in the 19th century to Ambedkar and Periyar and others in the 20th century, we can suggest that the following themes are common:

(1) In contrast to the 'economic nationalism' of the elite (which has been well researched), the focus was on what we might call socio-economic egalitarianism, emphasising a development in which the subject of development was not simply the 'nation', but the masses of the people.

(2) In contrast to the elite concern for industrialisation as the key to development, as well as to the Gandhian focus on the traditional village taken as an ideal of harmony, anti-caste movement intellectuals very often focussed on agricultural or agro-industrial development as a basis for all-around progress.

(3) In contrast to the simple concern to establish Indians instead of foreigners in positions of power, the anti-caste movement wanted representations for members of all castes and sections: Reservation was the main method adopted for this, and it was seen as connected with governance.

(4) In contrast to the concern for *swadeshi*, the anti-caste movement sought to meet foreign competition through all-around education, including technical education, and fought for universal compulsory primary education as well as higher education.

(5) A perspective of sustainable development and appropriate technology was put forward on environmental issues, which contrasted with Gandhism in its orientation to development of technology, but sought to utilise traditional production methods and skills as well to adopt the most sophisticated modern technologies.

6

Decoding Dalitism

Reflections on Dalit Literature in Maharashtra

S.P. Punalekar

The present essay is an exploration of underlying ideas and anxieties of Dalit masses revealed through Dalit literature. What are these anxieties about? Towards what socio-economic, political and cultural terrain are these anxieties directed? Dalit literature reveals that the anxiety and uneasiness essentially relate to their own social and economic life space, to their cultural landscape and the contradictions they face at every step (Ingle, 1975; Jog, 1985). They relate to their political past and present and also future.

Indeed, there is a need to fathom with care and sympathy the inner tensions of the Dalit masses, within their household and outside, i.e. in their neighbourhood, with peer groups, in school and community, on festive occasions, in the sugarcane fields or in roadside labour camps. One can also observe the replications in places like wayside inns, village Panchayats, village cultural events, and primary health centres or in factories (Pantawane, 1978).

Social scientists in India have just begun examining seriously some of these spots, but the present endeavour is as yet woefully short of capturing fully the essence of what is happening there in the Dalit existence and their perceptual world, and the intensity of those happenings (Guru, 1991). This shortcoming, if I am allowed to say so, relates to what we observe and record as social science practitioners. One may label it as an observational or perceptional lapse or inadequacy (Gupta, 1979).

Another aspect is that of interpretation or rendering meaning to what one sees and observes in the Dalit world, of course not in isolation, but in an interactive, participative mode. And here too, there are some gaps (sometimes critical, spurred by haste and over-enthusiasm). That deprives us of an opportunity to grasp in a reasonably coherent manner, the meanings behind Dalit action and reaction, their ambition and frustration. In other words, the complex domain of Dalit sense and sensitivity remain coded and obscure (Gupta, 1979; Punalekar, 1985). Decoding that sense and possibly the overall implications for other social units in particular, and potential social change in general, becomes an imperative task for social scientists interested in these issues (Human Rights Watch, 1999; Bodhirajkumar, 1988).

I do agree there are immense difficulties in overcoming these pitfalls. It is not an easy task to discover the inner world of the marginalised, be they Dalits or other similar social segments. Difficulties lie in the realms of theory and modes of gathering facts and insights. The problem is of a different kind—it is considered unnecessary or impertinent to decompose social realities into categories like Dalit and non-Dalit.

It is viewed as an overtly imagined construct, pregnant with possibilities of demolishing the domain of rational, scientific truths already attained through the existing repertoire of social science and its epistemological parameters (Zelliot, 1992; Waghmare, 1992). In other words, those who advocate such a view see no reason why such a categorisation is necessary. Upholders of this position have, in my view, a static and somewhat parochial view on the nature of social reality and the mode of collecting relevant material for analysis.

There is another angle and ideological position to buttress this view. This is the view that such categorisation (like Dalits and Adalits, Brahman and non-Brahman social formations) embodies the seeds of entanglement and dissension between groups which are otherwise living a non-antagonistic, non-combative existence, socially and culturally separate, yet together, if not physically, at least in a metaphysical sense. Unity, integrity, togetherness and harmony—these are the dominant values that guide such perception and analysis in sociological discourse (Punalekar, 1988; Omvedt, 1994).

> If the first view took shelter in scientism, the second took recourse to politics and ethics to justify their viewpoint. Let us admit that the concept 'Dalitism' is not alone to encounter such stiff opposition; others fighting for the question and cause of feminism, sustainable environment, alternative medicine, peace and human rights too have faced similar prospects in the evolutionary phase of their assertions.

Dalit literature in Maharashtra (and also in the states of Gujarat, Karnataka, Uttar Pradesh, Andhra and, more recently, Madhya Pradesh) brings to the fore, in my view, the need and urgency to confer an identity and independent status to Dalits not only in socio-political and economic terms, but also as a cultural and moral category. And this ought to be done not with a view to dismantle the supposed sense of unity, harmony or integrity, but to dismantle the hegemony of the ruling ideas of the socio-culturally entrenched groups and classes (Bagul, 1981b; Chavan, 1989; Fernandes, 1996). Dalit literature is principally for justice, equality and self-respect. It abhors and assiduously fights against values and practices of inhumanity and degradation, of indignity and caste-based hierarchies in present times.

At least in Maharashtra, and to some extent in Gujarat and U.P., it is evident that Dalit literature is largely fulfilling this role of uncovering the duplicity and decadence in the present social and cultural order. This is done through essays, short stories, novels, poetry and autobiographies. Dalit drama and journalism are two other forms of articulation that are slowly emerging on the scene in recent years, though they are yet to gather enough density.

Here, one may recall that Dr. Ambedkar, too, had taken the help of journalism in a decisive way to carry across his message of struggle and emancipation. His articles, speeches reproduced in *Mook Nayak*, *Janata*, and *Prabuddha Bharat*, are reminiscent of this mode of communication and its pervasive impact in the slums of industrial towns and cities like Sholapur, Nagpur, Pune and Mumbai. Even the rural hinterland of Maharashtra then was considerably influenced by the thoughts and teachings of Dr. Ambedkar. The Dalit households of Mahars, Mangs and Dhors living in the villages were especially keen to read or listen to the common readings of the journals brought out by Dr. Ambedkar (Bandhu, 1982; Pawar and Moon, 1978).

Bandhu Madhav, a noted short story writer, has written perceptively on the popularity of Ambedkar's Marathi writings among the hutment dwellers in Mumbai. A literate Mahar or Mang read out his journal to a group, and the others listened to him in rapt attention. The group consisted of the old and the young, men and women, and the time was always after 9 p.m., when all the day's labour and domestic chores were over.

I feel that reading Dalit literature is often a painful, self-introspecting experience. This is specially so for a non-Dalit, and especially for a Brahman, urban-bred and educated person. The degree of pain and injury may vary depending on the social and cultural proximity or distance between the characters in stories and novels and the readers, and their social background, which also includes their caste background. A lesser distance between the two may not diminish the sense of pain or injury, but it will certainly enhance one's awareness and knowledge. I may say that this is the beginning of the process of self-discovery and recognition. Some Dalit and non-Dalit intellectuals have frankly admitted to experiences of such consciousness (Anand and Zelliot, 1992; Phadke, 1977; Punalekar, 1997c).

The more the distance between the readers and the writer, the stronger grows the feelings of restlessness and self-questioning among the readers. And often one wonders about the stranglehold of age-old institutions like caste and religion, and cultural practices that defy the secular mandate of urbanisation and industrialisation, of democratic ethos and pluralism (Kothari, 1994). In other words, the whole thesis of modernism and modernisation became suspect in the eyes of some.

Of course, there are relieving features, too. Fortunately, Dalit literature is not eclectic or extremist. It does respond to forces of moral balancing. One can come across voices of reconciliation and amity in ample measure in some writings of the Dalits (Bagul, 1992; Kumbhojkar, 1994). This negates the thesis that Dalit literature is always about questions, about contradictions and constraints, about social decay and violence. Evidence such as this suggests that those who condemn the Dalit writings as invariably negative in content and destructive of social balance have really not shed their biases against this literature; or maybe, they are not inclined to decode the positive, emancipatory elements within this literature (Dangle, 1991; Maheria, 1988). Whatever be the reasons behind such castigation, Dalit literature does contain elaborate descriptions of acts and perceptions, reminding us of available spaces for social recovery and redemption (Punalekar, 1993; Salve, NA). To realise this, one needs to probe a little deeper beneath the anger and protest in the literature, or listen to the debates among them in the literary conferences held regularly since 1970.

Tryambak Sapkale, a leading Dalit poet, deeply struck by the removing the eyeballs of the Gavai brothers (they were untouchables), said in a pensive mood that his pains and pangs forced him to be vocal and vociferous. The days of silent suffering and resignation are over, he said firmly. Similar anguish and distress is present in the poems written by the Dalit poets who wrote on the riots in the BDD chawls in Bombay (now Mumbai), the atrocities on Dalits during the Marathwada agitation in the late 1970s and on the violence that erupted in Ramabai Ambedkar Nagar in North Mumbai (Anand and Zelliot, 1992; Dangle, 1992b). There are countless examples of major poets being in great agony caused by events of atrocities, humiliation and torture against Dalits (Dhongde, 1992; Joshi, 2001; Punalekar, 1994a).

What questions do they raise in their prose and poetry? The following topics dominate their writing:

(1) Why, despite decades of self-rule and freedom, Dalits are made targets of mindless violence and destruction.
(2) Why their huts are burnt, and why their cattle and domestic animals tortured.
(3) Why the books of their children are torn to pieces and trampled upon.
(4) Why their meagre means of livelihood such as bullock carts, sewing machines and flour mills are burnt to ashes.
(5) Why their men, aged and innocent, are paraded in the streets with face blackened and hair tonsured. And,
(6) Why their mothers, sisters and wives are molested in blatant violation of Hindu ethics and above all, the rule of the law (Bagul, 1981b; Guru, 1997; Lobo, 1988; Parmar, 1986 and 1996a).

They also question the veracity of the elementary principles of governance, and the connivance of the village headman, police *patils* or *patel*, police personnel and officials in the higher echelons in such incidents. Bondage and servitude masquerade in the name of freedom and justice; lawlessness becomes the rule of law; and even primary rights of shelter and livelihood are attacked in the name of 'restoration' of traditional rights and village culture. Why do such things happen in this modern, civilised world, they ask pensively (Rathod, 1988; Pawar, 1974; Valera, 1999).

And the reasons are not easy to locate, except in generalisations that the Dalits are not wanted (or they are dispensable) or that they will always remain objects of the hatred and humiliation of the upper castes. They have nowhere to go, they plead. The village elders whom they have been respecting for years are found failing in their duty to shelter and protect the Dalits, when under attack. Often, the poor *savarna* labourers working with the Dalits in the same fields are found behaving strangely in a crisis situation. They keep aloof from the Dalit labourers; sometimes, they are even found leading the group committing vandalism against their Dalit brethren (Valera, 1999; Patel, 1999; Lobo, 1994).

It is intriguing to learn that among Dalits themselves, there are instances of sharp division and divisiveness. Members of one Dalit caste separate themselves from the rest, and remain dormant watching the violence and atrocities committed on their neighbours, who hail from ex-untouchable, but 'other', caste groups. This has happened in the villages of Aurangabad, Jalana, Beed, Osmanabad, Latur, Nanded and Nashik districts of Maharashtra (Gupta, 1979; Punalekar, 1985). Such instances were visible in Gujarat state also. The cities of Vadodara, Ahmedabad and Mehsana witnessed factionalism among the Dalits themselves during crisis times. The Bhangis living in these urban centres remained dormant or passive when the Vankars or Mahyavanshies were being targeted (Lobo, 1994; INSAAF, 1995). In Maharashtra's villages and towns, the Mangs preferred to remain with the *savarna* Hindus when the Mahars were being hounded out from their houses and fields.

Contrary to our pet assumptions that urban centres are free from casteist tendencies or parochialism, this is not so. Dalit intellectuals and activists themselves are worried about the emergence and consolidation of such tendencies among urban Dalits (be they industrial workers or casual labourers, men or women, young or old). Why is this so? How long will this last? The Dalit writers pose such questions in their writings—in poems, short stories and self-narratives.

> Social boycott is another intermittent but powerful weapon with which Dalit masses are harassed and humbled. In Gujarat,

this phenomenon is popularly known as Hijarat, i.e. running away from one's native place. During the last 20 years, there are many instances of such Hijarat in Gujarat villages, and yet there is no let up or improvement in this situation. Village shopkeepers belonging to upper or middle castes refuse to sell them commodities or daily necessities; the savarna farmers refuse to employ them in their farm as daily wagers; the village women also belonging to savarna castes refuse to serve water from common wells to Dalit women; the common passage from the village street leading to their Basti (settlement) is blocked. This is nothing less than embargo and apartheid. Total ban on essential services make the living of the Dalit households worse than that of prisoners. Virtually, the survival of the Dalits is threatened. And then the Hijarat follows, where one and all Dalit families decide to leave that ancestral place for good, and move to towns or bigger villages, where they feel they are safe. Dalit literature does throw light on such exasperating events.

Barring a few instances of organised resistance and success, in nearly all the episodes, the Dalits have emerged defeated, accepting nearly all the demands of those whom they had intended to teach elementary lessons in the principles of democratic living and working. In my knowledge, Swamannagar in northern Gujarat is the only notable example of Dalit success. In this instance, the Dalits from Sabarada village fled and built their new settlement elsewhere. Magan Parmar, a Dalit professor from the Morbi Engineering College, was the leader of this movement, and he fought a long-drawn collective battle for the restoration of the human rights of the Dalits (Desai and Maheria, 1995).

It should also be remembered that many Dalit and non-Dalit intellectuals, activists and others stood behind Parmar and the Sabarada Dalit families. There were even some government bureaucrats who silently helped the process of resettlement. Journals like *Naya Marg*, *Nirikshak*, and *Disha* also enabled the poor Dalit families to make their cause visible through the media. The state government had to respond to this well-organised protest, and come forward to relocate them with civic amenities at the district headquarters.

But such instances are few and far between. The Dalit writers ask: Why, in the first place, do Dalit families have to leave their home and abandon their agricultural fields? What is their crime for which they are forced to take such a decision? Why are they treated as a cursed community? Can they not vote according to their conscience? Can they not dress well and enjoy the fruits of material life? Can they not buy a sewing machine, TV set, scooter, sofa set, and enjoy some comfort like others in their village? Can they not send their sons and daughters to high schools and colleges? Can they not celebrate Buddha Jayanti and Ambedkar Jayanti? Can they not invite city-level social workers and political leaders to their *basti* or settlement? (Punalekar, 1985 and 1988).

Daya Pawar, a noted Dalit writer from Maharashtra, then asks: "We have been living outside the village. Are we living outside the country?" This question unsettles and compels us to re-look into our definitions of national life, national integration, etc. Prahlad Chendvankar, in his poem, *Audit*, questions our past methods of identifying merit on the basis of caste alone, and warns that he would scrupulously audit the past deeds of our offensive actions against the Dalits who have been pushed into dark ghettoes and a sub-human existence.

But Chendvankar does not seem too harsh. At the end of his poem, he is in a reflective mood and moved by pity towards those who have been unkind to his Dalit brethren. He argues that if they (i.e. the *savarnas* who have been perpetrating socially degrading practices against the Dalits) genuinely admit to their chicanery and double standards, he (the Dalit poet) is ready to forget and forgive them. Chendvankar is essentially seeking transparency in the social and cultural dealings of the upper castes towards the Dalits. Other Dalit writers like Namdeo Dhasal and Arjun Dangle are more vehement and unflinching (Anand and Zelliot, 1992; Pawar and Moon, 1978).

They are not in a mood to forget the history of social injustice against the Dalits. Sometimes, they are in an indignant and abusive mood. Often such a situation has led to serious debate in Marathi literature and, on occasions, resulted in some unfriendliness and alienation of socially sensitive non-Dalit writers from the Dalit literary world (Zelliot, 1992).

What we can observe is that there is not a single, uniform, undifferentiated tendency of hatred, acrimony, anger, protest, or revolt in the Dalit literary expression. One can easily discern that the perceptions of the Dalit writers vary; their responses are dissimilar. If there is any definite ideological or political or moral statement in their script (which is there in some of the writings), that depends on their social and political moorings and angularities. Obvious examples can be found in the writings of Baburao Bagul, Annabhau Sathe, Bandhu Madhav, Keshav Meshram, Yeshwant Manohar, and Narayan Surve, though Surve is himself not a Dalit by background.

But that is what Dalit literature is all about. It contains plural tendencies, articulations and positions. No doubt there is some convergence, but there is also a richer terrain of diversities and differentiation. We hope that in future, social scientists will pay attention to this critical dimension and make new discoveries through the expressions (and also silences) of the Dalits, who lead a sub-human existence, either directly or through cultural memory.

There is another interesting aspect to Dalit literature, and that relates to the sincere attempts at expanding one's frontiers of knowledge and understanding, and linking one's agony and anguish with others located far beyond one's village, district or state. In a way, the effort is one of universalising one's voice against injustice, violence and destruction (Dangle, 1992b; Bagul, 1981b). This is indeed a remarkable quality found among Dalit poets, essayists and journalists. There are no regional or sub-regional boundaries in the identification and documentation of events in their writings.

In Maharashtra, some Dalit poets have penned moving, heart-rending poems on the murders and molestation of Dalits at the hands of the *savarnas* (and other socially dominant groups) in Belchi and Pantnagar (in Uttar Pradesh), in Bodh Gaya and Bhojpur (in Bihar), Golana of Gujarat, and Minakshipuram in Tamil Nadu. Similarly, now flourishing Dalit literature in Gujarat not only wrote about events in Golana, Sabarada and Ranpur (all villages in Gujarat), but they have also raised their voices against happenings in Maharashtra, Uttar Pradesh, etc. The poems and critical writings of Dalpat Chauhan, Joseph Mcwan, Sahil Parmar, Kisan Sosa, Karsan Lohar and others reflect these sentiments in ample measure (Lobo, 1988; Maheria, 1988).

In fact, there is also an attempt among the Dalit writers of Maharashtra and Gujarat to come together and share their perspectives on social, political and cultural issues. This process began in the mid-1980s, and continues till today. In fact, some journals like *Disha*, *Naya Marg* and *Swaman* have taken a lead in translating Marathi Dalit writings into Gujarati. This helps to widen and deepen one's understanding of Dalit issues and questions, no doubt.

Some Dalit writers have written with reverence about Martin Luther King. Some have brought out a whole issue of their journal on Nelson Mandela when he was released from the prison. This is evidence of the transnational sensitivity that exists among Dalit writers. Their affinity with black literature in the U.S. is already known. Janardan Waghmare (a Maratha and not Dalit by caste) has done excellent work in the field of critical works on themes like literature and social consciousness. His works on the Negro slave narratives and his efforts to compare the Dalits with the Negroes are now well received in Maharashtra. Baburao Bagul, Keshav Meshram, and Raosaheb Kasbe are the three other principal writers who have written with feeling on this subject (Kasbe, 1998; Waghmare, 1992).

Autobiographies are more potent and incisive documents on Dalit life and experience. Some Dalit autobiographies can be adjudged as sociological documentaries on the life of the marginalised class of Indian society. They carry immense insights into the social, economic, political and cultural fabric of our society. Daya Pawar's *Balut*, Laxman Mane's *Upra* and Laxman Gaikwad's *Uchhlya* can be singled out as examples of critical reflection on social values and practices among the Dalits and the outlook of others, the so-called elite within rural and urban society in western and southern Maharashtra (Punalekar, 1993). Joseph Macwan's *Angaliyat* in Gujarati is another example of the same genre.

These and a few other autobiographies depict Dalit life in meticulous details. They document the affection of the mother, the drunkenness and irresponsibility of the father, and the routine quarrels with cousins and caste fellows on petty property and status issues. Interestingly, in these self-narratives, one comes across a sense of anxiety on the part of the writer to search for a meaning in their everyday struggles (Mane, 1984; Pawar, 1985). The passionate search for a deeper meaning to their lives have enabled them to render convincing (and also pensive) accounts of Dalit lives and their visible and invisible struggles against the odds in their path.

What do these self-narratives (*atma-kathane*) reveal? Poverty is penetrating and painful. Hunger and starvation is a routine experience, forcing them to come up with ingenious ways of survival. Begging, borrowing, snatching, eating field rats, or stealing—they will do anything to survive. The Bhangis or scavengers made begging for leftover food their caste right. The village streets were meticulously distributed among them; and none was permitted to transgress these unwritten rules on begging jurisdictions (Parmar, 1996a and 1996b).

A marriage in an upper-caste family in a village meant a rare chance to fulfil the desire for a full belly. Dalit women, children and old men queued up outside the marriage *pandal* for food. Some even carried cloth bags and utensils to gather food that would see them through the next few days. One Dalit caste Berad (also called Santa Muchlar in Andhra Pradesh border villages) lived traditionally on lifting or snatching goods. The entire caste was earlier listed in the category of ex-criminals, and treated with indignity and suspicion. And this practice has not substantially declined as yet in the Marathwada region, which covers villages bordering Andhra Pradesh.

The Berads survived on their skills of shoplifting or thefts in the market or at *Melas*. But whatever they gained did not remain with them. Many respectable members of the village society and others like the village chieftain, police *patel*, *taluka*-level constabulary, lawyers, and even goldsmiths survived and grew prosperous on the shoplifting skills of the Berads or Santa Muchlars. Laxman Gaikwad belonged to this caste, and thanks to the encouragement of Vijay Tendulkar and the Granthali outfit, wrote an excellent self-narrative called *Uchchlya*. Gaikwad gives a list of this parasitical class at the end of his narrative.

Dalit literature also brings out the hurdles the Dalits face in the way of upward mobility and change. Their social and economic mobility is blocked, there are many bottlenecks in their path. The Kaikadis (a nomadic tribe in Maharashtra very similar to the Lamans or Lambadis elsewhere) cannot send their children to school. Children are born in the open fields, and not in their homes or a clinic. Who will certify their birth, and without an official birth certificate, who will admit them in school? Due to the hue and cry about this, now in Maharashtra, this condition is much diluted, and this is a good thing. Even if a child from a nomadic tribe is admitted in school, how can he continue in the same school when his parents move on, as per tradition? Most of these nomadic groups are constantly on the move for their survival, so their children's education becomes a rare and impossible dream.

Laxman Mane, himself from a Kaikadi community, wrote *Upra* (Outsider); he was the only male member to pass the class

12 examination in a community of over 1,00,000. This was the case in a progressive state like Maharashtra, where Karmaveer Bhaurao Patil initiated schooling among the peasants in the early 1920s, and Dhondo Keshav Karve strived for women's education. The education reform movements of the yesteryears bypassed the nomads, it seems.

The Kaikadis, Berads, Pardhis, etc., are called members of ex-criminal tribes. The villagers and their organisations do not trust them. Even ex-untouchable castes remain aloof from them, and join with other *savarna* groups in castigating them. They are suspect in their eyes, and often identified as offenders when thefts take place in the village. The police machinery also feels likewise. The policemen on duty take these so-called offenders to their *chowki* and beat them up mercilessly. Not only that, the policemen take away whatever they find useful from raids on their houses in the name of makingout a *panchnama*. Nothing is recorded and nothing ever returned.

Gaikwad tells us the story of how one Pardhi woman living in the slums of Latur town was treated by the townsmen and the police. She was interrogated in her hut when her husband was away at work. A shop in the town had been broken into, and she was suspected of playing a part in the theft. She was asked to part with a new sari and the foodgrains in her hut, despite the fact that both sari and foodgrains had been gifted to her by the district family planning centre, where she had undergone a tubectomy operation. She showed the papers to the police, who simply refused to look at the documents. What was the ground on which she was being faulted? Her fault seemed to be that being a Pardhi woman, she was not supposed to possess a new sari, and ten kilos of foodgrains. New clothes and storage of foodgrains were the privilege of the better-off sections of the society. That is the mindset of the ruling sections of society.

> What does Dalit literature stand for? It is difficult to answer this question in a hurry. Any straight jacketed profiling would

> betray the reality, which is too dense. There are too many complexities involved. Dalit literature is not a homogeneous, undifferentiated enterprise. It has many shades, many colours, and many meanings. Despite this diversity, one can discern some commonalities or set of uniform tendencies. What are these? What are the underlying urges, questions, and anxieties in Dalit Literature? How does this literature (and essentially the writers scripting their views and experiences) perceive Dalitism? We may attempt to address these questions.

Firstly, Dalit literature endeavours to encompass Dalits not merely as members of one particular caste group/s (say, Mahar, Chamar, Mang, Dhor, Berad, Kaikadi, etc.). They include all socially and culturally marginalised and suppressed castes in their narrative format, be they scheduled castes, scheduled tribes, nomadic tribes, or Muslims (Bagul, 1981a).

Secondly, to them, Dalitism is an encapsulating, multi-faceted concept embodying subjugation and control from 'above' in all spheres of living, be it social, economic, political, cultural or moral. To them, Dalitism stands for perpetual immobility and emasculation. It is an enclosure with complete denial of freedom, participation and decision-making. Dalit literature includes in its reflections the dominance of the household and the community (even their kith and kin). It also highlights the severity of violence against women, including their self-exploitation, and also abuse of children in the name of support to and stability for a dwindling family income (Jog, 1985; Joshi, 1986).

> Together it symbolises denial of the selfhood, and dignity and respect. They are reduced to chattel. The literature does castigate the parents and elderly persons in the Dalit family for their unconcern towards their women and children, their own drunkenness and other undesirable habits pushing the entire household into a debt-trap. Even their caste and community leaders are not spared for their social and moral lapses.

Thirdly, Dalit literature holds both external and internal forces responsible for their perpetual domination and loss of identity. Among the external factors, the principal ones are social and religious systems, mainly rigid applications of Hindu tenets that are outdated, but still remain part of social consciousness in towns and the countryside. They squarely condemn the conservative and fundamentalist forces within Hindu society that are out to deprive them of any access to open, democratic, competitive opportunity. They also single out politico-bureaucratic systems and processes as decisive factors in their manipulation (Maheria, 1988; Pantawane, 1978).

> More significantly they look inward and remain introspective about the role of their own family, their parents, caste fellows, leadership and educated Dalit classes. They believe that to a large extent these internal agencies like family, kinship, caste council, etc., have played a key role either by institutionalising these principles of hierarchy, control and manipulation (hegemonic tendencies within Dalits), or by silently suffering hardships and dishonour (Punalekar, 1994b; Salve, NA). In some writings, the elite Dalit class is rebuked for its dubious and diabolical role in caste/group humiliation and setbacks in their march in a more just and egalitarian direction. Bagul, Kasabe, Shankarrao Kharat and Murlidhar Jadhav are notable Dalit writers who hold such critical perspectives.

Fourthly, there is a considerable degree of anger, anguish and restiveness in Dalit literature. It is also said that Dalit literature smacks of negativism and defeat, self-pity and overstatement. But Dalit writings are not always negative. They have some ideas, however vague or nebulous they may be, on what freedom, equality and dignity mean. They worship hard work; they uphold values of gender equality and exhibit sensitivity towards upright, moral living. They, however, bemoan deeply the objective conditions that are so appalling and repulsive.

They are also aware that the obstacles, both material and cultural, are so strong and dense that the intentions and aspirations of the Dalit masses cannot be easily translated into a workable design of good, honest living in the current times (Bagul, 1981b; Omvedt, 1994). This painful awareness fully pervades the writings of Dalit writers such as Gaikwad, Daya Pawar, Sharan Kumar Limbale, Laxman Mane and P.E. Sonkamble. Their self-narratives, stories, poems and critical notes reflect this tendency in bold relief.

Fifthly, Dalit literature stands for change and social and cultural transformation, a change that will enrich the life of ordinary Dalits socially, economically and culturally. They value and plead for good education, responsive parenthood, a helpful neighbourhood, sensitive leadership, and a relatively non-hierarchical community life (Phadke, 1977; Waghmare, 1992). They pine for good food and drink, good reading material and sanguine and sensible moral advice. They are not against all traditions; they do care for resourceful and creative traditions among their own people. But they hate having to continue with the spurious and demeaning aspects of those rituals and practices that rob individuals of their basic human qualities.

And lastly, Dalit literature is not always clear on certain things, social or political. They are not against Brahmans, but are extremely critical about Brahmanical ways and mindsets, including that found even among their own Dalit relations, friends and leaders. When asked, they have plenty of questions, questions that are full of agony and discomfort. They ask about the nature and directionality of development; about the dominant notions on poverty and marginalisation and their content; about the contours and operative principles of freedom and justice (Guru, 1997; Jog, 1985; Pawar and Moon, 1978).

They talk about the persisting trends of hunger, starvation, homelessness, unemployment, and unsanitary conditions in their *bastis*. They talk about their aged parents, who are still slogging in the agricultural fields as wage labourers or as cobblers in an urban street. They raise nagging questions about their working mothers, who did not find rest till their death, and who had to mortgage their ornaments to educate their children in the town.

But when the barrage of such questions emerges, we ask them about their notions on the concept of change, or the alternative path, or paradigms. Some Dalit writers then get confused and befuddled; some of them feel restless and angry. But few of them come out quickly with suave formats and prescriptions, like us, better educated and westernised intellectuals.

My submission is: Are their questions less valid or relevant because they are merely questions, unaccompanied by neat answers. And who should be answering those questions? Should we not all be working together to pursue these questions seriously and to attempt to find answers to them? Decoding Dalitism entails also a task of decoding non-Dalitism, with all its underlying structures of values and practices. Both these tasks are linked intricately with one another, I believe.

References

Anand, Mulk Raj, and Eleanor Zelliot (eds.), 1992, *An Anthology of Dalit Literature*, New Delhi: Gyan Publishing House.

Bagul, Baburao, 1981a, *Ambedkar Bharat, Part One*, Pune: Rajhans Prakashan.

—, 1981b, *Dalit Sahitya: Aajche Krantividnyan*, Nagpur: Buddhist Publishing House.

—, 1992, 'Dalit Literature is but Human Literature', in Dangle, Arjun (ed.), *Poisoned Bread: Translations from Modern Marathi Dalit Literature*, New Delhi: Orient Longman.

Bandhu, Madhav, 1982, *Amhihi Manas Ahot*, Mumbai: Mukti Prakashan.

Bodhirajkumar, 1988, *Dalito, Laghumatio ane Binsampradayikta* (Gujarati), Ahmedabad: Gujarat Khet Vikas Parishad.

Chavan, R.N., 1989, *Bhatkya-vimuktanche Antarang* (Marathi), Pune: Sugava Prakashan.

Dangle, Arjun, 1991, *Dalit Vidroh* (Marathi), Mumbai: Granth Ghar Publication.

—, 1992a, 'Now, Now', translated by Jayant Karve and Eleanor Zelliot in Anand, Mulk Raj, and Eleanor Zelliot (eds.), 1992, *An Anthology of Dalit Literature*, New Delhi: Gyan Publishing House.

— (ed.), 1992b, *Poisoned Bread: Translations from Modern Marathi Dalit Literature,* New Delhi: Orient Longman.

Desai, Harshad and Chandu Maheria, 1995, *Sambardathi Swamannagar* (Gujarati), Surat: Centre for Social Studies.

Dhongde, Ramesh V., 1992, *Dalit Atmacharitre: Sahitya ani Samaj* (Marathi), Pune: Dilipraj Prakashan.

Fernandes, Walter (ed.), 1996, *The Emerging Dalit Identity: The Reassertion of the Subalterns,* New Delhi: Indian Social Institute.

Guru, Gopal, 1991, 'Hinduisation of Ambedkar in Maharashtra', *Economic and Political Weekly,* Vol. 26, No. 7, February 16, pp. 339-41.

Gupta, Dipankar, 1979, 'Understanding the Marathwada Riots: A Critique of Eclectic Marxism', *Social Scientist*, Vol. 7, No. 10, May.

Guru, Gopal, 1997, *Dalit Cultural Movement and Dalit Politics in Maharashtra*, Mumbai: Vikas Adhyayan Kendra.

Human Rights Watch, 1999, *Broken People: Caste Violence against India's 'Untouchables'*, New York: Human Rights Watch.

Ingle, Waman, 1975, *Dalit Muktiladha ani Dalit Sahitya*, Aurangabad: Kalchakra Prakashan.

INSAAF, 1995, 'Commission on Dalits and other Oppressed Classes', in Sandeeep Pendse (ed.), *At Crossroads: Dalit Movements Today,* Mumbai: Vikas Adhyayan Kendra.

Jog, V.S., 1985, *Marxvad ani Dalit Sahitya,* Mumbai: Subodhi Prakashan.

Joshi, Barbara (ed.), 1986, *Untouchable Voices of Dalit Liberation Movement*, London: Zed Books.

Joshi, Satyakam, 2001, 'Dalito par thati Hinsanu Sachot Dastavejikaran', *Arthat,* Vol. 20, Nos. 1 and 2, January-March, April-June.

Kasabe, Raosaheb, 1998, *Republican Paksha: Aikya, Vastav ani Bhavitavya* (Marathi), Pune: Sugava Prakashan.

Kothari, Rajani, 1994, 'Rise of the Dalits and the Renewed Debate on Caste', *Economic and Political Weekly*, Vol. 29, No. 26, June 25, pp. 1589-94.

Kumbhojkar, Lalita, 1984, *Dalit Kavita: Ek Darshan* (Marathi), Pune: Pratima Prakashan.

Lobo, Lancy, 1988, 'Angaliat: A Dalit Novel', *New Quest*, 69, May-June, pp.141-48.

—, 1994, 'Dominant Castes and Atrocities on Scheduled Castes in Gujarat', *Downtrodden India*, Vol. 1, No. 1, January-April.

Maheria, Chandu, 1988, *Dalit Sahityani Prabhavi Kuch* (Gujarati), Ahmedabad: Gujarat Khet Vikas Parishad.

Mane, Laxman, 1984, *Upra*, Mumbai: Granthali.

Omvedt, Gail, 1994, *Dalits and the Democratic Revolution: Dr. Ambedkar and the Dalit Movement in Colonial India*, Delhi: Sage Publication.

Pantawane, Gangadhar, 1978, *Dalitanche Prabodhan*, Aurangabad: Vivargranthmala.

Parmar, Rameshchandra, 1986, *Golana Hatyakand: Bhalne Bhale Kali Tili* (Gujarati), Ahmedabad: Bharatiya Dalit Panther.

—, 1996a, *Hathma Zadu, Mathe Mailu* (Gujarati), Surat: Centre for Social Studies.

—, 1996b, *Hun Bhangi Sadiothi* (Gujarati), Ahmedabad: Dalit Panther Prakashan.

Patel, Arjun, 1999, 'Dalit Samashyaoni Sachukli Ugra Rajuvat' (Gujarati), *Arthat*, Vol. 18, No. 3, July-September.

Pawar, Daya, 1974, *Kondwada* (Marathi), Pune: Magova Publications.

—, 1985, *Balut*, Mumbai: Granthalaya.

Pawar, Urmila and Meenakshi Moon, 1978, *Aamhihi Itihas Ghadvala* (Marathi), Mumbai: Granthali Publication.

Phadke, Bhalchandra, 1977, *Dalit Sahitya: Vedna ani Virodh*, Pune: Shree Vidya Prakashan.

Punalekar, S.P., 1985, 'Caste Ideology and Class Interests: Reflections on Violence in Marathwada Region', in Centre for Social Studies (ed.), *Caste, Caste Conflict and Reservation*, Delhi: Ajantha Books International.

—, 1988, 'Identities and Consciousness: An Overview of Dalit Literature in Maharashtra', *Man and Development*, Vol. 10, No. 4, December.'

—, 1993, 'Sociology of Dalit Autobiography', *Man and Development*, Vol. 15, No. 4, December.

—, 1994a, 'Dalitism and Gender', in P.G. Jogdand (ed.), *Dalit Women in India: Issues and Perspectives*, New Delhi: Gyan Publishing House.

—, 1994b, 'Atmakathan ani Samaj Darshan' (Marathi), *Marathi Samajshastra Patrika*, Vol. 3, No. 3, November.

—, 1994c, 'Protest Literature in Maharashtra', *Frontier*, November 19.

Rathod, Motiraj, 1988, *Bhatkya Vimuktancha Jahirnama* (Marathi), Aurangabad: By the Author.

Salve, Dinkar, NA, *Dalit Sahityachi Kondi* (Marathi), Pune: Krantisinh Nana Patil Academy.

Valera, P.K., 1999, 'Gujaratma Dalitopar Atyachar: Ek Dastavej ane Tena Lekha-Jokha' (Gujarati), *Arthat,* Vol. 18, No. 1, January-March.

Waghmare, Janardan, 1992, *Sahityachintan* (Marathi), Pune: Pratima Prakashan.

Zelliot, Eleanor, 1992, *From Untouchables to Dalits*, Delhi: Manohar Publications.

7

Conversion as Subversion of Hierarchy

Ambrose Pinto S. J.

Ideologically, the forces of the Sangh Parivar have opposed the minorities ever since their origin. To oppose the Muslims, Christians, Communists and the progressive forces in society is a part of the political agenda of the Rashtriya Swayamsewak Sangh (RSS) and its affiliates. Through fierce opposition to the other cultures of India, the Sangh Parivar has designs to build a 'Hindu India'. In this Hindutva, there is no place for anybody other than those who accept the hierarchical caste order. Of course, the Buddhist, Sikh and Jain religions, which had their origin in India, will have to agree to be a part of Hindutva to exist in the country. This means that while the different in faith, they must accept the system of *varna*. If they do so, they are considered a part of Hinduism. The two concepts that are utilised to legitimise the indigenousness of religions and differentiate them from the others are *pitrabhoomi* (fatherland) and *punyabhoomi* (holy land). For the religions that have their origin in India, the country is their fatherland as well as their holy land since the sacred places of their founders, their holy shrines and pilgrimage centres are in the country.

Both Islam and Christianity are religions of Asian origin. The immediate conclusion, therefore, is that the followers of these two religions cannot be patriotic and loyal to the country. Their *punyabhoomi* and *pitrabhoomi* are outside the country. For the Hindutva forces, therefore, religion becomes an important element in the construction of the nation. India is identified with Hindus and Hinduism is, therefore, the religion of the country. Only the Hindu is a real citizen of the land. The other religions that originated in India are a part of the country provided they accept being a part of Hindu culture.

Religion and Caste

However, the Hindu religion does not exist merely as a relationship with God. Hinduism determine's one's social position in society through the system of caste. "It is the cardinal faith of every Hindu that the Hindu social order is a divine order... This is called by the Hindus the *varna vyavastha*. It is the very soul of Hinduism. Without *varna vyavastha*, there is nothing else in Hinduism to distinguish it from other religions."[1] That is why all Indian religions must accept *varna vyavastha*.

And what is worse, "everyone who feels moved by the deplorable condition of the untouchable begins by saying: We must do something for the untouchable". One seldom hears any of the persons interested in the problem saying: "Let us do something to change the Hindu." It is invariably assumed that the object of the reclaimed is the untouchable as though untouchability was due to his depravity and that he alone is responsible for his condition. If there is to be a mission, it must be to the untouchable. Nothing requires to be done to the Hindu. He is sound in mind, manners and morals. He is whole, there is nothing wrong in him. He is not the sinner."[2]

And yet the real state of affairs is that it is the Hindu who discriminates, is unsound in mind and soul.

There is an absence of conscience in Hinduism. Human beings are not treated as humans. And this is legitimised by religion. "The sanction behind the caste system is the religious sanction, for, the caste as a new form of *varna* system derives its sanction from the *Vedas* which form the sacred books of the Hindu religion and which are infallible. I say unfortunately because anything which has a religious sanction becomes by virtue of it sacred and eternal. To the Hindu, caste is sacred and caste is eternal."[3]

The only way to escape from the curse of caste is to abandon Hinduism. Ambedkar was convinced there is no salvation within Hinduism for an untouchable. The Hindu religion has justified the treatment meted out to Dalits, though rationally, untouchability cannot be justified. The Hindus want the Dalits to remain untouchables. Any decision to move away from Hinduism is resented. And yet, the Hindu mindset does not change. They would not like to treat the untouchables any differently.

Ambedkar and Conversion

Ambedkar, therefore, rightly attributed the low status, degradation and low esteem of untouchables to Hinduism. That is why he holds that "one way to solve the problem of the untouchable is for them to abandon Hinduism and be converted to some other religion. At a conference of the Mahars held in Bombay on May 31, 1936, a resolution to this effect was passed unanimously. Although the conference was a conference of the Mahars, the resolution had the support of a very large body of untouchables throughout India. No resolution had created such a stir. The Hindu community was shaken to its foundation and curses, imprecations and threats were uttered against the untouchables who were behind this move."[4]

Why did Ambedkar convert, why did he choose Buddhism and why were the upper-caste Hindus so disturbed by

Ambedkar's move? His conversion had a lot to do with the evils of the Hindu religion. The major shortcomings in his perceptions of Hinduism were: (a) It deprives moral life of freedom and spontaneity and reduces Hinduism to a servile conformity to externally imposed rules. (b) There is no loyalty to ideas, only conformity to commands. (c) The laws are iniquitous in that they are not the same for all the classes. (d) The laws are not made by prophets or law-givers. (e) The Hindu code has been invested with the character of finality and fixity.[5] Ambedkar's contention was that a religion that favours some and curses others must be destroyed. There is nothing irreligious in working for the destruction of such a religion, he felt. "Hinduism and social union are incompatible. Hinduism—the traditional social structure—is the great obstacle to Hindu unity.... Hinduism creates an eagerness to separate."[6]

Ambedkar was clear that the caste factor dragged Hinduism into a religion of inequality. In his understanding, religion had to be rational, secular, moral, spiritual and personal. Hinduism was none of these. He found all these characteristics in Buddhism. There is no place for prayers, pilgrimages, sacrifices, rituals, belief in God and soul and propitiation of God through ceremonies in Buddhism. Buddhism strove to establish right relations among human beings. Each one had to strive for his own moral progress, social emancipation and personal transformation.

In fact, it is in Buddhism that Ambedkar discovered a counter force to Brahmanism. Buddhism had no priesthood and no caste. It believed in social equality and economic security. Knowledge was available to all in Buddhism. Hinduism, while because it upheld privilege and inequality, denied social equality. By denying freedom of a vocation and compelling people to serve ends chosen by others, Hinduism was against economic security. Hinduism does not recognise fraternity. The caste system and its hierarchical character are against fraternity.

Ambedkar's desire was to revolutionise Dalit politics through Buddhism. Buddha had repudiated the authority of the *Vedas*, denounced all rituals, sacrifices and rites, and opposed the caste system. Beyond a religious community, Buddhism stood for equality and fraternity and thus it was a social group. By converting to Buddhism, Ambedkar visualised a separate community outside the Hindu fold. What attracted Ambedkar to Buddhism was:

(a) Buddhism stood for living experience and a life divine, attainable here and now, not after death.

(b) It was a religion of realism and never an idealism.

(c) It upheld liberty, equality, truth and justice; it emphasised humanity, love and peace.

(d) It was dynamic, scientific and all-embracing.

(e) Its explanation of life and its meaning and purpose of birth and death and its aftermath were very clear, intelligible and logical.

(f) The human person was its centre and not anything outside of him/her.[7]

There were other reasons as well. In his thesis on the origin of indigenous people, Ambedkar made it clear that untouchables were once Buddhists. Talking to BBC London in May 1956, he said: "Buddhism gives three principles in combination which no other religion does. Buddhism teaches *prajna* (understanding) as against superstition and supernaturalism, *karuna* (love) and *samata* (equality)."[8]

Conversion was a Protest

Thus, for Ambedkar, conversion was a protest against Hinduism. At one point, in 1935, Ambedkar said that "though born a Hindu, (he) would never die as one". By discarding the ancient religion which stood for inequality and oppression and embracing Buddhism in 1956, he fulfilled that promise he had made to his people. Conversion was one of the high points of Ambedkar's life. In fact, for him, conversion was movement from an unequal social group to a social group of equality. And if thousands of others after Ambedkar have left the Hindu fold, it is because the Hindu superstructure is highly discriminatory, terribly iniquitous on the underdog and has, over the years, become fossilised into customs and rituals. The ugly exterior, which is all the underprivileged get to see, does nothing for them. Hinduism's biggest threat is from its steadfastness in believing that rituals and superstitions constitute the central message of the faith, its total reluctance to get rid of caste, and all these are important factors that make people denounce the system. Its condemnation of millions to a fate worse than anything imaginable for no other reason than that they were not born in a forward caste is enough reason to protest and join social groups outside the Hindu fold.

Objections Against Conversion

The Hindutvavadis have opposed conversion on flimsy grounds till now. While, on the one hand, the untouchables are not treated as equals, on the other, moving away from Hinduism continues to be resented. Various arguments have been offered against conversion. The following are the most important:

(a) Conversion makes no changes in the status of untouchables: For Ambedkar, this was a one-side view of religion. "Religion emphasises universalised social values and brings them to the mind of the individual who is required to recognise them in all his acts in order that he may function as an approved number of the society." Hinduism does not recognise the worth of Dalits as human beings. It does not stand for liberty, equality and fraternity. The wrongs to which the untouchables are subjected by the Hindus are acts which are sanctioned by the Hindu religion. They are done in the name of Hinduism and are justified in the name of Hinduism... The spirit and tradition which makes lawful the lawlessness of the Hinduism. How can the Hindus then ask the untouchables to accept Hinduism and stay in Hinduism?"[9].

(b) For the untouchable, conversion is not for economic or political gain: The gain is social since the untouchables will be members of a community whose religion has universalised and equalised all values of life. The untouchables need an end to social isolation and their inferiority complex. By establishing kinship with another community free from the spirit of caste, the untouchables can put an end to social isolation. Conversion can also put an end to their inferiority complex. "The inferiority complex of the untouchables is the result of their isolation, discrimination and unfriendliness of the social environment."[10] Religion can change this complex provided it provides an atmosphere in which one finds possibilities for feeling himself equal to all other human beings. That is why Ambedkar does not accept the argument that conversion can make no change in the status of untouchables. Moving from a social group that rigidly believes in hierarchy to a group that believes in equality is both psychologically and socially beneficial to the Dalits.

(c) All religions are equal: If all religions teach the same thing, there is no reason to prefer one religion to another. One can join any religion. There should be no ban or heartburn on conversion. Besides, Ambedkar's argument is that all religions are not equal. "One religion holds that brotherhood is good, another caste and untouchability is good."[11] How can they be the same then? There are religions that advocate violence. Some others hold on to non-violence. Since different religions have different beliefs, they cannot be equal. Buddhism believes in equality of all humans and Hinduism does not. How then can these religions be equal?

(d) Conversion is political in nature: Ambedkar felt this argument was an ill-considered one. While not denying that conversion could provide incidental political gain, Ambedkar held it could bring no new political gain. The untouchables have political rights as any other. "If they change their faith, the change is not to bring into existence political rights which did not exist before. Political gain has no connection with conversion. The charge is a wild charge made without understanding."[12] On the other hand, if politics is defined in terms of power, conversion can provide social power to the converts which they did not have in Hinduism.

(v) Conversion of the untouchables is not genuine: In Ambedkar's perspective, all conversions are genuine. Most people hardly make choices about their religion. "Religion has become a piece of ancestral property. It passes from father to son... What genuineness there is are such cases of conversion."[13] On the other hand, "the conversion of the untouchables, if it did take place, would take place after full deliberation of the value of religion and the virtue of different religions. How can such a conversion be said to be not a genuine conversion? On the other hand, it would be the first case in history of genuine conversion. It is, therefore, difficult to understand why the genuineness of the conversion of the untouchables should be doubted by anybody."[14]

Conclusion

For Ambedkar, therefore, conversion was a subversive activity. The purpose was to overthrow the existing Hindu caste social order and create a new one. While he denounced Hinduism all through his life and in his writings, he presented Buddhism as one of the alternatives because of its egalitarian character. The objection of the Hindutvavadis against conversion should, therefore, be looked at from the Ambedkarite perspective. By keeping the caste system as it was and by providing legitimacy through religion, the upper castes and classes have benefitted economically, socially and politically. Demolishing the caste order is not in the interest of the privileged castes. Attacks on *masjids* and churches cannot prevent conversions. What the self-styled defenders of Hinduism need to work at is the reform of their religion. Nobody wants to convert from a faith that treats them as equal human beings. However, such reform is not possible in Hinduism. Without caste, there is no Hinduism as far as the Ambedkarites are concerned.

The only way, therefore, left for Ambedkarites is to reject Hinduism, the kind of Hinduism propagated by the Hindutvavadis. All human beings need religion, a system of beliefs that provide a sense of meaning to life and empowerment. Such meaning and empowerment can be had in religions that treat human beings as equal, and with dignity and fraternity. Once people reject categories of pure and impure, high and low, touchable and untouchable, and embrace religions that propagate equality, fraternity and justice, subversion of the present social order is bound to take place. It is this subversion that the Hindutvavadis seem to be afraid of. The attack on egalitarian religions, therefore, must be viewed from their insecurity and the imagined threats to their economic and social interests.

The Hindutvavadis have stated that Buddhism is a part of Hinduism. This has been resented by Buddhists. In a statement, on December 12, 1999, in Delhi, Buddhist activists and scholars denounced Hindutvavadis for doing so and observed: "The effort by the votaries of Hindutva to coopt and absorb Buddhism into the fold of Hinduism is the most vicious of the designs to negate the existence of an entire religion and the people who constitute a sizeable proportion of population of the country. The Buddhists of India, and specially those of us from the Bahujan Samaj and other segments of society who have been victims of continuing caste oppression, proudly reassert our identity as Dalits. We reject any creed which preaches and practises inequality, brutal suppression, enslavement and persecution of crores of Indians."[15] While Buddhism is totally opposed to Hinduism in creed and belief, the attacks in the last two years have been on Muslims and Christians, the traditional enemies of Hindutvavadis. The cause is the same—both these religions define identity outside the Hindu fold and provide their followers with a sense of dignity and equality. Another additional reason for attack is that these two religions have their origin outside the country and, at least in profession, totally negate the concept of hierarchy in social life. The attack on Christianity has been more severe. The cause is that Christianity, an Asian religion identified with the West, provided the country a democratic form of government wherein all are treated as equals, a concept with which the Hindutvavadis were most uncomfortable. They would like to revive the age-old caste order. Rejection of hierarchy is denial of power to the dominant groups who have for centuries sucked the blood of the poor labour and exploited the untouchables in the name of religion. In the opposition to conversion, therefore, the economic and political interests of the upper castes and classes is paramount.

Notes

1. Kuber, W.N., 1991, *Ambedkar: A Critical Study*, New Delhi: p. 84.
2. Ambedkar, B.R., 1989, *Dr. Babasaheb Ambedkar's Writing and Speeches*, Vol. 5, Government of Maharashtra, p. 94.
3. *Ibid*., p. 103.
4. *Ibid*., p. 403.
5. Ambedkar, B.R., *Annihilation of Caste*, p. 72.
6. Ambedkar, B.R., 1945, *What Congress and Gandhi have done to the Untouchables?*, Mumbai: Thacker and Co. Ltd., p. 187.

7. Kuber, W.N., p. 93.
8. Keer, Dhananjay, 1965, *Mahatma Jyotirao Phule: Father of Social Revolution*, Mumbai: Popular Prakashan, p. 487.
9. Ambedkar, B.R., *Dr. Babasaheb Ambedkar, Writings and Speeches*, Vol. 5, p. 412.
10. *Ibid.*, p. 418.
11. *Ibid.*, p. 405.
12. *Ibid.*, p. 405.
13. *Ibid.*, p. 405.
14. *Ibid.*, p. 405.
15. *Annual Report*, Indian Social Institute, 2000, New Delhi, p. 68.

8

Conversion, Empowerment and Social Transformation

S.M. Michael

For the last few years, the word 'conversion' has been almost constantly in the news. It is one of the most important issues on which Christians are targeted. Almost every day, there is some news item in the Indian newspapers on the subject. A number of statements have been issued on the subject by different Hindutva organisations. For example, the 8th Dharma Sansad of the Vishwa Hindu Parishad (VHP) in February 1999 in Ahmedabad, demanded strict anti-conversion laws, and a white paper issued by the central government talked of the 'foreign conspiracy', behind conversions. Former prime minister, Atal Bihari Vajpayee demanded a 'national debate on conversion', implying that the attacks on Christians were due to their conversion activities. Vajpayee said: "If Christian missionaries continue religious conversions, the government cannot stop reconversions." VHP's Ashok Singhal argued that Professor Amartya Sen's Nobel Prize was a Christian conspiracy to open more missionary run educational institutions to convert the poor. It was alleged that missionaries use force, fraud and allurements to convert people to Christianity. Funds obtained for welfare activities are used for conversion. All the same, conversion from Christianity to Hinduism is encouraged and supported by the Sangh Parivar as *ghar wapasi* or homecoming.

Many of these pronouncements by various Hindutva oriented journalists, politicians and religious leaders call for a scientific study on conversion.

Sanskritic Hindus*, the Biggest Converters in India

We need to analyse the issue of conversion without prejudice. History teaches us that social change is an inevitable process. Inventions, discoveries, invasions, diffusions and assimilation have been affecting the lives of people all over the world throughout history. The anthropological and sociological process of conversions has to be seen in this wide perspective of social change. Usually, when conversion is discussed in India, it is done in the context of conversion to Islam and Christianity alone. But this has to be seen wholistically in the Indian historical context (see Michael, 1998). There have been many cultural and religious encounters and interactions over the ages. India is a subcontinent with a vast population and diverse levels of culture. The cultural inputs and influences coming from the ancient tribes of India, the urban centred Indus valley people, and the whole galaxy of new arrivals–Aryans, Greeks, Scythians, Parthians, Shakas and Huns before the eighth century, as well as Arabs, Persians, Turks, Afghans and Mongols between the 8th and 12th centuries–was part of a vital and living process of the many migrations into India since time immemorial. Among the different migrants in ancient India, it was the Aryans who vigorously imposed a hierarchical social order, the *varnashrama dharma* on the heterogeneous

---

* The twice-born Hindus who believe and practise the hierarchical values in their life and act as agents of the Brahman *dharma*.

population of India. It was then that the homogenisation process of the multicultural, multireligious and multiracial population of India along the lines of a Brahmanic or Sanskritic social order began.

What we today call and designate 'Hinduism' was not known till the medieval period. The term 'Hindu' originally derived from the name Indus and was used successively by the Achaemenids, the Greeks and the Muslims to denote the population living beyond that river. Anthropological studies on India show that sanskritisation took place in ancient India through a process of absorption, assimilation and conquest. This process continues even today with much political support. Adivasis (tribals) and other indigenous people are often drawn into the orbit of a Sanskritic world-view.

When Aryan immigrants entered the country, they called the original inhabitants Dasyus. The word 'Dasyu' was used to denote people different from themselves. In the early history of India, Aryan invaders began to exercise their superiority over the other racial people in India. This led non-Aryan tribals to either compromise with the Aryan social order or to run away to the deep forest (Sharma and Sharma, 1998:100). All through the centuries, Sanskritic Hindu dominance influenced and assimilated non-Aryans into different gradations of caste even to the level of untouchability in the Aryan social structure of *varna*. The observations of Bradley Birt, Baine (1891:118), Rislev (1901:98), O'Mallev (1911:235), Shoobert (1931:403), Elwin (1952:35), etc., also testify to the absorption of tribals into the Sanskritic Hindu culture.

During the long Sanskritic period of Indian history when Brahmans and other upper-caste people had so much influence over the lower castes, untouchables and tribals, the culture and lifestyle of many of these underprivileged groups submerged into that of Brahmanic Hinduism. Jayant Lele illuminates the process: "The Brahmanic world-view had succeeded on several occasions in the past in capturing the diversity of cults, deities, sects and ideas (by making many compromises) under the rubric of Sanatana Dharma. It had thus stabilised existing practices and subjected them to the supervision and patronage of a Brahman dominated economic and political order. Many of the tribal, low-caste deities to which Brahmanism had to adapt ended up as consorts or local incarnations of the pan-Indian patriarchal gods, thus investing these pan-Indian symbols with unprecedented power and potency for popular mobilisation" (Lele, 1995:xviii). The history of the lower strata of Indian society cannot be traced exactly, and here only historical anthropology, which includes popular beliefs, legends, myths, tales, short histories of local traditions, etc., can help us know about their past (Sharma and Sharma, 1998:101).

N.K. Bose also observes that "even in ancient times, Hindu law-makers were clearly conscious of the fact that various *jatis* were coming within their organisation and it was necessary to teach them Brahmanical morals and Brahmanical religious ceremonies in order to bring them closer to the rest of the population" (1967:211). According to Bose, "Hindus hardly left any economic freedom to the *jatis*, but they left intact the original social and religious culture of the tribes in so far as that was possible. Their policy was not to eradicate the old beliefs and practices where they were not inconsistent with Brahmanical moral ideas. But it was nevertheless necessary to do something in order to bring the tribal cultures in line with Brahmanism, as we have seen in the quotation from the *Mahabharata*. So they made a rule that each caste, on becoming a part of Hindu society, was to be served by Brahman priests during marriage, birth, initiation and funeral ceremonies. A close and living connection was thus established between the priestly class and the new recruits, and a means of direct infiltration of culture was thus successfully organised. The Brahmans modified the old culture where it went against the grain of their own ideas and left the rest intact. They added to tribal ceremonies certain items of their own, which were to be performed by Brahman priests on behalf of their new clients" (Bose, 1967:212).

In explaining this process of Brahmanic incorporation, reinterpretation, appropriation and assimilation of tribal and other cultures, Bose says: "Once a tribe came under the influence of the Brahmanical people and was converted into a caste enjoying monopoly in a particular occupation, a strong tendency was set up within it to remodel its culture more and more closely in conformity with the Brahmanical way of life" (Bose, 1967:214).

Jayant Lele traces the origins of Brahmanism as a hegemonic project (1995:51-80). He brings to light the struggles of some of the victims against that project and the resistance shown by diverse, self-conscious communities against its attempts to homogenise, reinterpret and control their diverse origins and identities. According to him, "popular memories of tribal, egalitarian communities and of aspirations for an enriched and expanded life of thriving interdependence, kindled during the early years of the Mauryan empire, were subsequently subjugated, reinterpreted and employed to justify a new hierarchical social order" (1995:ix). He also studied the resilience of Brahmanism during centuries of challenges and countermovements through the dual strategies of appropriation and exclusion (Lele, 1995:81-103). This was done by the Brahmans through a process of reinterpretation of tribal and other communities' histories, distortion of their folktales and disembodiment and rearrangement of their rituals and symbols. According to Lele, "an important step in ensuring the viability of this sort of exercise is to monopolise the institutional mechanisms through which information comes to life as knowledge and is validated as officially acceptable and true" (1995:x).

Jaiswal has thrown light on two processes that have contributed to the resilience of Brahmanism: (a) the incorporation of immanent critical impulses through their hegemonic reinterpretation, and (b) marginalisation of counter-cultural threats through their designation as permissible but quarantined deviance (*Vama Murga*). These processes seem to repeat themselves in subsequent periods (Jaiswal, 1981).

A few instances of the Hinduisation of tribals will confirm the state of affairs. In middle India, the Nagbansi Raja of Chotanagpur, who was the head of the Oranons and the Mundas, seeing the pomp and show of the Hindu Rajas of northern India, changed his surname of Rai into Shah of Shahi (around 1628 A.D.). He assumed the title of Maharaja and he began to imitate the ideal of royalty of the Hindu Rajas. A suitable palace was constructed. And Shahi Maharaja soon gathered Brahman priests, Rajput courtiers and *amlahs* and palace-hunters. The Oraons and Mundas resisted this and, as a consequence, more and more outsiders were called in by the successive Maharajas and the heavy cost had to be borne by the villagers. This period is also remarkable as being the period which saw the erection of a number of temples, such as the Jagannath Mandir and the Ram-Sita Mandir. The Bhils of western India also came into direct conflict with the local rulers and Marathi invaders (see Sharma and Sharma, 1998:106-110).

Even today, many of these tribal groups have been Hinduised through festivals and other Sanskritic symbols and rituals. This has been explained by Nirmal Kumar Bose as "the Hindu method of tribal absorption" (Bose, 1967; also Valiamangalam, 1996:129-146). After giving several examples of the Hindu method of tribal absorption, Bose observes: "But besides all these, it is absolutely certain that some *jatis* are undoubtedly of tribal origin; and this had been the result of a conscious plan of Hindu society to dominate over and absorb tribal groups within its economic and social framework. It may be recalled in this connection that some of the untouchable castes have cultural traits which clearly show their original affiliation and indicate their tribal origin" (Bose, 1967:208).

In spite of these efforts, because of the geographical isolation enjoyed by the tribals, some of them were still able to preserve to a great extent their socioreligious identity, faith and practices. But when the British introduced roads, the postal system and civil government, easier transport and communication were made possible within the tribal areas. This attracted traders and moneylenders. They were followed by Hindu missionaries. This led to the subsequent Hinduisation of the tribals. Before that, the tribals had kept up the purity of their blood because they did not intermarry with non-tribals. Since they did not practise untouchability, they were saved from loss of self-image.

The sacred traditions of the tribals were too far removed from the Vedic Dharma of Hinduism. But, the Hindu traders, money lenders and landlords, who became resident in the tribal area, were able to introduce elements of Hinduism into the tribal religion, paving the way for their assimilation into Hinduism (Bose, 1975).

Another way of assimilation of tribals into Hinduism is through close contact with lower caste Hindus, since they intermingle with tribals easily and pass on Hindu religious beliefs and practices (Bhuriya, 1992:17). The dominant Brahmanical religion, during its evolution through past centuries, subjugated and absorbed many tribal groups with their gods, religious rituals and customs (Bose, 1975). Priests and poets of the Brahmanical traditions succeeded in associating tribal gods with one of the deities in the Hindu pantheon. For example, the tribal god of Orissa, Lord Jaganaath, became identified with Vishnu, and Murugan of the Adi-Dravidians became identified with Skanda of the north Indian Hindu traditions. However, the biggest number of conversions was effected through the Hindu census enumerators. They were persuaded to enter tribals as Hindus in the census papers. G.S. Ghurye, an eminent sociologist, addressed tribals as 'backward Hindus' (1963:19). He promoted the idea that the tribals of India must refer to themselves as part of Hindu society and should not claim an autonomous culture of their own. According to him, "the only proper description of these people is that they are imperfectly integrated classes of Hindu society" (1963:19).

As the tribals were absorbed by Hinduism, the non-Aryan, i.e. the Sudras and Ati-Sudras were also incorporated and Sanskritised into Hinduism. The upper castes of a particular area exercised such a powerful influence and attraction on the lower castes and outcastes that they also wanted to be integrated into the caste hierarchy by adopting the values and practices of the castes. This process is described as sanskritisation by the eminent anthropologist M.N. Srinivas (1989:56). He defines sanskritisation as the process by which a 'low' caste or tribe or other group takes over the customs, ritual, beliefs, ideology and style of life of a high and, in particular, a 'twice-born' (*dwija*) caste. Orthodox Hindus frequently assert that Dalit Buddhists are really Hindus because the Buddha is a reincarnation of Lord Vishnu. Just as putting a snake over the head of the Buddha transforms him into an icon of Lord Vishnu, so too clothing statues of the Buddha's five first companions in the Mahabodhi Temple compound turns them into the five Pandavas, Hindu heroes of the great epic, the *Mahabharata* (Lynch, 1998:11).

Distortion of History to Make Believe Indigenous Origin of Aryans

Since the above facts of the social emergence of Hinduism in India go against the very interest of the Sanskritic Hindus, today, there are attempts to deny the Aryan migration (or invasion) into Indian soil. The Hindutvavadis are beginning to assertively propagate the idea that the Aryans are the indigenous inhabitants of this land. They founded the rich urban Indus Valley civilisation. This claim is very important for Hindutva oriented historians because it allows them to demonstrate that the present-day Hindus are the lineal descendants of the Aryans and the rightful inheritors of the land from time immemorial.

Since 1920, archaeological excavations at Harappa have documented that the rich urban civilisation of the Indus Valley is much older than Aryan culture in the Indian subcontinent. This left the Hindu nationalists with no recourse but to seek to incorporate the Harappan civilisation into the Vedic literary tradition. In this enterprise, the antiquity of the *Vedas* had to be pushed back several centuries and the Vedic river, Saraswati, had to be assigned greater priority than the Indus as a cradle of ancient civilisation.

But the numerous well-established linkages between the *Rig Veda* and the Avesta firmly rule out the Indian origin of the Aryans. Dr Stephen Fuchs' study on the 'Vedic Horse Sacrifice in its Culture-Historical Relations' (1996) also shows that the Aryans have been migrating from inner Asia in India and Europe and thus giving birth to the Indo-European language groups, which includes most European languages and many languages of western Asia, including Sanskrit and Hindi. "Equally definitively, it is simply inconceivable that the Harappan civilisation could have been Aryan. A number of arguments are advanced in support of this assertion, one among them being the absence in known Harappan sites of any well-testified remnants of the horse, a crucial animal in Vedic lore" (Muralidharan, 2000:75; also Mahadevan, 1977 and 2000; Thapar, 2000).

But, recently, the Hindutvavadis have claimed that the Indus script has been deciphered and that the language of Harappa was 'late Vedic Sanskrit' (see Rajaram and Jha, 2000; Rajaram and Frawley, 1997; Rajaram, 1999; Rajaram, 2000). They have also been claiming that the Harappan civilisation gives religious significance to the horse and thus should have been an integral part of Aryan civilisation.

These claims of RSS historians have been clearly refuted by international scholars. Recently, in a cover story article titled 'Horseplay in Harappa: The Indus Valley Decipherment Hoax', in the *Frontline* of October 13, 2000, Michael Witzel, a Harvard University Indologist, and Steve Farmer, a comparative historian, debunked the claims of N.S. Rajaram and N. Jha in their co-authored book, *The Deciphered Indus Script*. The book establishes a connection between the *Rig Veda* and the Harappan civilisation on the basis of, inter alia, a fabricated horse seal. In this question, international scholarship has been supported by the reputed Indian historian, Romila Thapar, and Iravatham Mahadevan, the leading Indian expert on the Indus valley script and one of the world's foremost scholars in the field (see *Frontline*, October 13, October 27 and November 24, 2000). The international scholars, Michael Witzel and Steve Farmer, have offered $1,000 to any Harappan researcher who is willing to defend Rajaram's claims. "Not one has taken up on our offer. So far as the scholarly world goes, nothing is left of Rajaram's Hindutva 'revisions' of history than as 'va-s ava-in plain English, a dead horse" (Witzel and Farmer, 2000:129).

These attempts of the Sangh Parivar to 'rewrite history' has come under great criticism by other eminent scholars and by the public (see The Times of India News Service, January 3, 2001:6; United News of India, January 1, 2001:4; Chattopadhyay, 2001).

With the above clarifications on the latest attempts to distort history, let us once more turn to our main subject of religious conversion in India.

Conversion for Empowerment and Upward Social Mobility

When we turn to conversion movements to Buddhism, Sikhism, Islam and Christianity by the backward and untouchable castes in India, we begin to understand the efforts of the underprivileged for social mobility and social transformation.

With regard to group conversion to Islam and Christianity, several Hindu fundamentalists complain that there have been forced conversions during the last several hundred years. Firstly, we have to assess different historical periods and different political regimes and the accounts are not the same for each. Further, the idea that missionaries came with the sword to convert, i.e. they always had the backing of the colonial state and the power to use military force to enforce conversions is seriously challenged by historical data. When we study the significant conversion movements in Indian Christian mission history, we have to take into consideration a multitude of significant factors. Conversion is never an isolated event.

Conversion has been a powerful religio-meaning system to protest and resist caste struggle even in pre-modern times. The existence of such a large number of Muslims in the country can have no other explanation. This has been accepted by even religious leaders like Swami Vivekanand. He says: "Why amongst the poor of India, are so many Mohammedans? It is nonsense to say that they were converted by the sword, it was to gain liberty from the *zamindars* (feudal lords) and priests" (*Collected Works*, Vol. VIII, p.330). With the advent of the Europeans, however, different forms of Christianity presented themselves as a major opportunity to equality and equal social treatment. The message of Christianity is that God is the father of all, that all humans are the children of God. Despite differences, we are all brothers and sisters in Christ. This had an obviously strong pull with the disinherited castes of India, often treated inhumanly by the dominant castes. The missionary efforts in spreading literacy and their assistance in times of material crises added the necessary existential and practical dimension. Mass conversions started in different parts and among widely separated communities of the country: the Mangs and Mahars of Mumbai, the Chuhras of Shahabad (Bihar) and Ballia (Uttar Pradesh), the hill tribes of the North East, the Karta Bhojas of Bengal, the Bhils of central India, the Mallas and Madigas of Andhra, and the Sambavars, the Shanars and Parayars of Tamil Nadu.

Studies on mass conversion to Christianity by Aloysius (1998) and Chatterjee (1994) and others "clearly indicate that these emerging communities did not 'accept' Christianity in 'cow-like' obedience, as the upper-caste nationalists claim, but indeed consciously and deliberately moved away from one set of religious symbolism, now perceived as sectarian and unjust, to another, again perceived as universal and egalitarian and hence suitable for the situation" (Aloysius, 1998:19).

While Hindu fundamentalist organisations, through their assimilation policy, claim that tribals and Dalits are Hindus, the tribals and the Dalits, on the other hand, reject this superimposed new identity. The upper-caste Hindus, while trying to get the services of the Dalits and tribals, paid little attention to alleviating their deprived conditions. They are addressed as 'backward Hindus' (Ghurye, 1963:19). Rejecting this identity, tribals and Dalits found their own ways to move up the social ladder of Indian society. The conversion movements among Dalits and tribals have shown the potential of social change in religion.

The Dalits, who tried to adapt first to the Hindu social structure of India, later experienced the burden of untouchability, unseeability and other oppressions of Hindu society. They gradually realised that they would never be able to attain their humanity in the Hindu *dharma*. Hence, they began to search for an alternative identity. Their search took the form of two types of cultural movements aimed at freedom from oppression (Shah, 1985:175). The first is reformative, that is, change within the Hindu system. It included the Bhakti movement, sanskritisation, and the non-Vedantic Dalit movements in Maharashtra, Tamil Nadu, and elsewhere. The initiative in a few of these movements came from the upper castes, but it was a response to pressure from below (see Fernandes, 1996:15).

The second type of movement includes alternatives from outside the Hindu fold. In some cases, these took the form of conversion to Christianity, Islam, Sikhism and other religions that preached equality (Sharma, 1976:219). Pickett sees one of the motives, and a quite legitimate one, in Dalit conversion, as the desire for social liberation (1933). Webster argues that conversion to Islam and Christianity represented rejection of a hierarchy which kept Dalits down (1992). Untouchable converts are often accused of being 'rice Christians', persons who embraced Christianity 'for a plate of rice', that is, material incentives. But is it so simple? It is true that in many cases, the missionary offered material help out of humanitarian considerations. However, Forrester (1980:74) and Fernandes (1996:17) point out that a deeper analysis of the conversion movements, made not from the missionary or upper-caste point of view, but from that of the convert, shows that to the untouchables, change of religion was not primarily a mode of economic and social improvement. It was, more than anything else, an effort to change social status, a search for freedom from caste oppression. Oddie asks: "If the desire for material advantage and protection was the only consideration, how does one explain the tenacity and perseverance of some converts who, in spite of material losses and persecution, still adhered to the mission?" (Oddie, 1977:19). Julian Saldanha has summarised the different studies on Christian conversion movements in India. He concludes, saying: "A sincere analysis of these conversion movements reveal that they were not the result of material inducements, nor were they exclusively religious events. They might better be described as socioreligious movements" (1996:79).

Further studies on conversion movements show that mass conversion of tribals to Christianity is related to the tremendous socioeconomic and cultural changes brought about by westernisation and modernisation (Natarajan, 1977). Snaitang, a Khasi studying *Christianity and Social Change in North East India*, finds that Christianity provided a means through which the tribals could accommodate themselves to the changes that were imposed through British administration and the process of modernisation it brought with it. In a situation where radical changes were taking place, Christianity provided institutions, a new lifestyle and ideology, which protected the tribal society from the danger of detribalisation and loss of identity. A new sense of tribal solidarity that transcended the traditional fragmented order was created. This was founded over the maintenance of the traditional kinship code, which was the only feature common to the tribals prior to the coming of the British (Snaitang, 1993). Forrester comments on motives: "The search for material improvement or enhancement of status is seldom if ever the sole or even the dominant motive in a mass movement. Dignity, self-respect, patrons who will treat one as an equal, and the ability to choose one's own destiny—all these are powerful incentives to conversion" (1980:75).

On the positive side, these movements represented an effort on the part of the Dalits to gain dignity, self-respect and the ability to choose their own destiny for themselves and their social group. There was a growing restlessness among them to have a fuller life of dignity for themselves and their children. John Webster (1992:71-76) observes that "the mass movements constituted the first stage in the modern Dalit movement"; they were initiated and led by them, and sustained by their heroism in the face of persecution. These were group decisions to belong to a new community which not only had a religious tradition comparable to that of the caste Hindus, but which also began to distinguish itself from the traditional caste community. On the negative side, they were a revolt against a socioreligious system which failed to provide a meaningful response to their needs and aspirations (Boel, 1975).

Two Opposing Views on Conversion

Sociologically, conversion is a process of change from one religion to another. The motive for a change of religion may be economic, social or religious. Conversion could be seen as a way to gain protection, education and status. It was something that could be used by the individual to move forward in society, above all through education, and by a group to free themselves from inherited shackles, to better themselves and their children. These shackles might be those of caste, of illiteracy, of economic slavery, of psychological apathy, of disease, or of a religion of fears and taboos (Wingate, 1997). But all these factors are always interlinked and none of them should be considered in isolation (Michael, 1983:40-52). Forceful conversion should be condemned. All the same, is it wrong if a group of people change their religion when they realise that their poverty and social degradation are due to the legitimised religious values and the structure of the majority society? The prospect of radical change can only seem subversive to those who are committed to the status quo. It is understandable that the beneficiaries of the status quo resent radical changes. But to the oppressed and downtrodden, change is the lever of hope.

Some critics who are opposed to Christian conversions take recourse to Gandhi's attitude to conversions. It is true that Gandhi was a great opponent and a critic of Christian conversions. All the same one is surprised to learn, with all due respect to the greatness attributed to Gandhi, that he equates the cow with untouchables and considers cows to be holier than the untouchables. We need to examine his attitudes on conversions. The controversy between Gandhi and Ambedkar brings out the two different approaches to religious conversions in India.

Gandhi's conversation with Dr. Mott on the conversion issue brings out Gandhi's prejudices against untouchables and Christian conversion. For the benefit of reading the original conversation of Gandhi with Dr. Mott, I reproduce the dialogue:

> *Dr. Mott*: I agree that we ought to serve them whether they become Christians or not. Christ offered no inducements. He offered service and sacrifice.
>
> *Gandhiji*: If Christians want to associate themselves with this reform movement, they should do so without any idea of conversion.
>
> *Dr. Mott*: Apart from this unseemly competition, should they not preach the Gospel with reference to its acceptance?
>
> *Gandhiji*: Would you, Dr. Mott, preach the Gospel to a cow? Well, some of the untouchables are worse than cows in understanding. I mean they can no more distinguish between the relative merits of Islam and Hinduism and Christianity than can a cow" (Gandhi, 1941:240-241).

When some missionary friends of Gandhi took exception to this comparison, he was unrepentant and did not relent, but confirmed that he felt no remorse for this analogy (Gandhi, 1941:98-101).

The issue of conversion remains incomplete and unresolved when looked at from the one-sided and biased position of Gandhi. The views of the untouchables themselves and those of Ambedkar on this issue are very necessary and relevant. Ambedkar's stand on conversion stands in sharp contrast to that of Gandhi.

Ambedkar tried his best to find a place in the Hindu social order. All the same, Ambedkar was clear that "we do not wish to live as *shudras* in the four-fold *varna* structure". With this direction in mind, he led the Chavdar Talav movement in order to have access to public drinking water, and he led the Kalaram Temple agitation in order to gain entry into Hindu temples. The violent reaction of the upper-caste Hindus to these agitations made him look towards other religions for the social empowerment of the untouchables. In 1929, Ambedkar advised the untouchables to embrace any religion that would regard them as human beings, that would give them an opportunity to break off from oppressive structures, and that would enable them to act, eat, walk, and live like men (see Wilkinson and Thomas, 1972:33). Following this, a group of untouchables from a village near Nashik decided to embrace Islam (Matthew, 1982:1031). In 1935, at a conference attended by 10,000 untouchables at Yeola, Ambedkar declared: "I solemnly assure you that I will not die a Hindu." He found in Hinduism the cause of his people's wretched condition because, he argued, it was Hinduism's sacred texts that defined untouchables as the lowest of the low and polluting. In addition, it was Hinduism's sacred texts that mandated the degrading, humiliating, and unjust treatment from which his people had suffered for centuries.

Ambedkar rejected Gandhi's views on Hinduism and conversion. Gandhi said: "I must say in all humility that

Hinduism as I know it, entirely satisfies my soul, fills my whole being, and I find solace in the *Bhagavad Gita* and *Upanishads* that I miss even in the Sermon on the Mount" (quoted by Chifford Manshardt). In Gandhi's perception, the ancient Hindus had already achieved an ideal social system with the varna vyavastha. So, according to Gandhi, "The law of varna means that everyone will follow as a matter of dharma or duty the hereditary calling of his forefathers ... he will earn his livelihood by following that calling" (Zelliot, 1992:154). Ambedkar believed that an ideal society had yet to be achieved in India. For him, the priority was not in making Hinduism or Hindu society 'shine forth', but building a new, equal, free, open, non-hierarchical, modern India. His own words best explain the sort of society he envisaged: "An ideal society should be mobile, should be full of channels for conveying a change taking place in one part to other parts. In an ideal society, there should be many interests consciously communicated and shared ... This is fraternity, which is only another name for democracy. Democracy is not merely a form of government. It is primarily a mode of associated living of conjoint communicated experience. It is essentially an attitude of respect and reverence towards fellow men" (as quoted by Shashi, 1992:130). Hence, Ambedkar realised that an egalitarian society couldn't be built in India without destroying the *varna vyavastha*.

Gandhi honoured cows more than the untouchables in keeping with the Hindu belief. Gandhi viewed the conversion attempts of the untouchables to egalitarian religions with disgust. Ambedkar, on the other hand, rejected Gandhi's views and criticised Gandhi for his attitude towards conversions to egalitarian religions. According to Ambedkar, Gandhi's arguments against Christian missions "are just clever. There is nothing profound about them. They are the desperate arguments of a man who is driven to the wall" (Moon, 1989:449). Ambedkar continues: "All these arguments of

Gandhi are brought forth to prevent Christian missionaries from converting the untouchables" (Moon, 1989:450).

Even now, the attitude of the upper castes and priests towards untouchables have not changed much. For example, the recent earthquake of January 26, 2001, killed thousands and rendered thousands homeless in Gujarat. But, even in this disastrous situation, the caste barriers remained firmly up. Tents were set up to protect the victims from the chill of the nights. But the lower castes and Dalits were not allowed to use these tents because of caste prejudices (Ghatwai and Vasavada, 2001:1).

With the rise of Hindutva politics in the last few decades, there have been great attempts to convert non-Hindu untouchables from other religions to Hinduism. Even here, the reconversion programme of the Hindus to their religion does not recognise the equality of the lower castes. For example, the Shankaracharya of Govardhan Peeth in Puri, Jagatguru Nischalananda Saraswati, converted 72 tribal Christians in Orissa in June 2000. Instead of accepting them as equals, he promised to build 'low-cost' temples, 'as prescribed in Hindu texts'. The Puri Shankaracharya's proposal to build separate Swastik temples of Lord Ganesha for the reconverts to Hinduism was strongly supported by the Vishwa Hindu Parishad. Priests at the famous Jagannath Temple declared: "The lower caste people, mainly from the Pana community, who had been converted into Christianity are known as Mlechha (untouchables) and they eat the flesh of cows. We cannot allow Mlechha people to enter the Lord Jagannath Temple at Puri, whether they are Hindus or Christians" (see Dash, 2000:7).

Conversion movements are not only towards Christianity, but also to other religions such as Islam, Buddhism and Sikhism. Sikhism, which drew heavily from Islam as well as Hinduism, attracted low-caste untouchables in big numbers. Many of them converted to Sikhism in the early part of the

20th century, despite stiff opposition from the Arya Samaj and other elite Hindu streams. Hence, the conversion issue should be studies in a holistic perspective, and not from the perspective of Christianity alone.

In constitutional negotiations, Indian Christians gave up the request for separate electorates, and came under the general voters' roll; this helped to ensure they were seen as Indians first and foremost, in a political sense, and not just as Christians. The critical part of the Constitution, adopted in 1949, was Article 25, under 'Fundamental Rights'. This said: "Subject to public order, morality and health and to the other provisions of the Part, all persons are equally entitled to freedom of conscience and the right freely to profess, practice and propagate religion."

Within this Constitution, there have been repeated attempts to regulate conversions. Prime Minister Nehru announced: "There should be no regulations of religious conversions. Such curbs will only lead to other evils" (Lok Sabha Address, December 3, 1955). He went on saying that votaries of every religion can overstep the mark. But it is Christian members of the house who should regulate Christian missionaries, not private members' bills. He ended resoundingly: "Christianity is as old in India as Christianity itself. Christianity found its roots in India before it went to countries like England, Portugal and Spain. Christianity is as much a religion of the Indian soil as any other religion of India."

Misinformation on Conversion and Distorted Identity of India

There is much misunderstanding and misinformation with regard to conversion. Interested parties with a view to malign minority communities spread stories of proselytisation. It is also highly politicised. Some of the fundamentalist organisations spread rumours and exaggerate things related to one or the other conversion event. Behind this politicisation, there is the big agenda of the Hinduisation of India. Some of the Hindu fundamentalists do not recognise the pluralistic nature of Indian society. India and Hindu are often equated when defining Indian culture (see Ludden, 1996; Dalmia and Stietencron, 1995; Basu and others, 1993; Andersen and Damle, 1987). Here, the conception of tradition is Brahmanical and textual, seeking to invert homogeneous traditions applicable to all Hindus. This process has been well explained by K.N. Panikkar. According to him, "the Brahmanical textual view of tradition overlooked the existence of multiple traditions even among followers of Hinduism. A majority of the Hindus were outside the 'great tradition', which in essence was the ideology of the upper-caste domination. The construction of scripture-based Hinduism by upper-caste reformers during the colonial period was in effect an attempt to universalise the Brahmanical tradition" (Panikkar, 1995:113). Hindu nationalism defines the Indian nation in a monocultural fashion as a Hindu Rashtra and seeks to displace and remove alternative, pluralistic definitions. In its efforts to unify India, Hindu nationalists give top priority to their opposition to Islam and Christianity. The Article 25 of the Indian Constitution grants every citizen the right to 'practise, preach and propagate' his faith. Let it not be forgotten that it was Sardar Patel (no mean Hindu or patriot) who insisted on including the right to 'propagate' in Article 25. It is a pointer to the dynamic vision underlying our Constitution, a vision that we have begun to resent!

The glorification of ancient India by nationalist historians meant the glorification of Hindu India. According to the well-known historian, Jha, this historiography is based on James Mill's three volume *History of British India*, first published in 1817. Mill divided Indian history into three periods, viz., Hindu, Muslim and British. Jha points out that the seeds of communal bias in Indian historiography were thus sown (see Jha, 1997:xv-xviii). To quote Jha, "Mill's periodisation, which is based on the wrong premise that ancient Indian kings from 1000 B.C. to 1200 A.D. subscribed to the

Hindu religion were wrongly portrayed as Hindu kings. Some of the major ruling dynasties like the Indo-Greeks, Shakas and Kushans, who were not Hindu, were ignored. For that matter, not even the Mauryans were Hindu. In fact, the ancient Indians never described themselves as Hindu. First used by the Arabs and later by others, the term Hindu stood for the inhabitants of Hind (India). The term is foreign to early Indian literature and passed into Indian nomenclature much later" (Jha, 1997:xvii).

In reality, Buddhism and Jainism were widespread in India, but today, they are reduced to small minority religions because of the missionary activities of Brahminic Hinduism. Hence, a deeper study will show that the idea of conversion is part and parcel of the Indian tradition. The Arya Samaj and other Hindu organisations like the Vishwa Hindu Parishad promote conversion and reconversion in their programmes not only in India, but all over the world (see Jordens, 1977). *The Ghar Vapsi* (homecoming) movement of reconversion of Christian tribals and Dalits to Hinduism initiated by Dilip Singh Judev, a BJP member of Parliament from Jashpur, targeting the Chotanagpur plateau in Madhya Pradesh (now in Chhatisgarh) and portions of Bihar, Orissa and West Bengal is well known (see *The Asian Age*, 1997:4). The Sikhs and Buddhists believe in a process of conversion towards human dignity and emancipation. In this context, the Hindu fundamentalists recognise as valid only one kind of conversion, namely reconversion to the Hindu fold. This attitude is out of tune with Indian tradition and contradicts the fundamental rights of the people of India.

Religious Freedom and Conversion: Human Rights Issues

India is a sovereign nation. It has a written Constitution, the solemn pledges of our founding fathers, it is a document especially treasured for broadness of vision and egalitarian values. This Constitution is drawn and promulgated in the context of the debate on the pluralistic nature of Indian society.

The founding fathers of the Indian nation were well aware of the multicultural, multireligious, multilingual and multiethnic nature of Indian society. Hence, it is very important to affirm the pluralistic nature of Indian society and its traditions, and that no religious group can lay claim to India as their exclusive property.

Conversions have been taking place all through Indian history. Anthropological studies on India show that through a process of absorption and assimilation and conquest, tribals and other indigenous communities have been drawn into the orbit of Sanskritised Hinduism. Even today, this process of Hinduisation is going on with political support from the state and central governments. Moreover, conversion is not only to Christianity but also to other religions. There is a lot of misinformation, rumours and political overtones with regard to Christian conversion. Hindu fundamentalists do not recognise the pluralistic nature of Indian society. Hence, they politicise even the very idea of conversion to Christianity. Therefore, the sweeping statements and vicious accusations often made against Christians on conversion require to be met with the real facts of history and an unprejudiced mind.

Conclusion

In opposition to the prevalent view, which conceives of society in terms of "functional coordination, integration and consensus", Ralf Dahrendorf has called for a reorientation of sociology toward "problems of change, conflict and coercion in social structures" (Collins, 1997; Zeitlin, 1996). The conflict approach to social change analyses social process in terms of the actors pursuing their interests.

The conflict approach assumes that conflict is the dominant process in society, that social arrangements represent the dominance of a powerful establishment over the masses, and that once the masses become aware of their plight, they will overthrow the prevailing order and establish a more just world. Charismatic leadership is very significant in this process.

Dahrendorf viewed societies as coordinated systems. Authority structures are an integral part of every social organisation, which leads to the formation of interest groups with a potential source of conflict. Various positions in society have different amounts of authority. There is differential distribution of authority, of positions, of domination and subjection. Those in positions of authority have legitimate rights to exercise control over others. Authority structures consist of relations of superordination and subordination. They define rights and obligations as well as sanctions to ensure conformity.

These positions hold interests that are 'contradictory in substance and direction'. Such distribution of authority leads to the formation of conflict groups with possibilities of conflict arising out of opposing interests. Those in dominant positions seek to maintain the status quo, while those in subordinate positions desire change.

In the traditional Indian society, the dominance of the upper-caste Hindus was legitimate. The lower castes permitted the upper castes to control them. When conflicts arose between the two groups, they were quickly resolved without disturbing the authority structures. Society returned to normalcy by maintaining the status quo, with the superordinate elements retaining their dominance.

The impact of the Christian mission, the process of industrialisation and urbanisation, and the British rule in India began to bring about changes in the power structure of traditional Hindu society. In the changed circumstances, the values of equality, fraternity and social justice began to influence the traditional Hindu social order. The pervasiveness of this ideology began to be a reality through the new structures of education and sociocultural empowerment brought about by social change in India. This affected and questioned the traditional authority in India. The Christian world-view of equality and fraternity had a strong pull obviously with the underprivileged sections of Indian society. The lower castes indeed took the opportunity to move away from one set of religious symbolism, now perceived as oppressive and unjust, to another, perceived as universal and egalitarian.

Actually, conversion has been a powerful religio-meaning system to prevent and resist caste struggle even in pre-modern times. As pointed out earlier, the persistence of such a large number of Muslims in the country can have no other explanation. Hence, the issue of conversion is very complex and it requires complex analysis in terms of the marginalised and the underprivileged seeking empowerment and social transformation.

References

Aloysius, G., 1998, *Religion as Emancipatory Identity: A Buddhist Movement among the Tamils under Colonialism,* New Delhi: New Age International Publishers.

Andersen, W.K. and S.D. Damle, 1987, *The Brotherhood in Saffron: The Rashtriya Swayamsevak Sangh and Hindu Revivalism*, New Delhi: Vistaar Publications.

The Asian Age, 1997, "VHP Plans Ghar Vapsi to Reconvert Christian Tribals", *The Asian Age,* October 25, p. 4 (Kolkata edition).

Baine, Sir A., 1891, *Census of India*, 1891, Report.

Banerjee, B.N., 1983, 'A Hindu Attitude to Conversion', *International Review of Missions*, No.287, pp. 393-397.

Basu, Tapan, and others, 1993, *Khaki Shorts Saffron Flags,* New Delhi: Orient and Longman.

Bhuriya, Mahipal, 1992, 'Reconversion of Tribal Christians to Hinduism in Madhya Pradesh', *The New Leader*, June 16-30.

Boel, J., 1975, *Christian Mission in India: A Sociological Analysis.* Amsterdam.

Bose, Nirmal Kumar, 1967, *Culture and Society in India*, Mumbai: Asia Publishing House.

—, 1975, *The Structure of Hindu Society*, New Delhi: Orient Longman.

Bose, Sugata, and Ayesha Jalal, 1997, *Modern South Asia: History, Culture, Political Economy*, Delhi: Oxford Publications.

Chatterjee, Partha, 1994, *Nation and Its Fragments*, Delhi: Oxford University Press.

Chattopadhyay, Dhiman, 2001, 'ASI projecting Vedic Civilisation the RSS Way', *The Times of India*, February 24, p. 9.

Collins, Randall, 1997, *Theoretical Sociology*, New Delhi: Rawat Publications.

Dalmia, Vasudha and H.von Stietencron (eds.), 1995, *Representing Hinduism, The Construction of Religious Traditions and National Identity*, New Delhi: Sage Publications.

Dash, Jatindra, 2000, "Priests Say No to Converts at Orissa Temple", *The Deccan Chronicle*, June 18, p. 7.

Elwin, Verrier, 1952, *The Loss of the Nerves: A Comparative Study of the Contact of People in the Aboriginal Areás of Baster State, Central Province of India*.

The Examiner, 1999, "The Other Cheek" by Prof. Ram Puniyani, May 20, p. 8.

—, 'The Endangered Species—I', May 20, p. 5-7.

—, 2000, 'Update: Attacks on Christians', September 16, p. 6-7.

Fernandes, Walter, Geeta Menon and Philip Viegas, 1987, *Forests, Environment and Tribal Economy: Deforestation, Impoverishment and Marginalisation in Orissa*, New Delhi: Indian Social Institute.

Fernandes, Walter, 1988a, 'The Draft Forest Policy 1987; The National Water Policy 1987', *Social Action* 38.

Frontline, 2000, 'Horseplay in Harappa, In the 'Piltdown Horse' Hoax, Hindutva Propagandists Make a Little Sanskrit Go a Long Way', *Frontline*, October 13.

—, 2000, 'Horseplay in Harappa', *Frontline*, October 27.

—, 2000, 'New Evidence on the 'Piltdown Horse' Hoax', *Frontline*, November 24.

Forrester, D.B., 1980, *Caste and Christianity: Attitudes and Policies on Caste of Anglo Saxon Protestant Mission in India*, London: Centre for South Asian Studies, University of London.

Fuchs, Stephen, 1979, *Anthropology for the Missions*, Allahabad: St. Paul's Publications.

—, 1996, *The Vedic Horse Sacrifice in Its Culture-Historical Relations*, Delhi: Inter-India Publications.

Gandhi, M.K., 1941, *Christian Missions*, Ahmedabad: Navjivan Publishing House, (2nd edition, 1960).

—, 1941, *Christian Missions*, Ahmedabad: Navjivan Publishing House, (2nd Edition, 1960).

Ghatwai, Milind, and Jignesh Vasavada, 2001, 'You Thought Death was the Great Leveller? Ask These Dalits', *Indian Express*, February 10, p. 1. (Mumbai edition).

Ghurye, G.S., 1963, *The Scheduled Tribes*, Mumbai: Popular Prakashan.

Gladstone, J.W., 1976, '19th Century Mass Movement in South Travancore: A Result of Social Liberation', *Indian Church History Review*, No. 1, pp. 53-66.

—, 1986, 'Christian Missionary Work and Socio-Religious Movements in Kerala: 1850-1910' Ibid., No. 1 pp. 30-42.

Gore, M.S., 1993, *The Social Context of an Ideology, Ambedkar's Political and Social Thought*, Delhi: Sage Publications.

Grafe, H., 1990, *The History of Christianity in Tamil Nadu in the 19th and 20th Centuries*, Vol.4, Part 2 of the Church History Association of India, *History of the Indian Church*, Bangalore, CHAI.

Hardgrave, Robert L. Jr., 1969, *The Nadars of Tamil Nadu*, Mumbai.

Jaiswal, Suvira, 1981, *The Origins and Development of Vaisnavism*, Delhi: Munshiram Manoharlal.

Jha, D.N., 1997, *Ancient India*, An Introductory Outline, New Delhi: Manohar.

Jordens, J.T.F., 1977, 'Reconversion to Hinduism, the Shuddhi of the Arya Samaj', *Religion in South Asia*, G.A. Oddie (ed.), New Delhi: Manohar, pp. 145-161.

Legrand, Lucien, 1996, 'Conversion in the Bible: A Dialogical Process', *Mission and Conversion: A Reappraisal*, (eds.) Joseph Mattam and Sebastian Kim, Mumbai: St. Paul's Publications.

Lele, Jayant, 1995, *Hindutva: The Emergence of the Right*, Chennai: Earthworm Books.

Ludden, David (ed.), 1996, *Making India Hindu*, New Delhi: Oxford University Press.

Lynch, Owen M., 1998, "Dalit Buddhism: The Liberate Bodh Gaya Movement", *Dalit International Newsletter*, Vol. 3, No. 1, February.

Mahadevan, Iravatham, 1977, *The Indus Valley Script: Texts, Concordances and Tables*, New Delhi: Memoirs of the Archaeological Survey of India.

—, 2000, 'One Sees What One Wants To', *Frontline*, November 24, p. 125.

Matthew, G., 1982, 'Politicization of Religion: Conversions to Islam in Tamil Nadu', *Economic and Political Weekly*, No. 25, pp. 1027-1034; No. 26, pp. 1068-1072.

Michael, S.M., 1980, *The Cultural Context of Evangelization in India*, Indore: Satprakashan.

—, 1983, 'Sociological Perspectives of Conversion in India', *Indian Sociological Review*, January, Vol. 5, No. 1, pp. 40-52.

—, 1996, 'The Cultural Context of the Rise of Hindutva and Dalit Forces', *Vidyajyoti: Journal of Theological Reflection*, May, Vol. 60, No. 5, pp. 294-310.

—, 1998, *Anthropology of Conversion*, IIC Occasional Papers, Mumbai: Institute of Indian Culture.

—, 2000, "Real Issues Behind the Violence", *Mission Today*, January-March, Vol. II, No. 1, pp. 9-22.

Moon, Vasant, 1988, *Dr. Babasaheb Ambedkar's Writings and Speeches*, Vol. 5, Mumbai: Education Department, Government of Maharashtra.

Muralidharan, Sukumar, 2000, 'Questions about the Aryan Identity', *Frontline*, December 22, pp. 73 75.

Natarajan, Nalini, 1977, *Missionary Among the Khasis*, New Delhi: Sterling Publishers.

Oddie, G.A. (ed.), 1977, *Religion in South Asia*, New Delhi: Manohar Book Service.

O'Malley, L.S., 1911, *Census of India*, Report.

Panikkar, K.N., 1995, *Culture, Ideology, Hegemony, Intellectuals and Social Consciousness in Colonial India*, New Delhi: Tulika Publishers.

Parpola, Asko, 2000, 'Of Rajaram's Horses', 'decipherment', and Civilizational Issues', *Frontline*, November 24, pp. 124-125.

Picket, J.W., 1933, *Christian Mass Movements in India*, Lucknow: Lucknow Publishing House (2nd Indian edition).

Rajaram, N.S., and N. Jha, 2000, *The Deciphered Indus Script: Methodology, Readings, Interpretations*, New Delhi: Aditya Prakashan.

—, 1999, *From Sarasvati River to the Indus Script*, Bangalore: Mitra Madhyama.

Rajaram, N.S., and David Frawley, 1997, *Vedic Aryans and the Origins of Civilization*, New Delhi: Voice of India.

Risley, H.H., 1901, *Census of India*, India Report.

Saldanha, Julian, 1996, 'Patterns of Conversion in Indian Mission History', *Mission and Conversion: A Reappraisal*, Joseph Mattam and Sebastian Kim (eds.), Mumbai: St. Paul's Publications.

Shah, Ghanshyam, 1985, 'Anti-Untouchability Movements', *Caste, Caste Conflict and Reservation*, I.P. Desai, et. al. (ed.), Delhi: Ajanta Publications.

Sharma, S.P., and J.B. Sharma, 1998, *Culture of Indian Tribes*, Vol. 1, New Delhi: Radha Publications.

Sharma, Ursula, 1976, 'Status-Striving and Striving to Abolish Status: The Arya Samaj and the Low Castes', *Social Action* 26.

Shashi, S.S. (ed.), 1992, *Ambedkar and Social Justice,* New Delhi: Government of India.

Shoobert, 1931, *Census of India* 1931, C.P. and Berar Report.

Snaitang, O.L., 1993, *Christianity and Social Change in North East India,* Shillong: Vendrame Institute.

Srinivas, M.N., 1989, *The Cohesive Role of Sanskritization and Other Essays,* New Delhi: Oxford University Press.

Thapar, Romila, 2000, 'Hindutva and History', *Frontline*, October 13, pp. 15-16.

The Times of India News Service, 2001, 'Amartya Hits Out at Sangh Parivar for Trying to 'rewrite History' ', *Times of India*, January 3, p. 6 (Mumbai edition).

United News of India, 2001, 'RSS Attempts to Rewrite History', *The Indian Express*, January 1, p. 4 (Mumbai edition).

Valiamangalam, Joseph, 1996, 'Conversion in Indian Religions', *Mission and Conversion: A Reappraisal,* Joseph Mattam and Sebastian Kim (eds.), Mumbai: St. Paul's Publications.

Vidyarthi, L.P., and B.K. Raj, 1977, *Tribal Culture of India,* Delhi: Concept Publishing Co.

Webster, John C.B., 1992, *Dalit Christians: A History,* Delhi: I.S.P.C.K.

Wingate, Andrew, 1997, *The Church and Conversion. A Study of Recent Conversions to and from Christianity in the Tamil Area of South India,* Delhi: I.S.P.C.K.

Wilkinson, T. and M.M. Thomas (eds.), 1972, *Ambedkar and the neo-Buddhist Movement,* Chennai: CLS.

Witzel, Michael and Steve Farmer, 2000, 'Horseplay in Harappa: The Indus Valley Decipherment Hoax', *Frontline*, October 13, pp. 4-14.

—, 2000, 'New Evidence on the 'Piltdown Horse' Hoax', *Frontline*, November 24, pp. 126-129.

Zeitlin, Irving, 1996, *Rethinking Sociology: A Critique of Contemporary Theory*, Jaipur: Rawat (reprinted).

Zelliot, Eleanor, 1992, *From Untouchable to Dalit: Essays on the Ambedkar Movement*, Delhi: Manohar.

9

Brahmanical Social Order and Christianity in India

Lancy Lobo

This paper intends to tease out the links between the Brahmanical order and Christianity in India. It also attempts to highlight the differences between them. Having described the character of the Brahmanical order, it goes on to explain the challenge posed by Christianity, as Christian missionaries were the only rival intellectuals to the traditional Brahmanical order. In the bargain, Christianity has internalised some elements of the Brahmanical order. Having discussed the challenges of Gandhi, Hindutva (Hindu nationalism) and Dalits to Christianity, it deals with the possible direction that Christians in India need to take to find their role in secular and globalised India.

I
Brahmanical Social Order

Varnashrama dharma, popularly known as the caste system, is the creation of Brahmanical Hindus supported by the scriptures of the Aryans such as the *Vedas* and *Manusmrti*. The Aryans were invaders and imposed their religion and hegemony on the conquered Anaryans (non-Aryans), Dravidians and indigenous populations. Eventually, they divided the population into *varna* categories by placing themselves at the top of the hierarchy of wealth, pow- position and privilege. The body metaphor of differen- place coming out in the different body parts of Brahma is icant because it indicates the differential impo- of different castes. belonging to the

There are claims of the Indus ci- nated by the Aryans Anaryans and later on being designed the caste system (Sharma, 1995:65). The A- they safeguarded their interests. (Ghurye, 1969:176) ig- ned everyone a caste, an occupation, a The caste system -al code, different sets of rituals for birth, rank, a behav- death, and assigned strictures and sanctions to marriage them. Stability was thus assured and institutionalised. enfor- Th- term Brahmanical is not restricted to the Brahman castes alone, but could apply to all upper castes. There was a clear separation between the producer, agriculturist, peasant, menial and those that undertook intellectual work. The latter were superior to the former.

The stability of the Brahmanical order was slightly disturbed during Muslim rule, but the former had an uncanny way of finding its feet and coping with any threat. Later, during the British rule, too, it faced certain challenges. Hindu or Hinduism is a 19th century construct. It is a shallow word that has gained flesh only recently under the Hindutva campaign, according to the noted historian, Romila Thapar. One must distinguish Brahmanical from non-Brahmanical Hindus; the Sanskritic (the twice-born Hindus who follow the hierarchical values) from non-Sanskritic Hindus; the Great Tradition from the Little Tradition of Hinduism. For instance, Kancha Ilaiah states: "In our childhood, all of us, the Dalit-bahujans of India, never heard the word 'Hindu' not as a word, nor as the name of a culture, nor as the name of the religion" (1996). Hinduism has never been monolithic as the Hindutvavadis are making it out to be. Religious Hinduism must be distinguished from political Hinduism. There was diversity in religious Hinduism. There was broadly sectarian and non-sectarian Hinduism. Non-sectarian Hinduism broadly belonged to the Dalits and Bahujans, which stressed caste rather than religion. Ilaiah has has be[...] convincing argument to the embarrassment of the [...]dis. He has exposed how Brahmanical Hinduism have been [...]off as mainstream Hinduism and how its traits their emulation. [...]n the intermediate and lower castes for

The lower castes [...] economic, social, political a[...]induism perpetually suffered were largely labourers who had [...]ous deprivations. They upper castes by working in their fiel[...]free services to the demeaning jobs. They lived in a segregated part [...]nd performing They could not be touched lest they polluted the upp[...]the village. They sought equality from the upper castes, but what they [...]castes. was only spiritual equality. Protest movements such as Buddhism, Jainism and the Bhakti Movement sought equality, but they too were in turn absorbed by the Brahmanical order. Since Brahmans did not serve them in ritual matters, they created their own priests (Brahmans of lower castes), a kind of replication of the Brahmanical order. The lower castes also replicated a kind of internal hierarchy among themselves.

II

SOCIAL BASE OF CHRISTIANITY IN INDIA

Christianity came to India around 52 A.D., but was confined to the southern tip of India, or Kerala, and composed of high-caste Syrian Christians. Colonial Christianity entered India from 16th century onwards, e.g. the Portuguese, the British and others. The Catholic Portuguese left behind a marine Christianity along the coastal lines of peninsular India consisting of people cutting across caste lines. The British period saw various denominations of Protestants working in many parts of India.

A large number of group conversions took place from among the lower castes and then tribes. The tribals of Chotanagpur and the north-east accepted Christianity. Thus, Christians in India are not at all homogeneous. They belong to three social bases: (a) the upper castes of Kerala, Mangalore, Goa; (b) the Dalits in many parts of India; and (c) tribals. Though initially, Protestant missionaries rooted for high-caste conversions, they were few to come by, and eventually, they accepted lower castes into their fold. The Roman Catholics by and large went for mass conversions or group conversions.

In general, it could be said that the missionaries were the only rival intellectuals in 18th and 19th century India for the traditional Brahmanical order. However, in their conversion drive, they showed preference for high-caste converts with the idea that the lower castes would automatically follow suit if the high castes accepted Christianity. But instead, the lower castes came in large numbers. The reason for this rush was the ill treatment they received at the hands of the upper castes who were either landlords or the priestly class. These lower castes wanted to escape the ignominy, indignities and exploitation meted out to them and both Islam and Christianity offered them visions of equality and dignity. The British period also brought about a lot of social consciousness among lower castes. There was an anti-Brahman movement led by E.V. Ramasamy Naicker in South India that spread up to Maharashtra. Large numbers got converted to Christianity, setting off alarms among the upper-caste Hindus. Reactionary movements like the Arya Samaj began to reconvert the low-caste converts to Christianity. So, today, of the 25 million Christians (2.4% of the total population of India), nearly 50 percent are estimated to be of Dalit origin, 30 percent tribals and the remaining 20 percent of upper-caste origin.

M.K. Gandhi, who was a Vaishnav Baniya (a higher form of Hinduism), while appreciating the selfless service of the Christian missionaries to the low castes, showed his unhappiness over conversions. He felt that health, sanitation, education and social uplift are good in themselves and are to be provided as good in themselves and their provision not used as means to realise other ends. In theological matters, Gandhi felt that each country or nation has an adequate religion and it needs no conversion to an outside religion. Hinduism, which has a multiplicity of gods, can accommodate Jesus as one more leader, teacher, god and revealer of truth to man.

After independence, the secular democratic Constitution of India put in generous clauses of affirmative action for the lower castes. The 'one man, one vote' policy flattened the merit of caste and there was no difference between the vote of a Brahman or a Dalit. For the lower castes, education and other institutional changes set off favourable moves for upward mobility in the class order. This meant loss of power, loss of opportunities for employment and loss of status for the upper castes. The upper castes felt that their privileges were encroached upon or thieved upon by the lower castes.

Over a period of time, the Dalit Christians found that their visions of seeking equality within the Church were not totally realised. Studies show that the Church and its resources dominated by the upper-caste Christians and its clergy hardly paid any attention to the felt needs of dalits. Satisfaction of spiritual needs alone was not sufficient. The Dalit question has brought to the surface the internal contradictions of Christianity in India. The Dalit question has become an embarrassment for the Church. The relevant issues to be addressed are: the nature of caste and Christianity in India; the Brahmanical order and Christianity; the Brahmanical order in Christianity; and religion and the socioeconomic order.

A criticism levelled at the Church in India by S.K. George, an eminent Gandhian and Christian, is the following: "Christianity has so far occupied only the byways of life, filling them with works of mercy, building schools and hospitals, sending out missionaries, and in these days providing refugee relief and sending food ships—but it has left the highways of life largely unoccupied; and it is along these highways that great injustices, cruel exploitations, racial discriminations, political dominations and other great evils stalk the world" (1939:90). He further states: "Religion has always had a tendency to be content with partial solutions, with encouraging charity instead of securing justice, with saving the individual and leaving the environment unredeemed" (1939:90-91). This suggests that mere charity is not enough, but that there must also be some fight for justice, perhaps through political action. What is needed is perhaps some kind of religious mass action rather than religious feasts and solemn assemblies.

III

CHRISTIANITY AND THE DALIT CHRISTIANS IN INDIA

As mentioned earlier, nearly 50 percent of India's Christians are Dalits, ex-untouchables. The Dalit Christians include the Pulayans in Kerala, Pariahs in Tamil Nadu, Tigalas in Karnataka, Malas and Madigas in Andhra Pradesh, Chamars (Ravidasis) in Madhya Pradesh, Uttar Pradesh and Bihar, Churhas in Punjab, Vankars in Gujarat and Mahars in Maharashtra ... converted during the last two hundred years. These conversions came to a halt after Independence. Christian Dalit issues cannot be considered in isolation from those of non-Christian Dalits. Such issues relate to religious changes leading to socioeconomic mobility, identity, differentiation, stratification, urge for self-determination, and movement towards viable, sustainable communities, reservation and discrimination as well issues relating to Dalit women, the official Church and its personnel.

There have been social movements among the untouchables in recent times—the Satnami movement of the Chamars in the Chattisgarh plains of eastern Madhya Pradesh, the Adi Dharam movement in Punjab (Juergensmeyer, 1982), the Mahar movement in Maharashtra (Zelliot, 1992), the sociopolitical mobilization among the Jatavs of Agra (Lynch, 1969) and the Anti-Brahman movement in South India. In all these, the untouchables were asserting their dignity and quest for equality either within or outside Hinduism. "To the untouchables," wrote Ambedkar in 1946, "Hinduism is a veritable chamber of horrors" (Zelliot, 1992). He further said in his conversion speech, "Choose any religion which gives you equality of status and treatment" (Elliot, 1992). Group conversions to Christianity by Dalits should be seen from this point of view. The Dalits saw visions of equality in Christianity.

Did the Christian Dalits achieve their visions? Yes and no. It is more no than yes for the following reasons: Christian Dalits have faced four-fold discrimination: (a) from the upper castes, (b) from the Church, (c) from the state, and (d) against Dalit Christians as they did with non-Christian Dalits. Most Dalits were economically dependent on the upper castes and on becoming Christian, there was no significant change in their economic status. The upper castes have not conceded any change. At the most, they call the Christian Dalits *Sudhrela* or civilised, educated Dalits.

The official Church has also discriminated against Dalit Christians. They are called at best neo-Christians. There are instances in some places in India of Dalit Christians being assigned a separate place during religious services, separate burial grounds, less decision-making power in church matters, and facing discrimination in their recruitment for the clergy. An estimate states that in the Pondicherry archdiocese, Dalit Catholics compose 80 percent of the population, whereas only 10 percent of the total priests in the archdiocese are Dalits, and none of them occupy any important post in it. In contrast, the priests from other minority upper castes comprise 90 percent and occupy high posts in the archdiocese (Raj, 1992:102).

The state has discriminated against the Christian Dalits in the sense that anyone reverting to the Hindu religion automatically becomes eligible for the reservation benefits that are available for scheduled castes. The argument is that Christianity, unlike Hinduism, has no caste. However, the state has granted reservations to Dalit converts to Sikhism and, later (1990), to Buddhists, but withheld it from Dalit converts to Islam and Christianity. In some states, Christian Dalits are placed in the OBC category. For instance, in Gujarat, they are labelled as 'Gujarati Christi'.

It should be stated that many religions such as Christianity, Sikhism and Islam do not believe in caste, but Sikhs, Muslims and Christians have castes. Most of the converts were from Hinduism and have not been able to shed their caste. And yet the state has thought it proper to give affirmative action to Sikh and Buddhist Dalits, but not to Christian Dalits. Perhaps political expediency has played a role in this.

Non-Christian Dalits, too, discriminate against the Christian Dalits. The former are worried about encroachment by Christian Dalits on their reservation benefits. Cultural differences are also creeping in among Christian and non-Christian Dalits.

After independence, the conversions from Dalits to Christianity and other religions have tapered off. This is partly due to the institutional changes that were set off by the democratic and secular Constitution of India. The ban on untouchability, protective discrimination and education have all assisted the Dalits to look up. But there have been instances of conversion like in Minakshipuram in Tamil Nadu in 1982. Conversion is still used as a weapon by dalits against the upper castes. Whenever Dalits are driven to the limit of their endurance, they threaten to change their religion. It is also true that upper-caste Hindus have subjected upwardly mobile Dalits to untold atrocities. For instance, during the anti-reservation riots spearheaded by the upper castes in Gujarat, only the upwardly mobile Wankar caste was attacked, not the Bhangis. The reaction of Hindu nationalists to conversions has been either to blame the missionaries or rush to appease the Dalits and cajole them into remaining within the Hindu fold.

Christian Dalits have experienced partial changes. A prefix or suffix has been added to the caste tag, e.g. Christi Mahar,

Wankar Christi, and so on. In the case of the Dalit Wankar caste, a comparative study shows that a creamy layer has emerged from among the Wankar Christi who are living in towns and cities, while the masses have remained in the rural areas without any socioeconomic change. However, the Christi Wankars have better literacy than the Hindu Wankars. There is some change in the living conditions and etiquette, too, among the Christi Wankars (Lobo, 1994).

Very few Christian Dalits have reverted to Hindu SC status to avail of reservation benefits. Most have opted to remain Christian despite a significant lack of change of economic status. This shows that the new identity of Christian has significance and made a difference, though not to their satisfaction. Becoming a Christian has made a difference to them. Today, many bishops, priests and nuns are recruited from Christian Dalits. One can say that the disabilities that Hindu Dalits faced in Hinduism are greater than those the Christian Dalits face in Christianity. The Dalit Christian movement in some parts of India has brought about great awareness in the Church about the discrimination the Dalit Christians faced.

The official Church is increasingly becoming conscious about the replication of the Brahmanical order within Christianity by the upper castes and its clergy. On their part, the Dalit Christians have mounted an anti-clerical stance seeking to participate in greater measure in the power, position and privileges of the official Church. The official Church dominated by the upper-caste Christians is taking note of the following:

(a) There is a cultural distance between the non-Dalit Christian clergy and Dalit Christians.

(b) The Church has taught docility to the Dalits instead of militancy to fight for their rights like in Buddhism and Islam.

(c) The Church has preached a kind of pietistic, ritualistic and cultic Christianity. What the Dalits need is a liberation theology component.

(d) The Church has offered a kind of terminal experience to Dalits in its parishes where they are born, married and die. The Church and its priests become the only reference. This has kept the Dalits from getting into the mainstream politics. The Church can no longer pretend to be a parallel state for Dalits.

(e) The economic support given by the Church to Dalits has not been communitarian, but selectively individual.

(f) The Church has been paternalistic rather than participatory in its interactions with the Dalits.

(g) In the context of patriarchy the Church has done little for Dalit women.

(h) One of the motives of Dalits in converting to Christianity was the upgradation of their socioeconomic status. The Church must throw its weight behind social justice rather than ritualism and religiosity.

(i) It is no longer sufficient to remain Christian Dalits or Hindu Dalits, they should all stand as Dalits first and then as Christians or Hindus.

The Church, conscious of its failure towards Dalit Christians, has mounted a sustained attack on the state for its discrimination against Dalit Christians. In recent times, in a number of fora, it has aired its displeasure. Rallies, meetings, memoranda and visits to dignitaries of the state have yielded little result. The state adamantly holds that Christianity does not believe in caste. The state must realise that the ground for reservation is socioeconomic backwardness, which cuts across religious boundaries. The state, in holding religion as the ground for reservation, is contravening the letter and spirit of the Constitution. Besides, the Constitution has outlawed untouchability and if caste and religion are the bases of reservations, then there is a clear violation of the Constitution by the state.

IV
Hindu Nationalism, Brahmanical Order and Christianity

During the last four years, atrocities against Christians have been on the rise in India. This appears to be an extension of atrocities on minorities like Muslims, Sikhs, Dalits, tribals and women. Modern citizenship is not based on primordial ties like caste, creed, language and region, it cuts across all of them. However, modern citizenship is seriously contested by the Brahmanic order whose traditionally held privileges and hegemony have been seriously under threat since the secular democratic Constitution was promulgated after Independence. Hindu nationalists must be distinguished from Indian nationalists. Indian nationalists stood for modern citizenship. The Hindu nationalism is a backlash to the Constitution of India. It is the Brahmanical hegemony that controlled the Congress Party, but when it became apparent that it was losing its hold, Hindu nationalism, through the Sangh Parivar, helped it to reassert itself. The minorities, Dalits and tribals became cannon fodder in this game. The Hindutva of the Sangh Parivar is a cover for a gradually rising fascism with the objective of foisting the Brahmanical order on the country.

India is for Hindus alone and minorities like Muslims and Christians either have to remain second class citizens or become Hindus. But then who is a Hindu ? There is no clear definition of a Hindu, except that one who is not a Christian, Muslim, Parsi, etc., is a Hindu.

In sociological literature, one finds that there are high-caste Hindus and lower-caste Hindus, Sanskritic and non-Sanskritic Hindus, Great Tradition and Little Tradition Hindus, Brahmanical Hindus and non-Brahmanical Hindus. The first category amounts to 20 percent and the second 80 percent of the Hindus. However, there are lower caste Hindus who would prefer not to be included in the Hindu fold, as, for instance,

Kancha Ilaiah (1994). Tribals, too, have been included among Hindus.

One must differentiate between political Hinduism and religious Hinduism. Hindu nationalists belong to the first category mentioned above (Brahmanical). They subscribe to political Hinduism. These have been upholding their hegemony and imposing it on the second category. There is no need to worry about Hindu nationalists if they extend dignity, human rights and equity to the Dalits and tribals. There is no harm in considering them Hindus either. But the whole project of political Hinduism is dubious as far as the minorities, Dalits and tribals are concerned.

It is the first category of Hindus who mounted anti-reservation riots and anti-Mandal riots against the Dalits and tribals. It is the same Hindu nationalists who are apologetic and want to modify the Constitution, which upholds democracy and secularism. It is doubtful if they will share their power, position and privileges with the Dalits and tribals.

It must be realised that given today's situation in India, we must ask the following questions which are in the interests of the Indian nation (Fernandes, 2000:4):

1. Are we promoting distributive justice in a rational and transparent manner among all sections of Indian society?
2. Are we applying secular, socioeconomic criteria in extending reservations to the weaker sections?
3. Are we mixing up communal and casteist considerations in what should be a humanistic, egalitarian enterprise devolving on the public authorities?

Conclusion

Indian Christianity has to shed its Brahmanical model in order to gain credibility to fight Hindu nationalists. Official Christianity tends to conform to the status quo in the established social order. It leaves much to be desired in the matter of social justice. Social historian Sarkar (1999:1696-7) has pointed out that in the past, the fight for justice was more of a fallout than conscious agenda in group conversions. The Church has to take cognisance of all pervasive caste structures as well as class structures in wider Indian society as well as among Christians. Contemporary Christianity in India, spurred by liberation theology, has found echoes in a number of episodes of social activist priests being murdered and nuns who fought on the side of the poor being killed or raped. In the face of these brutal attacks, Christian activists have not retreated into sectarian or fundamentalist shells, but continued to build bridges through joint work with secular, liberal and Left formations. Sarkar then concludes: "It is precisely these aspects of contemporary Christianity that arouse the greatest anger and fear among adherents of Hindutva" (1999:1698).

The Church needs to come out of its isolation and insulation in greater measure and get into the mainstream and strengthen civil society, rather than get burdened with institutions, be they educational, health or relief. It has also to reconsider its religious minority status. It has to raise its voice not just when a Christian is subjected to atrocities, but also when a non-Christian is subjected to such atrocities. What is at stake in contemporary India is not just Dalits, tribals and minorities, but democracy and secularism as enshrined in the Constitution.

References

Chowgule, Ashok, 1999, *Christianity in India: The Hindutva Perspective*, Mumbai: Hindu Vivek Kendra.

Fernandes, Lionel, 2000, 'Challenges before the Indian Christian Community', Seminar: 'Marginalised Communities: Social and Linguistic Problems', Mumbai: Department of Sociology, University of Bombay and Indian Institute of Culture.

George, S.K., 1939, *Gandhi's Challenge to Christianity*, London: George Allen and Unwin.

Ghurye, G.S., 1969, *Caste and Race in India*, Mumbai: Popular Prakashan (5th edition).

Juergensmeyer, M., 1982, *Religion as Social Vision: The Movement against Untouchability in 20th Century Punjab*, Berkeley CA: University of California.

Ilaiah, Kancha, 1996, *Why I Am Not a Hindu*, Kolkata: Samya.

Lobo, Lancy, 1994, 'Religious Conversion and Social Mobility', *ICSSR Research Abstracts Quarterly*, Vol. xxiii. No. 1 and 2, January-June, pp. 17-32.

—, 2000, 'Dalit Christians and Church Personnel in India', *Third Millennium*, Vol. III, No. 3, pp. 46-67.

—, 2000, 'Religion and Politics in India', *America*, Vol. 182. No. 5, February, pp. 7-10.

Lynch, Owen, 1969, *Politics of Untouchability*, New York: Columbia University.

Raj, Antony, 1992, 'The Dalit Christian Reality in Tamil Nadu', *Jeevandhara*, 22 (128) pp. 95-111.

Sarkar, Sumit, 1999, 'Conversions and Politics of Hindu Right', *Economic and Political Weekly*, June 26.

Sharma, R.S., 1995, *Looking for the Aryans*, Chennai: Orient Longman Limited.

Zelliot, Eleanor, 1992, *From Untouchable to Dalit*, Delhi: Manohar Publications.

10

Educational Stratification, Dominant Ideology and the Reproduction of Disadvantage in India

Padma Velaskar

A comprehensive critique of the Indian formal education system is long overdue not the least because of its rank failure to respond in any meaningful way to the needs and aspirations of the masses. The persistence of tremendous inequalities in educational access, retention, performance and outcome between oppressed sections such as Dalits and Adivasis and the rest of society, has laid bare the huge gap between the promise and reality of state sponsored education. Despite this, however, the mythology of education as the great equaliser persists in public and academic discourse and continues to shape policy, research and action. Even those who perceive education's failings and critique it, continue to repose faith in it and seek solutions to educational problems through policy change and reforms within the existing sociopolitical framework.

The social scientific study of education in India, too, has not escaped this naive faith. Educational research has been policy driven, and in obvious alignment with the state educational institutions. Sociologists of education, guided explicitly or implicitly by the structural functional paradigm in their modes of problem formulation have remained engaged in the task of investigating the functions and dysfunctions of education for society, their implications for economic, social and political development, and for the achievement of western modernity.[1] Even though the problem of inequality in education has been a central research theme, investigations have not ventured beyond questions of access and achievement, and explanations have been sought more in terms of the social origins and cultural background of the learners, and not in the way of the education system itself.

The general perspective adopted in this paper is that the role of education in society can only be grasped by viewing it historically, contextually and relationally. To understand the operation of the educational system in an unequal and hierarchical society, it must be located in the larger context of the structures and ideologies of power and domination and of the political economy. It is the contention of this paper that dominant ideologies and interests—which, in contemporary India, are predominantly rooted in caste, class and patriarchy, now increasingly in conjunction with those of the global capitalist economy—have got articulated through the state and largely determined the course of educational development, change and expansion in India. They have impinged upon the structure, content and process of education in socially significant ways, making it a complex political and ideological mediator.

This paper focusses on caste and class ideologies and structural processes, and explores their relationship with the educational structure of schooling in post-independent India. Its concern is with the plight of those historically excluded from and deprived of education, viz., the Dalits. More specifically, the paper examines the caste-class stratified structure of education and attempts to unravel the unstated values and assumptions that underlie it. The paper argues that the dominant cultural, social and economic values, both Brahmanical and capitalist, of the ruling classes are deeply embedded in the hierarchical design of the institution, making it a most significant source of inequality. It draws attention to the various ramifications of this dominance and the mechanisms through which educational stratification serves these dominant and influential caste, class and political interests and subverts the interests of the oppressed. Both external and internal structural features and internal hegemonic processes act as mediators of hierarchy and inequality. Apart from sustaining consolidating and perpetuating the historical condition of educational advantage and disadvantage, educational policy and practice has led to new divisions and hierarchies that breed new difficulties. Thus far, we have had fragmented critiques of individual aspects of the education system, but not systematic critiques examining society-school links and external and internal links within the system. A total structural analysis reveals how the system functions as a formidable force militating against the oppressed. Dominant ideology has also created a highly gendered institutional structure, which will not be explored in this paper. However, the analysis carried out here is fully applicable to girls belonging to Dalit communities.

Against a brief historical background of the ideological development and definition of the educational structure, the paper explores this relationship between caste-class structure and educational structure by: (a) systematically examining the caste-class linked character of the educational structure, (b) focussing on the political economy of educational provisions, (c) exploring trends in the current restructuring of the educational system in a globalising society and rapid changes in the meaning of education, and finally, (d) outlining implications and social consequences of the hierarchical system for the downtrodden castes of Indian society. In developing the framework of analysis and tentative propositions and arguments, I have drawn upon the indigenous anti-caste critiques, theoretical perspectives rooted in the critical and conflict traditions of the sociology of education and insights derived out of my own field based and historical research on education and Dalits in Maharashtra.[2] The limited secondary sources that throw light on educational inequality have also been utilised. There is an overall paucity, though, of meaningful historical and sociological research in education. Hopefully, the exercise conducted here will suggest a new direction for critical research in this field.

Ideological Roots of the Modern Education Structure

The sociohistoric roots of the modern educational structure lie in the colonial period. As is well critiqued and known, the colonial system reflected the power and educational needs of the colonisers. It was the sole powerful model on the educational scenario, having effectively destroyed the indigenous system (Kelly and Altbach, 1978; Carnoy, 1974.) In following a pernicious policy of religious neutrality, the British evolved a new educational system that seemed to rest on the traditional social order. The issue of which sociopolitical forces with what ideology have shaped the post-independence system has, however, not received much attention. In the post-independence period context of a political discourse that was dominated by national development, nation-building and nationalism, education came to be identified as a master instrument of change and development. The development agenda cast in western liberal ideology was that of Nehruvian modernity and Nehru called for the 'revolutionisation' of education to fulfil it. The dominant characteristics of the national paradigm were: massive industrialisation, the growth of science and technology in the service of an industrial civilisation, the creation of a scientific and rational temper, and instilling the values of secularism, liberty, equal opportunity and justice. Its chief proponents were the new social elites—the metropolitan, western educated upper and middle classes, the intelligentsia, predominantly all upper caste, who had benefitted from the colonial system. They were the architects of the 'new' national educational system, along with the right wing element of the ruling Congress' political and economic elite.

The 'revolutionisation' of education envisaged by Nehru, however, did happen. As the goals of national development were converted into those of capitalist development in agriculture and industry and any pretence of egalitarianism was crushed by the powerful presence of the old hierarchical structures, rooted in Brahmanical religio-culture, one saw the expansion of the colonial model of education which was earlier criticised by the very same nationalist elite. Due to the overwhelming Brahmanical domination in almost all categories of the ruling elite, Brahman ideology held sway in the shaping of the education system. As in older times, the Brahmans maintained close links with the economically and politically powerful, the latter, in turn, depending on them for intellectual and religious leadership. Having made the smooth transition from being a ruling class in the traditional feudal order, to being part of the ruling class in the colonial system, primarily on the basis of their knowledge power and literati tradition, the Brahmans had a particular stake in the maintenance and persistence of dominant colonial and Brahmanical categories. Education had been their traditional vehicle of domination and this was critical in the modern age, too, for self-preservation. Thus, as the predominant policy and decision makers, they advocated continuation of the stratified, lopsided educational structure that was tailor-made for the maintenance of sociocultural domination and for hegemonic use in the perpetuation of the dominant ideology. Not surprisingly, the opposing Phule-Ambedkarian ideology of education for enlightenment, mental awakening and social transformation towards a new humanist society found no place at all.

Though this area needs systematic historical study, the broad historical contours of educational policy making and action in the early decades after independence indicate how the foundation for educational stratification and inequality, (the rhetoric of mass education and action of mass expansion notwithstanding) was firmly laid during the time. For years, the Constitution of India was the only guiding light for extending mass education. A full-fledged education policy for the nation came into existence as late as 1968. In keeping with the elitist intents, higher education was given first priority in the efforts at reforming education towards fulfilling national goals (Kamat, 1989).[3]

The Brahmanical core of the decision-making element was most palpably evident in the staunch opposition to dismantling the hierarchical organisation of education in favour of a common school system based on the concept of a neighbourhood school. This was advocated by the Kothari Commission of 1964-66, but was bitterly opposed and rejected (Naik, 1977). The apparent contradiction between retaining a system (manufactured in the first place for exploitative use), and professing nationalist goals, can only be explained by the fact that these goals were only set for the ruling minority, to build and enhance their material and knowledge power.

The form and structure of the educational system was thus directly and almost autocratically determined by the interests and values of the dominant, who used it to attain hegemonic domination over the deeply divided, antagonistic Indian society. Curriculum and content as ideological apparatus have also been central to cultural domination-subordination through the educational system, but this is a separate and complex area, which will not be dealt with here. Suffice it to note here that modifications of content which aimed at indigenisation only meant Brahmanisation of the curriculum. In keeping with the strategy of agricultural and industrial modernisation, western science and technology assumed the level of 'high status knowledge'.

The only competing indigenous model of basic education was half-heartedly implemented. It, therefore, decayed and died a quick death. Now we look closely at the powerful structural features of the chosen system.

The Hierarchical Stratification of the Educational Structure

The external and internal hierarchical structuring of the system is of extreme importance in understanding how it actually functions in society—it serves as an instrument of internal domination/colonialism in the hands of the dominant classes, and serves to extend the caste/class handicaps and oppressions suffered by the subordinated in the home/community/village settings, right into the school.

All existing schools can be broadly classified into a four-tiered pyramidical hierarchy, which almost parallels the Varna of gradation. This hierarchical school system ranges from the exclusive, elitist public school that caters to the top of the social hierarchy, to the impoverished rural schools run by the local bodies that cater almost exclusively to the bottom, viz., the overwhelmingly poor SC/ST sections. It corresponds roughly, but definitively, to the hierarchical caste-class division of society into the high caste economic, social and political elites, the high caste, middle caste upper and middle classes, the lower caste-classes and the lowest class predominantly constituted by the lower Shudra, and Dalit castes and the Adivasis. It is important to note that the lower end of the hierarchy may signify not just the most inferior quality schooling, but no schooling at all.[4] Thus, the gradation in education terms of quality and social composition appears to rest on the traditional hierarchical system. The hierarchy may vary regionally in form and shape, depending on the general development of state or region, but there is a hierarchy nonetheless. In the context of the changing stratificatory order based on new criteria and principles, each new emergent stratum is fitted into an educational sub-system, which also gets increasingly differentiated to accommodate them.

The Internal Structure

The internal structure and culture of the colonial model of schooling has also remained unchanged. The defining features of the system are full-time attendance of specific age groups in teacher supervised classrooms for the study of graded curricula.

Whole day schools, unconducive time-spans of vacations and compulsory attendance have served as deterrent factors in households dependent on children for domestic work or other productive work to supplement household earnings. The fundamentally different economic situations, life aims and social circumstances of different strata households have not been given due cognisance in the selection of structure. In all, it has been particularly ill suited to develop the vast reservoir of the rural sector. Culturally, the educational norms of attendance, discipline, home work, tests and exams, the cognitively ethnocentric demands of concentration, comprehension, relating to and mastering what is being taught, are all problematic. The crucial factor of the content of education, the curriculum itself as a tool of cultural dominance and hegemony, has an alienating and intimidating impact.

Each stage of school education—primary, middle, secondary—leads to the next and is not terminal in itself. The design of the non-terminal internal structure is one that has negative consequences for the low-caste child or she is not suitably trained for upward advance due to the hierarchy. The few years of primary education are useful to gain the label 'educated', which is not adequate, however, as meaningful learning or preparation for gainful employment. For the child who succeeds beyond the primary level, absence of a middle or higher school in the vicinity puts limits to her motivation and aspirations. Public educational facilities at this level remain highly restricted till today. Thus, the overall though not terminal for the privileged, forces termination on aspirants among the underprivileged. Vocational training, which could be of some use to them, has remained a grossly neglected area. Overall, there is a drastic reduction in secondary school level opportunities, which appear to be meant solely for the middle classes.

At the school level evaluation practice, we have the great contradiction between the hierarchical structure and an equalitarian evaluation system in the form of the common school leaving exam. Children who school in sharply variant educational environments, especially Dalit children who also lack the 'cultural capital' of the caste Hindu children, are placed at an obvious disadvantage. The outcome is predictable—a vast gulf between types of schools in numbers attempting and qualifying the exam. There is vast difference in the educational levels attained and achievement levels of schools, which reflects difference by caste and class (Velaskar, 1992).

The Hegemony of Educational Values

The gross incongruence between operating such a hierarchical structure and the ideological values and assumptions claimed to be underlying the system *per se* has never been squarely confronted. The dominant liberal ideology that propagates education's prominent role in the creation of a just meritocracy has served well to camouflage the inherent injustice and unfairness of the system. As a result of the political rhetoric and social propaganda accompanying mass expansion, education's image as a neutral institution remains untainted in the public eye. The mythology of merit and achievement, productivity and efficiency, supposedly promoted by education holds, despite its stark ascription based foundations and practices, which reserve the best education for those with cultural and/or economic capital. The notion of merit becomes a convenient stick with which to beat protective discrimination policies, and their beneficiaries. What is needed is to problematise concepts of merit and intelligence and consider their social base. The characteristics that go into definitions of merit and IQ are not drawn from core values and knowledge of every strata, but from dominant strata. Dominant ideology plays a role in defining merit and the construction of merit itself is what upper classes can achieve easily ('pure' languages, maths and elite history), given the role of social origin and cultural property (increasingly economic property) in the attainment of merit.

New liberal values, thus, have been used to strengthen old patterns of cultural domination and legitimise them, rather than generate, create and nurture merit from the vast pools of talent that remain suppressed. In fact, the hierarchical designing of the educational system reflects unstated assumptions about the low social worth of the Dalits or Adivasis, their inferior natural intelligence and educational potential. Thus, there are limits set on the definition of their educational needs and the educational levels they can reach based on cultural assumptions regarding their preordained destiny as labourers and servants.

The Teacher as an Element in the Hierarchy

Following educationists, sociologists of education have treated teachers purely as an occupational category in research and theory. But teachers as social beings in an unequal society, must be sociologically seen as located in and representatives of, the caste/social class (and also gender/ethnic based) social order. In the Indian context, where the profession of teacher has been traditionally associated with the Brahman caste, and they along with other upper literati castes such as the Kayastha have dominated school and college teaching, this has been a major theoretical oversight. Unless we view teachers as products and bearers of caste/class cultures, we cannot make sense of the persistent set of negative findings regarding their overall poor functioning in mass schools. In particular, it should be useful to view the classroom in a poor, Dalit dominated backwater school as a dynamic site of caste antagonism, caste struggle and resistance. Otherwise, we are at a loss to explain the multiple findings regarding lack of teachers absenteeism, teacher apathy to teaching, low teacher motivation, teacher incompetency, teacher inability to cope, teacher attitudes, etc. Research studies are replete with such findings. There is need to go beyond such arbitrary collections of mundane facts, place teachers in their sociocultural contexts, examine the theories they hold on education and educating, and their social motives for entering the field. Most importantly, we need to investigate their stated or unstated assumptions about low-caste children, their deprived and deficient cultural backgrounds, their intellectual deficiencies, capacities and limits to learning, their discriminatory pedagogic practices of labelling, classifying and teaching styles, their 'realistic' perceptions of low-caste children's educational and life chances, in sum their attitudes and behaviours towards the downtrodden castes. What are teachers' levels of hostility and indifference to Dalit/tribal cultural traits, value systems and how does discriminatory behaviour manifest itself? While these issues have not been directly studied, empirical evidence that is available seems to suggest that teacher preconceptions and attitudes are the medium through which caste/class background dominates the educational process and contributes directly to low learning levels, dropouts and the creation of failure.[5]

The Political Economy of Expansion and Provision

The articulation of dominant politico-economic interests in the state has been amply evident in the pattern of educational expansion and financial provision, which provides sustenance to the hierarchical system. Politicians, policy-makers and bureaucrats as agents of the state, and private educational managements constitute the influential body of educational decision-makers and implementors. Their inter-relationships and actions determine the course of educational expansion (Rudolph and Rudolph, 1972; Rosenthal, 1972). We have little systematic study of the power relations that operate in policy framing and implementation, but it has been clear that there has been a grudging expansion of educational facilities of the mass variety and a particularly poor implementation of special policies made in the favour of the oppressed. Social reformist education's efforts launched during times of the nationalist struggles, withered away perhaps with the expectation that the state would take care of its constitutional commitments.

Along with the woefully inadequate educational infrastructure and the abysmal conditions of the schooling system meant for the lowly, we have a long history of apathetic implementation of all the schemes meant for the SC/ST/BC categories—freeships, scholarships, *ashram shalas*, hostels, etc.[6] Implementation is directly related to political action and where Dalit political and social consciousness and movements are strong, there has been pressure to put the schemes in operation and systems have been activated. Much energy has been spent on this translation of educational schemes into practice, thus even getting these measly provisions implemented has been an uphill task for the oppressed.

In contrast, traditional powerful elements and burgeoning sections of the urban and rural elite and middle classes in the post-independence period have advanced the systems of secondary and higher education under politico-ethnic leadership and patronage (Kamat, 1989). The new elite from the lower castes have also entered the fray and attempted to spread more education among their people, but this is happening to a very limited extent. Decentralisation has also served the purpose of expansion to hitherto deprived regions and sections, but quality has always remained questionable because of the extra-educational interests of those involved.

Educational investments and allocations have been commensurate with this deliberately created uneven and unequal pattern of growth. The difficult economic situation created by the overall severe under-investment in education has been aggravated by the lopsided financial priorities and allocations within education. The state, as the primary funder of primary, secondary and higher education, has clearly played favourites. The education of the entrenched elite and middle class segments of society receives a disproportionate share of valuable resources. The education of these segments at the secondary and higher education levels is subsidised, while mass education for the poor suffers. The priority given to primary education in the First Plan declined in subsequent years, till it had to be renewed in the Eighth Plan due to the glaring failures noted at this most basic level. Furthermore, the meagre resources allotted to primary education are largely spent on salaries, with a pittance allotted to capital expenditure on educational infrastructure (Tilak, 1997). Only 2 percent of the total capital expenditure on elementary education is for building, equipment, etc., and the backlogs are alarming as per NCERT reports.[7]

Furthermore, contrary to belief, state sponsored primary education has been free. Poor households spend large sums of money, including amounts on fees, books, uniforms (Tilak, 1996). In the context of the persistent existence of intense poverty, the costs of education have a definite deterrent impact on enrolment and retention.

Implications of Social Hierarchy and Political Economy of Education

The key implications for education of the oppressed that clearly emerge from the foregoing analysis are:

(a) The hierarchical system of education is a system of closure to the most socially valued, and most economically rewarded education. It organises for economic selection to take place on the basis of social ascription, while the façade is that of universalising access, democratising and opening up.

(b) The system either excludes the oppressed (through non-provision) or includes, but by employing the mechanism of tracking from the outset. Exclusion and tracking produce educational disadvantage.
(c) The system is thus caste discriminatory, which compounds the overall difficult socioeconomic conditions, making education a process full of struggle for the disadvantaged. Limits are set on how much education they will acquire and how far it will take them and where.
(d) The system involves closure to high-status knowledge and culture, yet it is an aggressively culturally homogenising and hegemonising system, which underscores and reinforces both the superiority of high castes and their culture and the cultural, educational inferiority of the oppressed. It socialises the opposing strata into roles of the exploiting and exploited (with an appropriate common or national civic consciousness), and legitimises this socialisation.
(e) Thus, the system is structured to guarantee unequal access and produce the unequal results in achievements and outcomes that it eventually does. Social hierarchy is converted into academic hierarchy.

Globalisation and the Restructuring of Education and Ideology

In the context of the powerful forces of the world global-capitalist economy, liberalisation and the quicker march towards the free market ethos, national development goals have undergone a sea change. The role of education has changed visibly and the earlier goals visualised for education have been transformed. The instrumental, economic goal has assumed pre-education, primarily as a means of individual, not collective, economic advancement. Citizen formation has given way to skill formation, national building to national economic competitiveness (Green, 1997). In India, in the context of the new consensus on the inevitability of the new economic policies, the new educational goals are obviously defined by the political and economic elite, who stand to gain the most by them. They are supported by the massive middle class, which is dependent on them for material betterment. Thus, new educational policies are masterminded by a new class of professional experts and assistants. The new instrumentalist ideology of education provides the legitimacy and impetus for (a) privatisation-expansion of private educational institutions, (b) narrow skill/knowledge based education geared to meeting the demands of the new economy, and (c) the concept of banking education to become dominant, in view of educational competition for individual success.

Privatisation refers to the increase in employment of non-public resources for providing education (tuition fees, donations, contributions). In the post-1980 regime, when liberalisation began, privatisation originated in higher education in the establishment of private engineering and medical colleges. The development signalled and reflected the change and a definitive move towards the privatisation of the public sphere.

Privatisation can be seen as a mechanism used by the powerful and the upward looking middle classes to be able to control/secure the conditions of their achievement and advance. It reflects a competition for credentials, which can be seen as a matter of power and exclusion in service of the reproduction of the middle class from one generation to the next in the new, lucrative economy. The present trends in the economy, provide a golden opportunity to further consolidate the hereditary advantage, now in neo-colonial collusion with the international agents of foreign investment and capital.

Privatisation as a dominant feature in higher education today is not delinked from caste interest. In Maharashtra, the Maratha political lobby is establishing Maratha hegemony though the use of educational institutions. The historical link between politics and education is old. Education has always constituted a micro-arena of politics. What is new is the unbridled expansion in response to the demand of upwardly mobile elements in specific castes and the predominance of the pure commercial motive (exemplified in the capitation fee). The consequence is the commercialisation and commodification of education. With the entry of the businessman-educationist, there is transformation of education itself into a big business. There is now open entry and access for commercial players in the field. Money power is central in the acquisition and expansion of education.

Hitherto, secondary education has largely been government aided private effort and primary education has been largely government run. Now in the continued search for upward mobility, there is great demand for private education at all levels. There has been a general proliferation of primary and secondary, recognised and unrecognised private schools. We do not have an idea of the exact size, but it is grossly underestimated (Kingdon, 1996). There is also a widespread proliferation of the parallel institution of the coaching class.

Along with the middle classes, the lower classes, too, demand private education in the struggle for mobility. Only a minority, however, can access it. In keeping with their lowly status, the quality impacted to them is poor. Private education for the poor is available at exorbitant rates and the sacrifices made eventually do not prove worth it, as they remain at the bottom of the hierarchy.

The Growing Dependence on Foreign Resources

With liberalisation began the foreign funding of primary education, made dependent through foreign loan aid. The historical Jomtien Conference on 'Education for All' in 1990 was the beginning of a structurally adjusted political economy of education. In actuality, Jomtien was the venue of a public ceremony at which the poor were introduced to the "nasty new world of post cold-war capitalism". After this, Jomtien, rather than the Indian Constitution, has become the origin of the concept of universal schooling. (Kumar, 1995). Moreover, education is now a component of the Social Safety, Net Adjustment Credit financed by IDA. Social Safety, as is well apparent to the perceptive, is the new façade of the welfare state. The actual goals remain social control and containment of growing discontent and frustration in the lower classes.

In the new primary education programme, NGOs will replace the state primary delivery mechanisms link between the bureaucratic and industrial elite. In a scenario which has seen the depoliticisation of NGOs through funding, the goals of the new programme are vague and elusive, such as capacity building. Monitoring through psychometric techniques of learning achievements seems to have a hidden agenda (Kumar, 1995).

The renewed rhetoric that emphasises the ideology of universalisation of primary education, camouflages the contradictory reality of receding expenditure on education of the poor and intensification of the inherent tendency of elitism in education. Mass education is being advocated as a tool to project the human face of adjustment. Similarly, in the new context of the human rights discourse, social justice and equal opportunity have become unfashionable, outmoded concepts.

This is the new political economy of primary education. The desperate situation of the education of the poor notwithstanding, in the context of the new political economy of privatisation, fees hitherto of marginal importance are being viewed as the most potent source of educational financing even with respect to primary education. This financial cutback will have a direct impact on opportunity at the most basic level.

Conclusions: Educational Stratification and the Reproduction of Disadvantage

Focussing on educational stratification by caste and class, this paper has argued that the hierarchical structuring of education itself fundamentally restricts hopes of equal opportunity that the socially oppressed people may have. We have attempted to problematise the manner in which the issue of educational disadvantage of these sections has so far been posed and laid the blame squarely at the door of the educational system itself for determining the very pattern of opportunity. Further, we have attempted, through an analysis of the ideology, structural features and mechanisms of differentiation of this structure and the political economy of education, to expose the full manifestations and implications of this hierarchy.

In this concluding section, we may briefly outline the impact of these structural processes in order to grasp the full import of how children from these groups are made victims of this highly unjust, inegalitarian, alienating and dehumanising system. The impact of educational stratification, summed up in the following points below, indicates how it has reproduced and produced the educational disadvantage suffered by those historically excluded from education.

(a) The adoption of the mass education system has represented a shift from mass exclusion to mass inclusion which is however an incredibly weak and highly discriminatory inclusion. Dominant ideology and caste and class interests have kept alive the Brahmanical principle of closure, cooling out most of the oppressed at the primary level itself.

(b) Educational deprivation, failure and low achievement for the oppressed sections are thus inbuilt in the system. As a result, there is a continued effective exclusion or the achievement of low levels of education, which do not necessarily reflect learning. This achievement level is an overall poor qualification in the labour market. With levels of learning officially declared to be at a minimum level for the disadvantaged, there is a further dilution in their learning. In contrast, the privileged are scaling newer heights of elitism in education. The situation of disadvantage thus will not only persist, there will be an increase in the relative gap between the advantaged and the disadvantaged in both the quantity and quality of education.

(c) The inevitable, therefore, has happened. Low education levels have not been of much consequence in raising the status of the oppressed. And with growing job ceilings, the pool of educated unemployed is expanding rapidly. But this large pool, which should be considered truly meritorious for having braved it through a hostile educational process, is not considered capable enough to be admitted in the open category.

(d) Thus, the painful process of education eventually may not result in social recognition or reward.

(e) The psychological, intellectual and cultural consequences are damaging. At the psychological level, unequal schooling and the failure mark it puts on these children, creates a range of negative impacts: low self-concepts, low motivation, low aspirations, which in turn serve to instill a fear and dislike for schooling. The school, more than the home, actively contributes to produce this condition of educational disadvantage, demotivating and alienating the students from the learning process and channeling them to varied other arenas not necessarily beneficial to them.

(f) In all, to view it from the perspective of the oppressed, they go through much anguish for such little education. They are damned if they get education and damned if they don't.

(g) From any angle one looks at it, educational backwardness is the dominant reality, but contrary to the general assumption and belief, it is a backwardness kept alive by the system itself. It would be futile to expect otherwise—that a hierarchical system would function as a harbinger of equal opportunity.

(h) On the positive side, education for those who have been able to secure it, has fetched dignity and self-respect. The achievement has been of immense symbolic value in itself, but its substantive social value in terms of fetching equal social status is, as we have seen, questionable.

(i) Thus, to make the crucial point clearly and emphatically, the true character of the educational system is that of a powerful bastion of caste and class inequality—an arena of institutionalised casteism, where hierarchical ideology prevails in several collective acts of omission and commission in educational provisions which make for a stratified educational system. Educational stratification is thus the fundamental basis of unequal opportunity on which the hierarchies of educational content and classroom process are maintained. Together, structure, content and process act to produce and reproduce educational disadvantage, which, in itself, given the poor economic capital or political power base of the oppressed masses, is conditioned enough to produce and reproduce social disadvantages.

Education thus helps maintain the hierarchical social system and also serves as its chief legitimiser. By corollary, it itself serves as a central obstacle in the democratisation of education and in the propelling of emancipatory impulses towards educational and societal change. In the contemporary environment where educational needs and demands are increasingly dictated by international market forces and imperialist designs, national goals and the Constitution itself are under threat by reactionary forces, and there is growing state repression of any countervoice, the problems of the oppressed, both educational and others, seem destined to intensify.

Notes

1. See for example the approaches of the Surveys of Research in Education published periodically by the NCERT.
2. In the main, I have drawn upon the theoretical work of Althusser, 1971; Apple, 1979, 1986; Bourdieu, 1973, 1977; Giroux, 1983; McCarthy, 1997; Sarup, 1978 and Sharp, 1980.

3. Early educational policy-making has suffered from inadequate attention. The priorities have been lopsided from the outset and the most crucial recommendations of important Commissions have been ignored and rejected. Educational expansion, thus seemingly ad hoc, has proceeded along the lines desired by the powerful (Naik, 1972).
4. For an overview of descriptive studies documenting inequality and hierarchy in schooling, see Velaskar, 1992.
5. See studies by Kumar, 1989; Banerji, 1997; Bhatty, 1998.
6. See the Commission of SC/ST reports, in particular the one authored by B.D. Sharma, published in 1987.
7. See the Survey of Education published periodically by NCERT. Most recent evidence comes from the series of Education for All studies published by NIEPA, New Delhi. See NIEPA, 2000.

References

Acharya, Poromesh, 1988, 'Is Macaulay Still Our Guru?' *Economic and Political Weekly*, Vol. XXIII, No. 22, May 28, pp. 1124-1130.

Aloysius, G., 1997, *Nationalism Without A Nation in India,* Delhi: Oxford University Press.

Althusser, L., 1971, 'Ideology and Ideological State Apparatuses, Notes towards an Investigation', *Lenin and Philosophy and Other Essays*, New Left Books, pp. 242-273.

Apple, Michael, 1979, *Ideology and Curriculum,* London: Routledge and Kegan Paul.

Apple, Michael, 1986, *Teachers and Texts: A Political Economy of Class and Gender Relations in Education,* New York and London: Routledge and Kegan Paul.

Banerji, R., 1997, 'Why Don't Children Complete Primary School?: A Case Study of a Low-Income Neighbourhood in Delhi', *Economic and Political Weekly*, Vol. 32, No. 32, August 9, pp. 2053-2063.

Bernsten, M., 1987, 'Obstacles on the Path to School: Educational Problems of Backward Class Children', *New Quest*, July-August.

Bhatty, K., 1998, 'Educational Deprivation in India: A Survey of Field Investigations', *Economic and Political Weekly,* Vol. 33, No. 27 and 28, pp. 1731-1740; 1858-1869.

Bourdieu, Pierre, 1973, 'Cultural Reproduction and Social Reproduction' *Knowledge, Education and Cultural Change: Papers in the Sociology of Education,* (ed.) Richard Brown, London: Tavistock Publications, pp. 71-112.

Bourdieu, Pierre, and Jean-Claude Passeron, 1977, *Reproduction in Education, Society and Culture,* London: Sage Publications.

Brown, P., A.H. Halsey, Hugh Lauder and Amy Stuart Wells, 1997, 'The Transformation of Education and Society: An Introduction', (eds.) A.H. Halsey et al., *Education, Culture, Economy, Society,* Oxford: Oxford University Press, pp. 1-44.

Carnoy, Martin, 1974, *Education as Cultural Imperialism,* New York: David McKay Company, Inc.

Cornia, G.A., Richard Jolly and Frances Stewart, 1987, *Adjustment with a Human Face Volume I, Protecting the Vulnerable and Promoting Growth,* Oxford: Clarendon Press.

Dangle, Arjun (ed.), 1992, *Poisoned Bread,* Bombay: Orient Longman.

De, Anuradha, Manabi Majumdar, Meera Samson and Claire Noronha, 2000, *Role of Private Schools in Basic Education* in Education for All Series, New Delhi: NIEPA.

Ghosh, A., 1993, 'Structural Adjustment and Education', *Economic and Political Weekly,* Vol. 28, No. 31, July 31, pp. 1561-1562.

Giroux, Henry, 1983, 'Theories of Reproduction and Resistance in the New Sociology of Education: A Critical Analysis' in *Harvard Educational Review,* Vol. 53, No. 3, August, pp. 257-293.

—, 1983, *Theory and Resistance in Education, A Pedagogy for the Opposition*, New York: Bergin and Garvey.

Green, Andy, 1997, *Education, Globalisation and the Nation State,* London: Macmillan Press Ltd.

Kamat, A.R., 1985, *Education and Social Change in India*, Mumbai: Somaiya Publications.

—, 1989, *Studies in Educational Reform in India Volume I: Perspectives for Educational Reform in India,* Mumbai: Himalaya Publishing House.

Karabel, J., and A.H. Halsey, 1978, 'Educational Research: A Review and on Interpretation' *Power and Ideology in Education*, (eds.) J. Karabel and A.H. Halsey, Oxford: Oxford University Press, pp. 1-85.

Kelly, Gail P. and Philip G. Altbach, 1978, 'Introduction', *Education and Colonialism,* (eds.) P. Altbach and Gail P. Kelly, New York: Longman Inc., pp. 1-44.

Khora, Sthabir, 1999, 'Privatisation of Education in Maharashtra', Paper presented at Seminar on 'Fifty Years of Indian Education: A Critical Review', Department of Sociology, University of Pune, Pune, January 7-8 (unpublished).

Kingdon, G.G., 1996, Private Schooling in India: Size, Nature and Equity-Effects, *Economic and Political Weekly*, Vol. XXXI, No. 51, December 21, pp. 3306-3314.

Kumar, Krishna, 1983, 'Educational Experience of Scheduled Castes and Tribes', *Economic and Political Weekly*, Vol. 17, Nos. 36-37, September 3-10, pp. 1566-1572.

—, 1989, *Social Character of Learning*, New Delhi: Sage Publications.

—, 1991, *The Political Agenda of Education: A Study of Colonialist and Nationalist Ideas*, New Delhi: Sage Publications.

—, 1995, 'Learning and Money: Children as Pawns in Dependency Game', *Economic and Political Weekly*, Vol. 30, No. 43, October 28, pp. 2719-2720.

—, 1996, 'Agricultural Modernisation and Education: Contours of a Point of Departure', *Economic and Political Weekly*, Vol. 31, Nos. 35, 36 and 37, Special Nos. September, pp. 2367-2373.

Kurrien, John, 1983, *Elementary Education in India, Myth, Reality, Alternative*, New Delhi: Vikas Publishing House.

Lieten, G.K., 2000, 'Children, Work and Education—Field Work in Two UP Villages', *Economic and Political Weekly*, Vol. 35, No. 25, June 17, 2000, pp. 2171-2178.

McCarthy, Cameron, 1988, 'Rethinking Liberal and Radical Perspectives on Racial Inequality in Schooling: Making the Case for Nonsynchrony', *Harvard Educational Review*, Vol. 58, No. 3, August, pp. 265-279.

—, 1997, 'Nonsynchrony and Social Difference: An Alternative to Current Radical Accounts of Race and Schooling', *Education, Culture, Economy, Society,* (eds.) A.H. Halsey et el., Oxford: Oxford University Press, pp. 541-556.

Mendelsohn, O. and M. Vicziany, 1997, *The Untouchables—Subordination, Poverty and the State in Modern India,* Cambridge University Press.

Naik, J.P., 1965, *Educational Planning in India,* Mumbai: Allied Publishers.

—, 1972, *Equality, Quality and Quantity: The Elusive Triangle in Indian Education*, Mumbai: TISS.

—, 1997, *The Educational Commission and After,* New Delhi: APH Publishing Corporation.

NIEPA, 2000, *India* in Education for All Series, New Delhi: NIEPA.

Ogbu, John, 1978, *Minority Education and Caste, The American System in Cross-Cultural Perspective?,* New York: Academic Press, Inc.

Rosenthal, Donald, 1972, *The Expensive Elite*, Berkeley: University of California Press.

Rudolph, S.H. and Rudolph, L., 1972, *Education and Politics in India, Studies in Organization, Society and Policy*, Delhi: Oxford University Press.

Sarup, Madan, 1978, *Marxism and Education,* London: Routledge and Kegan Paul.

Sharma, Rashmi, 1997, 'Dynamics of Learning Three R's in Madhya Pradesh', *Economic and Political Weekly,* Vol. 32, No. 17, April 26, pp. 891-901.

Sharp, Rachael, 1980, *Knowledge, Ideology and Politics of Schooling: Towards A Marxist Analysis of Education*, London: Routledge and Kegan Paul.

Sujatha, K., 2000, *Education Among Tribals* in Education for All Series, New Delhi: NIEPA.

Tilak, J.B.G., 1996, 'How Free is 'Free' Primary Education in India?' *Economic and Political Weekly*, Vol. 31, No. 6, February 10, pp. 355-366.

—, 1997, 'Five Decades of Underinvestment in Education', *Economic and Political Weekly,* Vol. 32, No. 36, September 6, pp. 2239-2241.

—, 2000, *Financing of Elementary Education in India* in Education for All Series, New Delhi: NIEPA.

Troyna, Barry, 1993, 'Racism and Education: Research and Perspectives', *Modern Educational Thought,* Buckingham: Open University Press.

Velaskar, Padma, 1992, 'Unequal Schooling as a Factor in the Reproduction of Social Inequality', *Sociological Bulletin*, Vol. 39 Nos. 1 and 2, pp 131-146.

—, 1998, 'Ideology, Education and the Political Struggle for Liberation: Change the Challenge among the Dalits of Maharashtra', *Education Development and Underdevelopment,* (eds.) S. Shukla, and R. Kaul, New Delhi: Sage Publications, pp. 210-240.

Velaskar, Padma and G.G. Wankhade, 1996, 'From Old Stigma to New... Exploring the Changing Identity of Urban Educated Dalits', *The Indian Journal of Social Work,* Vol. 57, No. 1, pp. 115-134.

Wankhade, G.G. and Padma Velaskar, 1999, *The Post-Matric Scholarship Scheme for SC/ST in Maharashtra and Goa: An Evaluátion* (mimeo), Mumbai: TISS.

Yadav, M.S., Meenakshi Bharadwaj and others, 2000, *Learning Conditions for Primary Education: A Review* in Education for All Series, New Delhi: NIEPA.

Yadav, M.S., Meenakshi Bharadwaj and others, 2000, *Learner Achievement in Primary Schools* in Education for All Series, New Delhi: NIEPA.

Young, Michael F.D., 1973, 'Curricula and the Social Organisation of Knowledge', *Knowledge, Education and Cultural Change: Papers in the Sociology of Education,* (ed.) Richard Brown, London: Tavistock Publications, pp. 339-392.

11

Confronting Caste Inequality

What Sociologists Must Do To Reorient Social Policy

Satish Deshpande

For sociologists interested in the history of their discipline, there is a puzzle that still awaits a satisfactory explanation. As in the famous Sherlock Holmes story where the crucial clue is that a dog does not bark, this puzzle too involves accounting for an event that ought to have taken place, but did not. The basic problem is the following: Given that (a) state programmes and initiatives towards equity enjoyed enormous political legitimacy in the Nehruvian era; (b) that involvement in such programmes brought prestige, power and resources to academic disciplines; and (c) that the institution of caste was the source of deep and widespread inequalities, why didn't Indian sociology try to leverage its intellectual ownership of (c) to lay claim to (b) by getting involved in (a)? [1]

The answer to this question is long and complicated, and it involves at least the following elements: orientalist and anthropological constructions of the caste system as the antithesis of modern (western) values; consequently, the defensiveness about caste among Indian intellectuals since the early 20th century; the stance towards caste taken by influential anthropologists such as Louis Dumont and M.N. Srinivas, which tended to downplay the material aspects of caste inequalities; the broadly anti-policy position adopted by dominant sections of the profession; the methodological biases of Indian sociology, which were both caused by and in turn helped reinforce the anti-policy stance; and, finally, the fact that deep-rooted sociocultural institutions like caste—with close links to entrenched religious orthodoxies—present a very inhospitable terrain for statist social policies: Legal-bureaucratic organisations are not best suited to intervene in such contexts.

But this paper does not develop these arguments, which I have tried to do elsewhere (Deshpande, forthcoming). Here, I am concerned with the more immediate question of what sociologists can and should do to shape the context in which social policies aimed at caste inequality are designed and debated. Accordingly, this paper is about the *ideological and conceptual preconceptions*—both implicit and explicit—that have framed discussions about how to redress caste based inequalities. I believe that Indian sociology has not done as much as it should have done to enable policy perspectives to transcend popular common sense. What follows is only the outline of an argument being presented for criticism and comment; this paper does not enter into a detailed discussion of the pros and cons of the relevant evidence.

I

Caste Inequality, Common Sense and Sociology

Today, a decade after the bitter controversy over the Mandal Commission report, we may be better placed to appreciate the irony in the fact that this controversy offered us—albeit by accident—a rare window of insight into Indian sociology. Given the centrality of caste, an undeniably 'sociological' subject, one would normally have expected the discipline to shed light on the controversy rather than the other way around. Of course, such expectations were not entirely belied.

But while its practitioners did manage to enter the mainstream of public attention in a way that had never been possible before, the discipline itself was largely unable to take advantage of this historic opportunity to enhance its prestige and authority.

Sociology's inability to raise itself in public esteem did not stem from the fact that sociologists adopted unpopular stances. In fact, most prominent sociologists were vocal in their support for the anti-Mandal position which dominated urban middle class perceptions of this issue and received wide and strongly sympathetic coverage in the metropolitan media. But regardless of whether these stances brought public praise or derision, they did not bring respect because, by and large, sociologists were unable to say anything that went beyond popular common sense.

Despite being the acknowledged experts on caste, sociologists were no different from all the journalists, politicians, administrators, other academics or legions of self-proclaimed pundits commenting on the subject. Like everyone else, they too concentrated their attention on the *possible consequences of implementing the Mandal Report*. Forgotten were the questions that ought to have come first, at least for a discipline claiming specialised knowledge of caste as a social institution: Is caste discrimination still practised in contemporary India? Does it continue to breed inequality? What is the nature and extent of such inequality today? How has it been changing since independence?

It may seem painfully obvious that problems must be discussed before solutions are debated, but exactly the opposite seems to have happened during the Mandal controversy. What is most remarkable, however, is that sociologists should have shared in and helped accentuate such a perverse response. By addressing crucial questions which the overnight experts are unable to answer, sociologists could have demonstrated that their discipline provides insights that common sense cannot. But it seems in retrospect that the sociologists' silence on questions of caste inequality was not so much perverse as prudent. As a matter of fact, despite all its claims to expertise on caste, Indian sociology did not have the answers, never having shown much interest in macro analyses of caste inequality. The important point, though, is that this lack of interest was itself invisible because it was so much a part of business as usual in Indian sociology.[2] It took a national crisis as big as Mandal to alert us to this blind spot, and to goad us into recognising that despite being the academic experts on this question, what we had to say on it hardly went beyond established common sense.

Common Sense on Caste Inequality

It would be misleading to suggest that there is any one homogeneous common sense view of caste inequality. Nevertheless, most urban, educated, middle class (and therefore largely upper caste) Indians would tend to think of caste inequality in ways that would include the following elements:

(a) Caste inequality is a social evil, in fact a rather terrible thing, and we have to admit that it used to be very bad in the past. However, after independence, things have been changing rapidly, even if not as swiftly or comprehensively as might be desired. The condition of the lowest castes and tribes is improving steadily; the link between caste and occupation is weakening, and members of every caste are now engaged in a much wider variety of occupations than before. Reservation has provided very real benefits to the SC/ST group, but this is being monopolised by a minority within the group. Reservation policies and the like have now become involved in the electoral arithmetic of votebanks and so are extended and continued in all sorts of contexts where they are not warranted.

(b) Caste has been given a new lease of life by its encashability in politics. Backward status is now something advantageous and is fought for by all sorts of castes. Since politics is dominated by the numerically stronger lower and middle castes, the upper castes are now facing very real reverse discrimination.

(c) There is very great variation in the economic and social status of members of every caste group. This variation makes it misleading to use caste per se as a criterion to decide backwardness or forwardness. More objective criteria sensitive to individual contexts are needed. The time may have come when caste is no longer particularly useful as a criterion, economic and other criteria being more relevant. Particularly with regard to job reservations, the principle of compensatory preferences has been overextended, and this has resulted in the 'murder of merit'.

(d) Socially and culturally, the main aspect of caste discrimination, namely, untouchability, has already been outlawed, and legislatively, there is not much more to be done in this area. Whatever prejudices remain are due to the stubborn attitudes of a few diehards. Such attitudes should be condemned and people should be educated to transcend them, but laws cannot really change the way people think. By and large, the upper castes have given up their prejudices and moved beyond/out of caste. Ironically, today it is the lower and middle castes who are the main props for the continuance of this pernicious system.

There is much that is true in this common sense story, but there is also much that is not; most important, perhaps, are the questions that remain unasked. For example, it is perfectly true that, by and large, when compared to the situation prevailing at independence, the condition of all social groups, including the lowest castes and tribes, has improved today. But by how much has it improved? How have the lowest castes/tribes fared in comparison to the rest of the population?

Again, it is almost a truism to say that, today, the variety of occupations and professions among all caste groups is much wider than it was fifty years ago. However, this does not change the massive social reality that the overwhelming majority of those in the 'highest' or most preferred occupations are from the upper castes, while the vast majority of those in the most menial and despised occupations belong to the lowest castes. In short, while it is indeed significant that *some* members of the lowest castes are now able to occupy very high positions, or that *many* members of high castes are being forced into menial occupations today, this does not by itself demonstrate that caste and occupational status have been delinked. We must also ask if particular occupations continue to be dominated by particular caste clusters, and whether this makes for a recognisable pattern systematically linking privilege and disprivilege to caste. In other words, the caste composition of the privileged groups in society is a critical yardstick: As long as this continues to reflect the dominance of the upper castes, it does not matter even if the majority of the members of these castes are themselves poor or disprivileged. This would only demonstrate that while caste remains a necessary precondition for making it into the privileged group, it is not in itself a sufficient condition to ensure entry. Thus, the first requirement in order to go beyond common sense is to look for and assess the available evidence on caste inequality in contemporary India.

II

Caste as a Determinant of Life Chances in Independent India

The first and most important point to be noted when considering the evidence on caste inequality is that there have been no systematic attempts to collect it. Indeed, the optimism of the Nehruvian era prompted scholars and administrators to take at face value the stridently declared intention of building a casteless society with a caste blind state. The explicit constitutional injunction to ignore all differences of caste, creed, religion and so on has been most faithfully followed in the case of caste. Thus, except for the constitutionally sanctioned scheduled tribes and castes, no official statistics have been collected on caste in independent India. Despite the fact that both language and especially religion have proved to be 'divisive' issues sparking violent conflicts, and even though it was the British who began this exercise, the Census of India has quite rightly continued to collect information on them. But ever since independence, the Indian Census has resolutely refused to ask citizens their caste, on the grounds that the new state was 'caste blind', and that previous attempts to collect such data were part of the imperial 'divide and rule' policy. So, until very recently, the only reliable data we had on caste is restricted to the three-way classification of 'Scheduled Caste', 'Scheduled Tribe' and 'Others'. This data can only tell us about the caste of one-fourth of the population, the remaining three-fourths being lumped together in the residual term 'Others', which includes non-Hindus and persons with no caste.

This active post-independence antipathy towards caste was the joint product of, first, the nationalist movement and its campaign against caste distinctions, and, second, a reaction against what were seen as deliberate colonial policies to create and sharpen divisions among the Indian people. As recent scholarship has shown, neither of these factors is simple or straightforward. First of all, it is a gross simplification to speak of the nationalist movement with a singular and unequivocal position on caste. The angularities and ambivalences of the exclusively upper-caste nationalist leadership are seen even in Gandhi. Easily the most visible and effective campaigner against untouchability, the Mahatma also believed that there was something to be said for the varna system, which divided society into a hierarchy of segments. The second factor, too, is more equivocal than it appears to be. Although it is easy to believe that a colonial power would foster institutions that produced divisions among the subject population, it is quite difficult to disentangle 'imperial invention' from 'indigenous inheritance' in the history of caste. Moreover, the motives and intentions of the colonial state are by themselves never enough to ensure the successful reproduction over centuries of so widespread a phenomenon as caste.

Whatever the merits of the antecedent causes, the post-independence backlash against caste was strong and sustained. It ensured that one of the paradoxical lessons of modern governance—that the state must measure whatever it wishes to eradicate—would not be learnt. As a result, the data that we have on caste inequality are not only meagre, but also *reluctant*, so to speak, needing to be coaxed into existence, and dependent on the accidents of scholarly interest and statistical convenience. What needs to be emphasised is that unlike other comparable situations, the paucity and poor quality of these data is the result of wilful, if well-intentioned, neglect: We refused to collect such data because we thought we should not collect them and did not need them. However, the irony is that the end result is not very different from what might have been the case had there been a giant conspiracy to suppress evidence of caste inequality.

It is against this background that we must evaluate the many shortcomings and silences of the available data on caste inequality.

The Available Evidence

The National Sample Survey Organisation (NSSO) has offered the most broadbased data sets that can provide relatively direct evidence on economic inequality across caste groups. However, for the reasons already mentioned, the NSSO has always restricted itself to the constitutionally sanctioned categories of the Scheduled Tribes and Castes, with everyone else being thrown together into the vast and immensely diverse residual group of 'Others'. Because it is unable to distinguish between the very different sorts of people included in it (such as the Other Backward Castes, the forward castes, and non-Hindus who may or may not have a caste identity), this category is an analytical nightmare, with arguments based on it being forever vulnerable to a host of statistical and logical objections. Nevertheless, flawed as they are, the NSSO data have demonstrated that caste continues to be a major fault line of economic inequality in contemporary India.

The last phrase is particularly important. I have taken up the most recent data available precisely in order to emphasise that we are indeed speaking of contemporary times, not of the bad old days: Caste is alive and well today, a half-century after its official abolition. In the tables below, I present data from the last quinquennial (five-yearly) 'round' of the NSSO, the 55th Round conducted during 1999-2000. The five-yearly or 'big sample' rounds of the NSSO are mammoth year-long surveys involving a huge, carefully selected sample of about a hundred and twenty thousand households from twelve thousand villages and urban blocks all over India. Although academics and policy makers have been concerned about the impact of some changes in the methodology of the 55th Round, there is no reason to believe that this will affect a single time-point comparison across social groups, which is what I am doing here.[3]

Moreover, the 55th Round is a historic one because it is the first to provide data separately for the 'Other Backward Castes' (NSSO 2001b). This allows us, for the first time since independence, to disaggregate the 'Other' category. In conjunction with the data on religious communities (published separately in NSSO 2001a), it is possible to construct rough estimates of what in statistical terms has been the most elusive group in modern India, namely upper-caste Hindus.

Details of household consumption expenditure are the most basic and widely used data collected by the NSSO surveys. Since consumption expenditure is arguably the most reliable proxy for income (which is notoriously difficult to measure directly), this is the main database used to estimate poverty levels in the country. The NSSO reports typically divide the range of monthly per capita consumption expenditure into twelve different size classes, and tell us what proportion of the rural and urban populations of each social group (caste or religion based) falls in each of these classes. The twelve size classes are much too detailed for the purposes of this book, so I have consolidated them into four main classes: below the official poverty line (defined as Rs 329 per person per month for rural India, and Rs 458 per person per month for urban India); from the poverty line to the next three size classes above—this may be called the 'above the poverty line' class; the next three size classes above this, which can be called the 'less poor' class; and finally, the top two MPCE classes, which can be called the 'non-poor' or the least poor.[4]

For someone seeking to understand caste inequality, a severe limitation of the NSSO data—though an understandable one, given the policy concerns it was designed to address—is that it is heavily tilted towards the poor. It is important to understand what this means in concrete terms. For example, if we imagine a family of five members, then the poverty line for 1999-2000 would include those with a monthly income of about Rs 1,650 or less in rural India and about Rs 2,300 or less in urban India. However, even at the upper end of the MPCE scale, the top two classes include all families of five with monthly incomes of Rs 3,875 or more in rural India, and Rs 7,500 or more in urban India. To put this more starkly, the highest urban class in the following tables stretches from a family of five earning Rs 7,500 a month right up to families like the Ambanis or the Tatas—they are all lumped together in the same category. That is why we are forced to use extremely vague grab-bag categories like 'less poor' or 'least poor' which conceal much more than they reveal. This is in part a technical problem because the rich—or even the middle classes—are such a small proportion of the population that it is difficult to ensure that they are adequately represented by standard sampling techniques designed to cover the entire nation. In fact, the NSSO has been making special efforts to 'oversample' the urban non-poor households to ensure that enough of them are covered.[5] While we cannot blame the NSSO data for doing what they were designed to do, namely provide a detailed profile of poverty, we can and must do two things: first, remind ourselves that even in its present form, the NSSO data offers plenty of evidence pointing to the continued existence of a massive caste divide in India on the eve of the 21st century; and second, look for more direct evidence that is able to confirm or deny the presence of caste inequality among the privileged sections of the population.

NSSO 55th Round Data on Social Inequality

Because the 55th Round data on consumption patterns have been published for both caste groups and for religious groups, and because this round also separately provides, for the first time ever, data for the OBCs, it opens up the unprecedented possibility of producing a comprehensive profile of inequality in Indian society. This includes the possibility of being able to track the most elusive category of all, namely the Hindu upper castes—i.e. those Hindus who do not belong to the SCs, STs or OBCs. However, in order to do this reliably, it is necessary to obtain household level data from the NSSO and manually extract further information which is not provided in the published reports. This information has to do with overlapping categories, i.e. those who belong to more than one social grouping (Christian STs, or Muslim OBCs, for example).

A further complication here is that unlike the Census, which uses very strict statutory definitions that regulate overlapping categories, all the NSSO survey data on social categories is based on self-reporting.[6] In other words, the NSSO simply accepts whatever is stated by the head of the household surveyed with regard to membership in categories like ST, SC, OBC or religion. Thus, there is much greater potential for overlaps in the NSSO, and until we have access to data on those belonging to multiple categories, it is not possible to accurately measure a category like Hindu Upper Castes.

However, I have gone ahead and provided rough estimates for this category because it is crucial to the analysis. So it is very important to emphasise that the data on Hindu Upper Castes in Tables 1-4 is only a rough estimate. However, we can get a rough idea of the degree of inaccuracy in the figures: This depends on the size of categories like Dalit Christian, Muslim OBC, and so on. Since all religious minorities other than Muslims are only a very tiny percentage of the population, they will only produce small errors. The most significant category—one that may lead us to underestimate the numbers in the Hindu Upper Caste columns—is likely to be that of Muslim OBCs. In short, the Hindu Upper Caste figures are almost certainly underestimates, particularly at the lower end of the economic spectrum. One should always keep this in mind when reading the tables, and this caveat is entered in bold letters at the bottom of each table.

Table 1 shows us the MPCE-class composition of each social group for rural India. There are four such classes as explained earlier: Rs 329 or less, which is Below the Poverty Line (BPL); Rs 329-470, which is Above the Poverty Line (APL); Rs 470-775, which includes the next three classes of the Less Poor; and finally the topmost class of Least Poor, which is everyone above Rs 775. Thus, the column for Scheduled Tribes shows that 50.9 percent, or almost 51 percent of the community belongs in the BPL group, while 2.7 percent or less than 3 percent is in the Least Poor group. We can similarly read down the column for any group to see its class composition—the percentage of its population that belongs in each of the four MPCE classes. The last column provides the class composition of the population as a whole.

However, the class composition of caste groups (i.e. what percentage of each caste's population is BPL, APL, and so on) tells us only half the story. We must also ask about the caste composition of class groups—that is, of all the people who are BPL, APL, and so on, what percentage belongs to the ST, SC or other caste/community groups? Table 2 provides us this information. It is computed by mapping the percentage distribution of Table 1 to the population totals for each social group. These

Table 1

Social Groups Stratified by Monthly Per Capita Consumption Expenditure Classes, Rural India, 1999-2000

MPCE Class	*ST*	*SC*	*OBC*	*Muslim*	*Christian*	*Sikh*	*Other Religions*	*Hindu Upper Castes ?*	*All Groups*
Below Poverty Line	50.9	42.9	33.7	37.5	24.1	6.1	42.6	16.9	33.6
Rs 329 to Rs 470	30.8	34.4	35.8	34.9	27.8	20.9	28.1	32.5	33.8
Rs 470 to Rs 775	15.6	19.2	24.5	22.2	32.5	46.1	22.0	36.6	25.3
Rs 775 or More	2.7	3.4	6.1	5.5	15.6	27.0	7.2	14.0	7.3
ALL CLASSES	100.0	100.0	100.0	100.0	100.0	100.0	100.0	100.0	100.0

Source: NSSO Report Nos. 468 and 469, September 2001.
Figures for Hindu Upper Castes are only rough estimates.
Last row subject to rounding off errors.

Table 2

Social Composition of Monthly Per Capita Consumption Expenditure Classes, Rural India, 1999-2000

MPCE Class	*ST*	*SC*	*OBC*	*Muslim*	*Christian*	*Sikh*	*Other Religions*	*Hindu Upper Castes ?*	*Total*
Below Poverty Line	15.3	23.0	37.5	11.8	1.6	0.4	0.8	9.6	100.0
Rs 329 to Rs 470	9.2	18.4	39.6	10.9	1.8	1.2	0.6	18.4	100.0
Rs 470 to Rs 775	6.2	13.7	36.2	9.2	2.8	3.6	0.6	27.6	100.0
Rs 775 or More	3.7	8.4	31.1	7.9	4.6	7.4	0.7	36.3	100.0
% of 1991 Popn	10.1	18.0	37.4*	10.5	2.2	2.0	1.4	18.4**	100.0

Source: NSSO Report Nos. 468 and 469, September 2001.
Figures for Hindu Upper Castes are only rough estimates.
* Population data for OBCs based on 55th Round estimate;
** Population data for Hindu Upper Castes obtained as residual.
Last column subject to rounding off errors.

Table 3

Social Groups Stratified by Monthly Per Capita Consumption Expenditure Classes, Urban India, 1999-2000

MPCE Class	*ST*	*SC*	*OBC*	*Muslim*	*Christian*	*Sikh*	*Other Religions*	*Hindu Upper Castes ?*	*All Groups*
Below Poverty Line	42.6	43.1	36.0	46.5	16.3	15.0	24.7	4.9	28.5
Rs 458—Rs 775	32.6	39.2	39.7	35.9	31.8	36.4	30.9	34.8	37.4
Rs 775—Rs 1,500	19.1	15.9	20.7	15.1	36.0	34.3	31.3	43.2	26.3
Rs 1,500 or more	5.7	2.0	3.7	2.5	15.9	14.4	13.0	17.1	7.8
ALL CLASSES	100.0	100.0	100.0	100.0	100.0	100.0	100.0	100.0	100.0

Source: NSSO Report Nos. 468 and 469, September 2001.
Figures for Hindu Upper Castes are only rough estimates.
Last row subject to rounding off errors.

Table 4

Social Composition of Monthly Per Capita Consumption Expenditure Classes, Urban India, 1999-2000

MPCE Class	*ST*	*SC*	*OBC*	*Muslim*	*Christian*	*Sikh*	*Other Religions*	*Hindu Upper Castes ?*	*Total*
Below Poverty Line	6.0	22.7	33.9	28.0	1.7	0.9	2.1	4.7	100.0
Rs 458—Rs 775	3.5	15.7	32.7	16.5	2.5	1.7	2.0	25.4	100.0
Rs 775—Rs 1,500	2.9	9.1	24.2	9.8	4.0	2.3	2.9	44.8	100.0
Rs 1,500 or more	2.9	3.8	14.6	5.5	6.0	3.3	4.0	59.8	100.0
% of 1991 Popn	2.3	12.0	31.4*	16.7	2.9	1.8	2.3	26.6**	100.0

Source: NSSO Report Nos. 468 and 469, September 2001.
Figures for Hindu Upper Castes are only rough estimates.
* Population data for OBCs based on 55th Round estimate;
** Population data for Hindu Upper Castes obtained as residual.
Last column subject to rounding off errors.

population totals in turn are obtained by taking the 1991 Census data on each social group (what percentage of the total population were the STs, SCs, and so on, in the 1991 Census) and applying it to the 2000 population projection. Table 2 is organised in terms of the four rows for each MPCE class. Thus, the row for Below the Poverty Line tells us that the BPL population of rural India was composed of 15.3 percent STs, 23 percent SCs, 37.5 percent OBCs, and so on, across the row. Tables 3 and 4 provide the same data for urban India and are organised in exactly the same way.

To establish the continued existence of sharp caste inequalities in contemporary India, we need go no further than a comparison of the four caste groups that appear on Tables 1 and 3—ST, SC, OBC and Hindu Upper Castes. In rural India, as Table 1 shows, more than half of the ST population lives below the poverty line. This proportion is only slightly less for the SCs at about 43 percent, and lesser still for the OBCs at about 34 percent. However, the Hindu Upper Castes (HUCs) are markedly different, with only about 17 percent BPL. At the other end of the class spectrum, if we look at the Rs 775 and above class, then there is a reverse effect: The HUCs at 14 percent are way ahead of the STs and SCs (both around 3%) and also of the OBCs at 6 percent. In other words, the Least Poor are a much smaller proportion of the lower caste population and a relatively much higher proportion of the upper caste population. The opposite is the case with the poorest or BPL class: The lower castes have a huge proportion of their population here, while the upper castes have a relatively much smaller proportion.

In urban India, as Table 3 shows, these inequalities are even more stark. Only about 5 percent of the HUCs are BPL, while the figures for the lower castes are much higher: 43 percent for both STs and SCs, and 36 percent for the OBCs. Conversely, the HUCs have a much larger proportion of their population among the Least Poor category (or those with MPCE levels of Rs 1,500 or more)—17 percent—compared to the single digit figures of 6, 2 and 4 for the STs, SCs and OBCs, respectively.

Coming now to the question of the caste composition of the different income or MPCE classes, we see that Tables 2 and 4 confirm the grim picture presented by the previous two tables. The general pattern is as expected in rural India, but Table 2 tells us one important fact, namely, that in rural society, the OBCs are the only social group with a remarkably even presence in all economic classes: They constitute 30 percent or more of each MPCE classes from the BPL to the Least Poor. As against this, the STs and SCs are underrepresented among the Least Poor and overrepresented among the BPL. The opposite is the case with the HUCs—they are overrepresented among the least poor and underrepresented among the BPL. Thus, while arguments about rural OBCs need to be made with care, the case for continuing caste inequalities is very strong.

However, it is in urban India—the seat of genuine privilege—that the inter-caste differences are at their starkest. The most striking feature of Table 4 is the figure in its bottom right hand corner—Hindu Upper Castes constitute almost 60 percent of the Least Poor urban class. The urban OBCs do not resemble their rural counterparts and are much closer to the STs and SCs in profile. In fact, urban OBCs account for more than one-third of the urban BPL population. Tables 2 and 4 provide us with yet another sobering fact: In the year 2000, STs, SCs, OBCs and Muslims together account for 91 percent of the urban BPL population and 88 percent of the rural BPL population.

Let me emphasise, in closing this discussion of the NSSO 55th Round data, that these are very significant facts. Common sense may tell us that the lower castes are now ruling the roost, but the facts are otherwise. Despite the major phenomenon of the rural OBCs—itself a residual, unexamined category that deserves more detailed attention—caste inequality is alive and flourishing in both rural and especially in urban India. These data are from a very large, national survey; they report proportions averaged across hundreds of thousands of cases—they cannot be dismissed as being due to inter-individual differences, or because of statistical accidents. The differences between caste groups are too strong and too stable to be artefacts. We have to make the necessary effort to transcend the common sense view and re-examine the question of caste inequality seriously.

Caste and Privilege

The feeling that the spirit of the times not only favours the lower castes, but is actively opposed to the upper castes, is entrenched in the minds of the largely upper caste urban middle classes. So much so that when confronted with the incontrovertible evidence that most enclaves of privilege are still dominated by the upper castes, they can only insist that this merely shows how cunningly anti-upper caste biases are being hidden.

Consider, for instance, the social composition of the government sector. In a country where less than 10 percent of the workforce is in the 'organised sector'—which includes both public and private sector employment—a government job has been and continues to be among the most coveted. But as Table 9 shows, the lower castes still tend to be significantly underrepresented in the government sector, and particularly in its upper echelons. Thus, despite the combined quota of 22.5 percent for the SCs and STs, only about 6 percent (or roughly one-fourth of the reserved quota) of Class I officers of the Central government are from these groups. The representation of the Other Backward Classes—the non-upper caste, non-SC/ST castes who are considered to be 'socially and educationally backward'—is even lower, at under 5 percent.

One may quibble about these data because they are based on the Mandal Commission's initial ('ad hoc') definition of the OBCs, which required them to meet *both* the caste criterion (i.e. belonging to the Shudra castes) *and* the educational

Table 5

Representation of Scheduled Castes, Scheduled Tribes and Other Backward Classes in Central Government Services, 1979-80

(Percentage shares in class totals)

	Class I		*Class II*		*Class III and IV*		*All Classes*	
	SC/ST	*OBC*	*SC/ST*	*OBC*	*SC/ST*	*OBC*	*SC/ST*	*OBC*
Ministries and Departments	7.2	2.6	13.7	4.0	31.0	8.4	16.8	4.8
Autonomous Bodies, Subordinate Offices	6.6	5.1	18.2	11.7	20.8	21.0	18.1	14.4
Public Sector Undertakings	4.5	4.6	18.7	9.9	31.7	15.8	20.0	10.6
TOTAL	5.7	4.7	18.2	10.6	24.4	19.0	18.7	12.6

Source: Second Backward Classes (Mandal) Commission Report, Appendix VIII, Statement 1

backwardness criterion (neither father nor grandfather studied beyond primary school).[7] One may argue that the educational criterion is a rather stringent one, and that there may well be other members of the Shudra castes in government employment who do not meet it. This is certainly possible, but it seems unlikely to change the numbers significantly, for other sources also confirm the broad picture conveyed by Table 6. For example, Santosh Goyal's study (Goyal, 1992a) of the social composition of the Indian Administrative Service shows that, in 1985, the Shudra castes account for *less than 2 percent* of this elite cadre, in which Brahmins were 28 percent and Kayasthas 11 percent. Goyal's data are based purely on the caste criterion (as identified from the last names of officers in the Consolidated Civil List) and are therefore exempt from the objection that might be raised against the Mandal Commission data. However, the caste of about 21 percent of the officers cannot be identified by her method; of these, about 10 percent are likely to belong to the SC/ST categories (being direct recruits above the general cut-off age of 26), which leaves about 11 percent with ambiguous last names who could belong to any caste group. Even if we make the rather unrealistic assumption that *all* the unidentified officers belong to the Shudra castes, this still gives a maximum possible percentage share of 12.5 percent, which is at most about one-third of their share in the general population, and quite probably even less than that. If we make the somewhat more reasonable assumption that the unidentified officers are equally divided among the forward, backward and scheduled castes, then we get a maximum Shudra share of between 5-6 percent, which is very near the Mandal Commission estimate for the Class I services in Table 5.

It has to be reiterated yet again that the messiness and uncertainties that plague this data are the product of deliberate decisions. In fact, the government refuses, except under duress from statutory bodies like the SC/ST Commissions, to publish even the data relating to these constitutionally recognised categories. As Goyal points out, it is impossible to estimate accurately the aggregate numbers of SC-ST officers in the IAS because the home ministry does not release this data, so that there is no authoritative source of information on whether or not the reserved quotas are being filled. All the indications are that there has been a significant carried forward backlog of unfilled reserved posts during the 1970s and 1980s, especially for the Scheduled Tribes (Goyal, 1992a:426-27). As already seen, the situation with regard to the Other Backward Classes is much worse, with hardly any reliable data available.

Table 6
Caste Composition of Top Corporate Officers, 1979-80

Castes	*Chairman President*	*Managing Director*	*General Manager*	*Director Ex. Director*	*Total*
Brahman	135 (36.0)	144 (35.2)	408 (46.2)	171 (41.3)	858 (41.2)
Vaishya	83 (22.0)	103 (25.1)	122 (13.8)	64 (15.5)	372 (17.9)
Shudra	6 (1.6)	24 (5.9)	35 (4.0)	22 (5.3)	87 (4.2)
Lingayat	1 (0.3)	4 (1.0)	7 (0.8)	1 (0.2)	13 (0.6)
Mallick	1 (0.3)	0 (0.0)	1 (0.1)	1 (0.2)	3 (0.1)
Singh	8 (2.1)	6 (1.5)	11 (1.2)	12 (2.9)	37 (1.8)
Khatri	70 (18.7)	69 (16.8)	165 (18.7)	81 (19.6)	385 (18.5)
Kayastha	26 (6.9)	35 (8.5)	119 (13.5)	47 (11.4)	227 (10.9)
Marwari	45 (12.0)	25 (6.1)	15 (1.7)	15 (3.6)	100 (4.8)
Total Caste Identified	375 (100.0)	410 (100.0)	883 (100.0)	414 (100.0)	2082 (100.0)
Total Caste Unidentified	168	274	380	225	1047
Grand Total of Employees	543	684	1263	639	3129

Source: Santosh Goyal, 1990, p. 540, Table IV.5 (Figures in parentheses are percent of Total Caste Identified).

If this is the case with the government itself, one can hardly expect the corporate sector to be different. Goyal's valiant attempt (Goyal, 1992b) to profile the social composition of this sector is reported in Table 6. The data in this table cover 3,129 officers of 1,100 large companies (in both the private and public sectors) that accounted for over 90 percent of the turnover of the Indian corporate sector as a whole in 1979-80. The designations considered are the topmost in the corporate hierarchy—Chairman/President, Managing Director, General Manager and Director/Executive Director. The caste of the officers is ascertained by the last name (comparing them to the lists published in the 1931 Census, and also by consulting scholars from different regions around the country). The castes of approximately two-thirds (66.5%) of the employees is ascertainable by this method, while the remaining 33.5 percent are either non-Hindus or of unidentified castes.

As can be seen from Table 10, Brahmans are once again the dominant caste, accounting for more than 41 percent of the total identified names, and about 27.4 percent of all employees (including non-Hindus and Hindus of unidentified caste). They are well ahead of all other castes, the next highest being Khatris (18.5%), Vaishyas (17.9%) and Kayasthas (10.9%). In fact, these four castes together comprise almost 89 percent of the caste identified names. Shudras are once again very low at 4.2 percent, while the SCs and STs are totally absent among the caste identified names.

Apart from such formal, if severely handicapped, attempts to gather data on large areas of public life such as government service and corporate management, there is also less formal or micro-level evidence that the lower castes are severely under-represented in all the modern professions. As M.N. Panini has pointed out, 'caste clustering', usually implying the overwhelming dominance of the upper castes, continues to be true of professions such as engineering, medicine, banking, journalism, and academics (Panini, 1996:32-36). In short, in every field that may be considered to offer a promising career in the contemporary world, the upper castes dominate and the middle and lower castes are more or less severely under-represented. Almost two generations after independence, it is no longer possible to evade these realities as being the byproduct of historical inequities. We have to face up to the uncomfortable truth that caste inequity has been and is being *reproduced* in independent India. What is most crucial is that this reproduction is accompanied by a systematic 'misrecognition' so that caste inequality becomes invisible even as it pervades our present.

III

Caste Inequality and Social Policy: A Lack of Elective Affinity?

It may be useful to reiterate the implications of the sort of evidence cited above. Drastic and sustained differences in *shares* and *proportions* averaged across very large numbers of individuals from different social groups cannot be explained in terms of differences in individual abilities or circumstances. As Emile Durkheim demonstrated long ago, although every individual suicide is undoubtedly an intensely personal event, the average rate of suicide in a society is a social fact. Explanations for differences in the rates of suicide in two different societies or social groups (numbering in the millions) cannot be sought at the individual level—we must look to social factors that affect the group as a whole. This is why, the common sense approach that seeks to turn data on the under-representation of the lowest castes in the privileged sections of society into evidence of the 'lack of merit' of these castes is sociological nonsense. An individual member of any caste may do well or not depending on his or her innate abilities, but when we speak of *rates* of representation for whole communities with millions of members, all such inter-individual differences in innate ability are averaged out. Unless we wish to resort to genetic explanations—and that should not be possible in this day and age—the only reasonable explanation is in terms of *social* mechanisms and processes that are *systematic* (i.e. not random or accidental) and *systemic* (i.e. beyond the intentions of individuals).

If inter-caste inequalities are social, systematic and systemic, why have they failed to generate policy initiatives commensurate with their nature and scale? To answer this question, one needs to look at the historical-ideological context that has framed the question of caste inequality in modern India.

There are three main factors that have shaped perceptions of the question of caste inequality since the late 19th century. These factors continue to be at work today, but have not received enough explicit attention—they tend to operate more like background assumptions that are taken for granted by all the actors concerned.

Regional vs. National Dimensions

One of the most crucial aspects of the caste question in public life is that this has been a region specific issue. Whenever it has been dealt with on the national stage, regional considerations have been the prime movers of policy in practice, although this fact is often obscured from view. By and large, until the 1980s, the policy campaign against caste inequality has been dominated by peninsular India, especially the southern states and Maharashtra. This has been somewhat anomalous given that notions of the 'national' have traditionally given disproportionate weight to the north, especially the Hindi heartland. When interpreting events and trends around this issue, it is important to keep this factor in mind: The national is an abstractly constructed notion that is often misleading in its evenhanded representation of all regions.

For example, when we look at the nationalist movement and how it attempted to deal with this question, region is an all-important factor. The framing as well as the outcomes of major national events such as the 1932 Poona Pact between Gandhi and Ambedkar, or the Mandal controversy of 1990-91 have to be viewed in this light. To what extent was the relative bargaining strength of Gandhi and Ambedkar influenced by regional considerations? Despite the obvious universal moral justification claimed by the Dalit movement, did Ambedkar's position get weakened vis-à-vis Gandhi because of his localised mass base being effectively restricted to the Mahars of Maharashtra? Was Gandhi able to drive a hard bargain because he faced little political pressure on this issue from the northern heartland? Similarly, although it was treated as a national issue, the Mandal controversy was driven by the regional realities of northern India. The anti-Mandal campaign was able to project the reservation policies approved by the V.P. Singh government as a national disaster in defiance of the fact that even stronger policies had been in operation in several southern states for nearly three decades, and that these states were among the most developed ones in the country.

In short, the basic point is that national decisions and policies may actually be the net outcome of varying regional considerations. It is important to look to these factors if we are to understand the history of national policy on caste inequality.

The Uniquely Negative Image of Caste

Among the peculiarities of caste from a policy perspective is that it has from the beginning been locked into an exclusively negative image. It is only in the 1970s that the possibility of caste identity providing a positive political resource for mobilisation first gained recognition. Before this, caste occupied an illegitimate position as something that, regrettably, continued to shape political practice, but could not be acknowledged in principle. Unlike other aspects of our past traditions, caste was *only* a 'social evil'—there was no redeeming aspect to this institution. Hence, in moral-political terms, caste got fixed into a simplistic model, where the only possible thing to be done with caste was its abolition. The point is not that such a goal was undesirable, but that it failed to acknowledge the resilience of caste, prevented a more nuanced understanding of caste identities, and concealed the need for an interim policy on caste until the goal of abolition was actually reached.

The mainstream attitude to caste was essentially that of the liberal upper caste person who was embarrassed by the unearned and unjust privileges that the institution had conferred on him/her. People imbued with this mindset dominated the nationalist movement. For such people (including major leaders like Gandhi and Nehru) the only possible response to their own caste identities was to disown them in favour of a more modern and progressive egalitarianism that suppressed all 'ascriptive' identities. In establishing these attitudes as the political norms of the nationalist movement, the leaders of the day failed to recognise the assymmetries of caste as a social institution. They did not allow for the fact that persons from the other end of the caste spectrum might have a more complex relationship with their caste identities than the simplistic upper caste variety. As with all oppressed or disadvantaged groups, the very fact of having been unjustly treated provides a powerful identity that is also a potent source of political mobilisation. But given the optimism of the times and the pressures of wanting to appear modern and progressive, these nuances were hardly noticed.

This unequivocally negative image of caste had the consequence of painting the polity into a corner. Since caste was by definition an illegitimate category, any policy initiatives that were addressed to it necessarily acquired a defensive and apologetic aura. Moreover, the upper caste attitude of suppressing or denying caste identity could occupy the moral high ground vis-à-vis caste based leaders or movements, who could be discredited for being casteist. Even Gandhi was not above exploiting this subtle advantage in his confrontation with Ambedkar. As a consequence of this exclusively negative positioning of caste and the fact that it is seen as a traditional, culture based institution, policy initiatives that address caste are always vulnerable to the charge that they help perpetuate the very phenomenon that they are designed to eradicate.

A comparison with poverty, also a phenomenon independent India had resolved to abolish, brings out the peculiarities of caste very clearly. Anti-poverty programmes are often criticised for their failure, which is sometimes also seen as perpetuating poverty. But caste based programmes are open to this charge even when they are successful, perhaps even more so than when they fail. It is taken for granted that anti-poverty programmes ought to measure and track poverty, whereas caste based programmes face a lot of opposition when they try to do the same for caste inequality. Finally, it seems self-evident that anti-poverty programmes will be needed as long as poverty exists. By contrast, caste based policies are seen as embarrassing compromises with meritocratic principles and are therefore always thought of as temporary or time-bound. (That they keep getting extended is, in turn, seen as evidence of the cynical opportunism of the political classes.)

Implication in the 'Hindu Majority' Question

A third framing factor is that at critical junctures in recent history, the caste question has been enmeshed with the larger political-cultural question of a 'Hindu majority'. The events and processes associated with caste have thus been complicated by their planned and unplanned intersections with other agendas and issues.

The confrontation between Ambedkar and Gandhi prior to the Poona Pact of 1932 is a classic instance of the imbrication of caste questions in the broader politics of constructing a Hindu majority in the Indian polity. Gandhi is absolutely clear that a separate electorate for the Depressed Classes will deal a deathblow to the political future of the Congress because it will undermine the decisive nature of its claim to represent the vast majority of Indians. If the newly created category of Hindu is deprived of its residual status—which ensures that everyone who is not a Muslim, Christian or other minority religion is automatically a Hindu—then it becomes just another (albeit slightly more numerous) group fighting for political recognition from the colonial power. It is therefore imperative to keep the Depressed Classes in the Hindu fold by any means necessary.

This is the background against which the special concessions to the Scheduled Castes and Tribes are included in the Indian Constitution. This is the price that the dominant sections of the Hindu leadership are forced to pay in return for the dropping of the demand for separate electorates. So, the most important social policy initiative addressed to caste inequality is the direct outcome of electoral arithmetic and the construction of minorities and majorities in 20th century India.

Although the communal basis of politics appeared to recede during the first few decades of independence, it has returned with a vengeance in recent decades. Once again, the question of caste inequality is being implicated in the question of a Hindu majority. The consequences of such intersections are not straightforward, and they are also constantly being altered in response to unfolding events and processes. Nevertheless, this is a framing factor that needs to be kept in mind when thinking about social policy in relation to caste inequality.

IV

Preliminary Tasks for Social Scientists

Given these framing factors, what is it that sociologists and other social scientists should be doing to reorient policy perspectives on caste inequality? Two preliminary tasks are particularly important in my opinion.

A. Focus Attention on the Contemporaneity of Caste Inequality

In India, social policy on caste inequality is founded on the presumption that it is compensating for the past injustices suffered by these communities. This is in keeping with the dominant mainstream understanding of the reservations policy as a regrettable departure from the desirable norm of meritocracy and blindness towards all ascriptive attributes. The Constitution is clear that this exception to the rule of equality of status is made necessary by the undeniable historical fact of severe discrimination and oppression suffered by the Scheduled Tribes and especially the Scheduled Castes. The defensive orientation of reservations policy (as discussed above) is underlined by the compensation-for-past-discrimination justification. Such a justification seems to invite a time limit, and more generally, is vulnerable to the questions commonly asked by the opponents of affirmative action: For how long should these compensatory policies continue, especially since caste has been legally abolished in independent India? Why (and to what extent) should the present generation (of non-scheduled castes) pay for the alleged sins of their ancestors? Or conversely, why (and to what extent) should the present generation of SCs and STs be compensated for discrimination practised against their forefathers?

But, as the evidence discussed in the second part of this paper clearly demonstrates, it is a fallacy to think of caste inequality as a relic of the past. The fact is that it has been reproduced quite successfully in independent India, and it is this *contemporary caste inequality* that our policies should address. There is a clear and self-evident rationale for having policies for the redressal of these inequalities for as long as they exist rather than any arbitrary time limit. Thus, the task of sociologists and other social scientists is threefold: First, collect existing data on contemporary caste inequalities and profile its nature, extent and changes over time; second, design and implement studies that will produce more such reliable data; and third, debate the design of policy initiatives that can successfully tackle the inequalities identified by research.

It must be emphasised, however, that the social scientists' task is not restricted merely to discovering such inequalities as exist—it also extends to documenting those inequalities that may have progressively diminished or even disappeared over time. It is conceivable that some caste groups have succeeded in overcoming their past disadvantages and are now no longer in need of protective discrimination. It is as much the duty of social scientists to point this out and argue for the cessation of benefits to these groups as it is to argue for the continuation or enhancement of protection to other groups whose degree of disadvantage may be increasing or constant. Similarly, it is also our duty to examine and report on the intra-group inequalities within particular castes or caste groupings (for example, across the many castes included in the ill-defined category, Other Backward Classes, among the different castes constituting the Scheduled Castes, within a single caste community like Brahmins or Vokkaligas or Yadavs, and so on). Each of these courses of action will of course invite the wrath of different vested interests.

Overall, the important task is to place our understanding of caste inequality on a rational footing, based on carefully collected evidence that can be publicly debated and critiqued by scholars and activists. We have to thoroughly rethink all our received categories and labels in the light of such evidence—including (for example) such 'holy cows' as the 1935 Schedules, the lists made by various state governments, notions like 'upper caste', and, of course, unviable hold-all categories like OBC.

B. Research the Mechanisms by which Caste Inequalities are Reproduced

The second major item on the immediate agenda for social scientists ought to be the investigation of the concrete mechanisms and processes by which caste inequalities have been reproduced in independent India despite the legal ban on the institution.

It is indeed ironic that recent calls for renewed attention to social institutions, networks, values and norms have come from economists (most notably Amartya Sen and his work on the sociocultural aspects of development) and political scientists (as in Putnam's much-cited notion of 'social capital') rather than sociologists. It is time that sociologists too devoted attention to the micro-processes through which caste privilege and disprivilege are being reproduced across generations in a modern social context that was presumed to be less hospitable to traditional institutions like caste.

Although our theoretical apparatus for tackling this issue remains relatively underdeveloped, we need to remind ourselves that it is sociologists who have pioneered this area. However, the well known attempts to theorise cultural capital (such as those of Gouldner or especially Bourdieu) need to be adapted and modified before they can speak to the Indian situation.[8] In pursuing this project of adaptation and repositioning, our objective should be to try and understand the ways in which caste functions as cultural capital, and to answer the crucial question of whether, and in what manner, such capital embodies *processes of socially legitimised exclusion*.

The starting point in our investigation has to be the preparation of an inventory of all the 'tacit knowledge' that people accumulate by virtue of their membership in social groupings like caste.[9] If we agree for the moment to use the label, 'cultural capital' to refer to this tacit knowledge and 'unlearnt' (or unconsciously learnt) skills, the contentious question is whether this capital confers *unfair* advantages or disadvantages—that is to say, does it constitute an *unjust* cause of inequality?[10]

This amounts to asking if cultural capital may be usefully treated as a form of property on par with other forms like land, wealth, or other assets. Although they are not exclusively concerned with caste, let me provide some tentative illustrations of the varied assets, aptitudes and competences that might constitute cultural capital.[11]

(a) The command of language and the language of command: Bernard Cohn's felicitous phrase summarises an important component of cultural capital, namely ease and familiarity with the dominant language, both in a narrowly linguistic sense—English, Sanskritised or otherwise caste inflected versions of Indian languages, etc.—as well as in the broader sense of the social idiom in which dominant groups express themselves (Cohn, 1985). One might say that those endowed with cultural capital are native speakers of 'power'.

(b) Family, kin and friendship networks: Such networks yield access to important information, skills or other collective resources outside formal institutional structures. A particularly useful concrete example (because it makes visible in a benign way something that may become socially invisible in another context) is the Indian students' 'mafia' commonly found in Anglo-American universities, especially in faculties like engineering, computer science, management and economics. While the category of 'Indian' can no longer suppress perceptions of internal difference within the community, it is still true that membership of this network provides access to all kinds of resources and skills, besides valuable training in survival techniques.[12]

(c) 'Technologies of the self' rooted in the caste habitus: By this I mean various ways of treating, training or disciplining oneself, techniques which are the product of a particular sociocultural milieu. Perhaps the most ubiquitous example is the technique of the examination. Examinations loom large in the social imagination of the middle class in India, especially its lower, parvenu segments.[13] Thus, the techniques associated with being a successful examinee are matters of considerable anxiety, and enormous investments of time, energy and money. Such a technology is strongly inflected by caste in the sense that the ethos of particular castes may ingrain this as a central aspect of socialisation and attaining personhood. However, the correlation between caste and this kind of technology would be considered benign or even overlooked because of conflation of cultural capital with the notion of individual merit or intelligence, as also the more straightforward misrecognition of the one as the other.

Needless to say the illustrations given above, besides being far from exhaustive, invite numerous doubts and queries. If we nevertheless proceed to ask whether something like what has been described above can constitute a form of property, the prima facie answer seems to be yes. Such a notion of cultural capital fulfills at least three attributes of property: It confers tangible and psychological benefits; it can be privatised, that is, others can be excluded from enjoying its benefits; and, finally, it can be transmitted across generations.

But the main problem with cultural capital is that it does not look like capital at all; rather, it takes the form of 'merit', a peculiarly Indian word which, it is relevant to remember, is also the common translation of the Hindu notion of *punya*. As the harvest of past virtuousness or disciplined striving and renunciation, then, cultural capital is fortified by a much stronger and deeper claim to legitimacy—to having been *earned and deserved*—than any other form of property. This 'thicker' claim to legitimacy derives from the peculiarities of cultural capital—its inseparability from the person and conduct of its owner, so that it is most often deployed in a 'performative' mode; its dependence on prolonged apprenticeship and training involving extensive investments of time, effort and money; its imbrication in crucial, highly legitimate institutions such as the family; or its tendency to deflect attention from itself by constantly taking on the appearance of other (often co-present) factors such as innate ability, skill, training, competence, and so on.

It is entirely plausible—though as yet undemonstrated—that their caste habitus has allowed the upper castes (especially the so-called 'literate castes' like Brahmans, Kayasthas, etc.) to successfully accomplish a certain kind of 'primitive' or 'original accumulation' in the Marxist sense. If so, this would help explain a major aspect of postcolonial social history in India, and that is why we urgently need more research in this area.

NOTES

1. Satish Saberwal was the first to draw attention to this puzzle in an important article first published in 1978 (Saberwal, 1999). However, it is interesting—and also perhaps an indication of the low priority attached to the subject—that this article itself seems to have dropped below the threshold of disciplinary notice.
2. This is despite the proverbial exceptions that prove the rule, including especially the work of Andre Beteille. See Beteille, 1991a and 1991b; see also the collection edited by K.L. Sharma (Sharma, 1999).
3. The problems have to do with changes in the 'reference period' for the 55th Round Survey (the period over which respondents are asked to report their consumption of various commodities). It is feared that these changes may make the 55th Round data incompatible with the previous rounds, so that comparisons across time cannot be made reliably. However, I am not comparing across time, but across caste/community groups within the same round, and there is no reason to believe that different castes/communities will be differently affected by the changes in the reference period.
4. The NSSO's rationale for determining class intervals has generally followed the standard statistical logic of dividing the distribution into evenly matched percentile segments (e.g. 5% or 10% 'slices' of the population, etc.). As Report No. 383 for the 43rd Round states, the grouping of MPCE classes was based on a trial tabulation and is designed to 'obtain approximately 5 percent of the population in each of the first two and last two classes and 10 percent in each of the middle eight classes' (pp. 15-16). This procedure implies asking the question: By how much must MPCE rise in order to cover the next 10 percent (or 5%, etc.) of the population?

   In re-arranging the size classes, I have followed a somewhat different logic, where the MPCE limits (in absolute terms) are determined first, without worrying about how much of the distribution they will cover. The logic for taking the poverty line as the lowest (consolidated) class is self-evident. (The poverty line estimates are from Planning Commission data.) I have tried to locate the highest class as high on the MPCE scale as possible. The middle two classes simply try to split the range between the lowest and highest MPCE into two convenient halves. This strategy serves to highlight the uneven distribution of the population among these classes both within and especially across social groups like SC, ST and 'Other'.

5. But perhaps the problem would persist even if these technical issues were not involved, for, as social scientists all over the world know only too well, it is much more difficult to study the rich and powerful than it is to study the poor and powerless. Unlike 'normal' subjects of research, people of higher economic and social status than the researcher are usually able to simply deny access to or, at the very least, shape the conditions and results of research.
6. According to Census classifications, persons belonging to the Scheduled Tribes may simultaneously be enumerated under any religion; however, persons belonging to the Scheduled Castes may only be enumerated as Hindus, Sikhs or (since the passing of the Constitution (Scheduled Castes) Order (Amendment) Act of 1990) Buddhists. Thus, Dalit Christians and other such groups are not recognised in the Census.
7. See the letter from S.S. Gill, secretary of the Commission, requesting this information reproduced in Appendix VII of the Mandal Commission Report.
8. The point is not that such work is inapplicable to India because it is simply 'western' in some essential sense, but that it is unable to address the *specificities* of the Indian context. For example, it is well known that Bourdieu developed his notion of symbolic capital as an ethnographer of Algeria. But Bourdieu's important work—while acknowledging symbolic capital to be a crucial form of property—treats it as a characteristic feature of a *pre-capitalist* social system, thereby implying its irrelevance for a capitalist society. On the other hand, his development of this notion through his (later) ethnographic work on French society, where cultural capital is recognised as producing 'distinction' in a contemporary capitalist setting, is overly aestheticised and distanced from the operations of the economy, so that its property-like aspects are underplayed. This obviously requires a much fuller discussion which I cannot enter into here.
9. Although much more systematic work needs to be done on this, readers may see two very different versions of something like such an inventory in the works of M.N. Srinivas (1996) and Kancha Ilaiah (1996).
10. Some causes of inequality are considered legitimate, or at least not unjust, such as intelligence, ability, hard work, and so on. Obviously, the basic problem is the high probability that one form will be actively 'misrecognised' as another (to use Bourdieu's term).

11. The subsequent examples are taken from Deshpande (1998). See this article for a more detailed discussion of this issue, albeit in the context of the language of rights.
12. For example, membership of this network could prove decisive in the following areas: 'doing well' academically, given the training provided by 'seniors' on how to deal with the academic system, especially tests and examinations; access to affordable and convenient housing; financial assistance, especially short term loans; information on job prospects and active help in securing jobs, and so on.
13. As is well known, examinations begin at the age of three for children born into this class. A social history of the examination in modern India is one of the many items that ought to figure urgently on the agenda of the contemporary social sciences.

References

Beteille, Andre, 1991(a), 'Distributive Justice and Institutional Well-Being', *Economic and Political Weekly*, Annual Number, Vol. 26, Nos. 11-12, March.

—, 1991(b), 'The Reproduction of Inequality: Occupation, Caste and Family', *Contributions to Indian Sociology*, n.s., Vol. 25, No. 1, January-June.

Deshpande, Satish, 1998, 'The Current Impasse in the Language of Rights: A Note on Questions of Context', *Economic and Political Weekly*, Vol. 33, No. 5, January 31-February 6, pp. PE11-15.

—, forthcoming, 'Caste Inequality and Indian Sociology: Notes on Questions of Disciplinary Location', *Recasting Indian Sociology: The Changing Contours of the Discipline*, (ed.) Maitrayee Chaudhuri, New Delhi: Orient Longman (in press).

Goyal, Santosh, 1992(a), 'Social Background of Officers in the Indian Administrative Service', Appendix II, *Dominance and State Power in Modern India: Decline of a Social Order*, (eds.) Francine Frankel and M.S.A. Rao, Vol. I, Delhi: Oxford University Press, pp. 425-33.

—, 1992(b), 'Social Background of Indian Corporate Executives', Appendix IV, *Dominance and State Power in Modern India: Decline of a Social Order*, (eds.) Francine Frankel and M.S.A. Rao, Vol. II, Delhi: Oxford University Press, pp. 533-44.

Ilaiah, Kancha, 1996, *Why I Am Not a Hindu*, Kolkata: Samya.

National Sample Survey Organisation, 2001(a), *Employment and Unemployment Situation among Religious Groups in India 1999-2000*, Report No. 468, September.

National Sample Survey Organisation, 2001(b), *Employment and Unemployment Situation among Social Groups in India 1999-2000*, Report No. 469, September.

Panini, M.N., 1995, 'The Political Economy of Caste', *Caste: Its Twentieth Century Avatar*, (ed.) M.N. Srinivas, New Delhi: Viking Penguin, pp. 28-68.

Saberwal, Satish, 1999, 'Sociologists and Inequality', *Social Inequality in India*, (ed.) K.L. Sharma, (originally in *Economic and Political Weekly*, Annual Number 1979).

Sharma, K.L. (ed.), 1999, *Social Inequality in India*, (revised 2nd edition), Jaipur and New Delhi: Rawat Publications.

Srinivas, M.N., 1996(a), *Indian Society Through Personal Writings*, Delhi: Oxford University Press.

Index